Hot Mettle

SOGAT, Murdoch and me

Hot Mettle

SOGAT, Murdoch and me

Brenda Dean

POLITICO'S

First published in Great Britain 2007 by
Politico's Publishing Ltd, an imprint of
Methuen Publishing Ltd
11–12 Buckingham Gate
London
SW1E 6LB

1

A CIP catalogue record for this book is available from the British Library.

ISBN 978-1-84275-200-5

Typeset by SX Composing DTP, Rayleigh, Essex
Printed and bound in Great Britain by MPG Books Ltd, Bodmin, Cornwall

Contents

Introduction	vii
Chapter 1	1
Chapter 2	10
Chapter 3	18
Chapter 4	26
Chapter 5	43
Chapter 6	59
Chapter 7	68
Chapter 8	74
Chapter 9	85
Chapter 10	104
Chapter 11	120
Chapter 12	135
Chapter 13	152
Chapter 14	167
Chapter 15	182
Chapter 16	195
Chapter 17	200
Chapter 18	210
Chapter 19	225
Chapter 20	235
Chapter 21	249
Chapter 22	258
Index	270

I did not really wish to write this book and could not have done it without the assistance of my husband, Keith McDowall, as with so much in my life. But he argued persuasively that the 'other side' of the Wapping clash and my personal role needed to be properly recorded. He also made a very strong case that once it had been done, our home could at last be cleared of the thick, dusty box files containing the full drama of this sad era.

B.D.

Introduction

Flying aboard Concorde is not something that would normally be expected of a trade union leader in the United Kingdom. Certainly not on one operated by Air France. But despite the novelty my thoughts were far away from the speed at which I was returning to Europe from John F. Kennedy airport in New York, and the delights of the cuisine on board. I knew the crunch was coming fast now on the violent year-long dispute at Wapping, on the north bank of the Thames in east London, between the trade union I led and Rupert Murdoch's News International.

We were beaten – that was the harsh truth of the matter. And now somehow I had to persuade my members to face the fact that the union was at the end of the line.

So was this to be the end of the line for Brenda Dean too? Was this how a career would conclude which had gone from a junior secretary in a Lancashire print firm to becoming the first woman ever elected to lead a major British industrial trade union? Would the left-wingers who had schemed to prevent me winning the election, tried repeatedly to wrongfoot me and fabricated dirty stories about me now have the last laugh?

The date was Tuesday 27 January 1987. The Wapping dispute was in its fifty-second week. For virtually a year it had filled the TV screens and the front pages of the newspapers and had dominated the radio news – an international epic tailor made for tabloids about power, money, brute force and, yes, sex. Me. So every news conference I held was packed with up to eighty newspaper, radio and TV journalists of every nationality reaching out for another instalment of 'Media mogul battles it out with union blonde'. My face had gone right round the world several times. And it all had gone on for nearly a year.

But for how much longer, I had to ask myself.

At my side on Concorde was Bill Miles, the union's national officer, who had been there throughout the highs and lows of the Wapping clash and was the only other officer in the union who knew of our mission. But even Miles had been thrown when I told him that as soon as I got back from a meeting with the union's Newcastle branch we would make a secret dash to New York for a final face-to-face with Murdoch's right-hand man, Bill O'Neill, and try to settle it all. And no one else was to know.

To avoid a leak we would go via Paris, buying our tickets secretly through the union's lawyers so that no one in the union, the Society of Graphical and Allied Trades – SOGAT – would find out. One premature leak before I could lay all the facts before the assembled members of the union executive and I would be completely wrongfooted by the hardliners who wanted confrontation to continue. And who wanted to oust me if they could and so prise open the moderates' slender grip on the issue – and on the union.

In what I call a 'plastic hotel', quite a basic one near JFK airport, we met in the coffee house with O'Neill. It was time, I said, that we both laid our cards on the table. Was it true that News International was considering taking our union back to the court – after previously seizing our funds and reducing the union to impotence? And was it now about to go back to the judge to have SOGAT fined even more heavily for contempt of court and see all its assets seized? In effect that would be the end of the union. I could see the headlines in my mind's eye – 'Woman union chief sees her union closed down'. What an epitaph.

O'Neill, a straight-talking Australian with whom I had always enjoyed good relations, sat back in his chair. 'Yeah, it's on the cards. We're talking to the lawyers about it. Why?'

I prided myself on coolness in negotiation but this time my heart was thumping as I heard myself say: 'Well, if you take us for contempt I will have to tell my executive what they now face.' What I wanted now was to negotiate an end to the dispute and try at least to get some money for people who had lost their jobs. It had been a long, bitter twelve months which had seen the jobs and livelihoods of nearly 4,300 SOGAT members go without warning or compensation. This hadn't affected just those in the print operation or distribution, who had lived well out of it, but also lower-paid people such as the cleaners at the *Sun*, the dedicated librarians at the *Times*, filing clerks in Bouverie Street and all the other back-of-office people who were flung out of work and blacklisted.

In the year that had gone by nine people had died just waiting for the strike to end. One young child fell to her death accidentally by slipping through the open staircase steps at Congress House, the TUC's headquarters. Appalled, I had watched in horror as the Metropolitan Police deliberately rode their horses into our pickets on the Highway outside News International's Wapping plant. Yet I had also been uplifted by the decision of the Bishop of Southwark's industrial chaplain to hold a special service for us in a church at Blackfriars, in the heart of printland, as it was before the dawn of so-called new technology.

Such were the twists and turns of a year of industrial warfare which was to prove to be the high-water mark of British trade unionism's so-called industrial muscle – always something of a myth to me – and final proof that Margaret Thatcher's chains on the freedom to combine were well and truly in place. So while every fibre in me urged 'fight on' I knew that the time had come for me as the person leading the union now to lead it out of the morass of the Wapping dispute.

I had thought about the timing extremely carefully. The twelve-month anniversary of the lock-out was due within a few days and there was a danger of the left staging a major confrontation and forcing through a decision to intensify the dispute if possible. That would get us into contempt of court again anyway, with a massive fine inevitable.

But there were also distinct signs from outside the capital that the members there did not want to see their union, which could trace its roots back 200 years, sacrificed for one London dispute. The dread that lurks within every trade union leader – splitting their own union – I had managed, with a lot of thought, to avoid. Comparisons with Arthur Scargill's fate of splitting his own union were all too obvious. I had so far managed to keep the union's provincial membership on board. But they were beginning to realise that their union was being wrecked for what was essentially a narrow London issue. There were some implications for Manchester and Glasgow newspaper production, but it had little to do with general printing, bookbinding, papermaking and the many different ways in which our members earned their daily bread far away from the supposed glamour of Fleet Street. In these places, what had become new technology had repeatedly been accepted and introduced without the Luddite and bully boy clashes within national newspapers, which were an embarrassment to the whole trade union movement.

With the backing of most of the SOGAT executive, we had held the membership together because there had been a national ballot in favour but despite it the union had virtually ceased to operate. Murdoch's lawyers had cleverly used the Thatcher government's anti-union legislation to seize our funds, close down our offices and take away our cars, while all the time the golden goose of News International, the *Sun* newspaper, had appeared each day at Wapping and successfully achieved its distribution. And so fund the expanding Murdoch empire.

Hence the dash by Concorde. But that was not the only secret flight I had to make in the dispute. Some months earlier, again with Miles, I had driven to a remote part of Heathrow airport, away from prying camera lenses, to board Murdoch's private jet and fly by way of Anchorage to meet him at his home in Beverly Hills in Los Angeles. I wanted to size him up and he wanted the same with me. We both wanted to see if we could cut a deal. The only other person present was the head of Murdoch's operation in London, Bruce Matthews, with whom Miles had kept up contact, and they had set up the meeting. But they slipped away. Murdoch barbecued lamb chops for the pair of us – making notes on the back of the packaging – as we sat by his swimming pool in Beverly Hills in the warmth of the California sunshine.

One aspect I probed was how genuine his offer was to give us any compensation at all. What I wanted was compensation in hard cash for the way my people had so brutally seen their livelihood and their ability to provide for their families snatched away. No employer was going to get away with that if I could do anything to prevent it – that was my personal bottom line.

As we talked it all through, so we got to know each other better. I have to say

I liked him. Printing ink is clearly in his blood – as I feel it is in mine – and all he wanted to do was produce newspapers, even, as he had shown, being prepared to sacrifice his nationality to do it. That evening we continued talking as Murdoch collected us from our hotel and drove us in his car to a downtown restaurant. His then wife, Anna, who was extremely friendly and gracious, also came along. By the end of the meal we had virtually agreed the dispute had to come to an end.

And, yes, there would be compensation for those of my members who had lost their jobs, if and when I could find a way to force the final confrontation by my colleagues of the Wapping issue. This was an important consideration for me because legally none of our members was entitled to a penny. But I was determined to get more than the basic Redundancy Payments Act allowance, even though under the Thatcher laws the SOGAT members had broken their contract, and had lost all entitlement as soon as the strike action began. This was notwithstanding the work from Gray's Inn Road and Bouverie Street being transferred overnight to dockland Wapping, several miles away. Thus had Thatcher loaded the dice against working people.

One condition I did stress to Murdoch was that I had to have terms acceptable to my members and as there had been a ballot to start the strike I wanted them to have another to call off the dispute if possible.

We seemed to be on the same wavelength and after a remarkably relaxed dinner Murdoch drove us around his newly acquired Fox studios in Hollywood, enthusing at the huge libraries of film they held – material which soon would be used, he predicted, to fuel the explosion of demand from TV channels worldwide. Once again Murdoch demonstrated to us how his thinking was far, far ahead of its time. And showed us what a forceful business manager we had taken on.

The chairman of News International and I had met only briefly before. The first occasion was at a dinner arranged to introduce me, newly elected as general president, the number two in SOGAT, and likely to be taking over as general secretary. He asked me point blank if I could take control of the Fleet Street situation and 'could I deliver?'. I was not in the easy-promises business but remember looking him straight in the eye. 'I don't know – it's a mess and matters may be quite beyond anyone's control but I have to find out. If you will give me three months I will come and tell you.'

Apparently afterwards Murdoch confided to his colleagues that he liked the look of me but didn't think I 'had the bottle' to take on the greedy people he regarded as holding his printing operations in London to ransom. So while I tried to persuade him to give me a fresh chance to negotiate he really wanted the freedom to make his own deals without any union pressure.

So he was ready to give the green light for the secretively planned Wapping confrontation to begin.

Another meeting with Murdoch occurred when Tony Dubbins, the leader of the National Graphic Association, and I, accompanied by two other officials, went for a taking-stock meeting at News International's headquarters, then in Gray's Inn Road. Dubbins promised full co-operation for the management to bring in the changes it wanted but Murdoch clearly did not trust him. 'The tune has changed', he told us, 'but the dance stays the same.' Now as the sun bounced off the pool, Murdoch knew he had been right but at a price. We may not have won the war but we had certainly carried the public relations battle and had succeeded in projecting News International and its chairman as unworthy bullies.

The company had calculated and planned its secret operations at Wapping extremely well, importing American computer print-setting equipment. Training its operatives for the new computerised typesetting had been conducted in great secrecy in Woolwich; secret negotiations with the Electrical, Electronic, Telecommunications & Plumbing Union had planned for busloads of newly trained recruits to be driven into News International's new print works by coach; the logistics company TNT (in which Murdoch had a stake) would distribute the newspapers by road, so bypassing traditional wholesalers and the railways, both of which were union dominated.

All this was protected by the nation's own police force, quite unashamedly abandoning any attempt at impartiality, willing to become anti-trade unionist shock troops – even to the extent of removing identifying numbers from their collars as they wielded their truncheons. Indeed those responsible had planned it all extremely well – except for a new young woman union leader able to articulate the dispute in a way which came across to the ordinary people of Britain to win their sympathy and support. The tabloid project of The Poor Beauty and the Ugly Thug was an image those handling the media inside Wapping found hard to combat all around the world.

There was a price – I completely lost any anonymity I had once possessed, even to the point of being followed round Marks and Spencer's vegetable counters one day in Islington to be told how I was getting my message across.

Yet after a horrendous year here I was flying back to Europe, via Paris again to retain secrecy, mapping out in my mind how to bring down the flag. And how – undoubtedly interpreted by some as failure – it was to be done.

I didn't sleep . . .

Chapter 1

It was a long way to the first-class lifestyle of Concorde from a two-up, two-down terraced house at 74 Davis Street, Eccles, Lancashire, lacking a bathroom and with an often cold outside loo. That was where I was born and where I lived until I was twelve years of age. My father, Hugh, was a signalman and a proud, lifelong member of the National Union of Railwaymen, but trade unions were seldom discussed in our home. I only had the faintest awareness of the union movement when I started out to work. My mother, Lillian, worked in a carpet factory.

As my dad worked shifts and my mother was at the factory all day I carried the front door key around my neck – we were known as 'latchkey kids' in the tabloids at the time – and it was often my responsibility after school to go home, let myself and my younger brother, Bobby, in and get tea for us both. Nevertheless, my parents gave my brother and me a secure family life and taught us, I think, to be self-reliant and resourceful.

Bobby was a lively little boy, wiry like his dad, and frightened of nothing – least of all his elder sister. So sometimes exerting discipline at teatime had its tense moments and probably gave me my earliest tests in gaining control and exercising some kind of authority, to which I can almost hear my brother saying: 'Well, she was always a bossy boots.' I don't think I was, but I am conscious that even then I liked to have everything sorted out, tidy and organised, a characteristic that has stayed with me all my life. Because I was always asking questions, my father nicknamed me Brenda Why.

I was always determined to have the full picture. I wanted to know what was going on and I am told that even as a very young child I nagged my father to know each day where he was going and what he meant by 'going to work'.

What *was* work, I wanted to know. Maybe that is why I am sometimes accused of being a 'workaholic', which I do not accept. I actually enjoy being on top of events, to have my ducks in a row, as the saying goes, and have been taught never to leave my desk until all is tided up. It's difficult to change the habits of a lifetime.

And soon I found out about work, as I rode on the back of Dad's bike to see the signal boxes where he would work out his shift, often with no other company than a stray cat adopted to keep down the rats. If it was near enough I sometimes walked along the trackside to take Dad his dinner and soon I was working out his hours of overtime so that he could make his weekly claim. Little did I know that one day I would be calculating that sort of thing for hundreds of my members, to whom a rise in the hourly rate meant everything.

But although I had confidence in myself it seems that I did not show it at school or with my friends, so much so that my parents sent me to tap dancing classes at weekends to try to 'bring me out', as it was put in those days. It probably explains to this day why I like nothing more than a good song-and-dance musical on stage or on the screen. Maybe I needed bringing out because I had been born in April 1943 in the middle of an air raid and I had learned from then on to keep quiet!

At St Andrew's Junior School, Eccles, again an apparent lack of confidence showed in me and I was marked as a borderline case for the 11-plus exam. But not for the last time someone stepped forward who was to have a major influence on my life.

He was a rather stern teacher named George Booth, of whom we were all terrified at the school. But when the exam result came through he refused to accept it. Instead Mr Booth came to my home and persuaded my parents to let him coach me privately, and when I was thirteen he enlisted me for the entrance examination to Stretford High School for Girls. I passed – Mr Booth's dedication and interest had paid off.

Many years later, when I was made a member of the House of Lords, I received a letter from him and was delighted, one weekend when in Suffolk visiting relatives, to seek him out. The kindly Mr Booth – not stern at all, I found out – had been following my career for many years. He really was enchanted to discover that one child, among quite a few, I suspect, had benefited from the interest he showed in them. Proof – as many of us realise in later life – that a teacher in one's younger days can indeed have a profound effect and impact.

I also took the time to go back to St Andrew's when I was at the top of the union and was delighted to see the children in the very classroom I remembered. I tried to repay the teachers by telling the children about my life and how St Andrew's had influenced it. Over many years I have given as much time as I could manage to visit schools, present prizes if asked, and to get across that the chance is there if one is willing to seize it. If I can do more I do, but I always try to make at least two school visits in the country a year. I have visited schools as diverse as Stowe, City and Islington Sixth Form College, Brandeston Hall Preparatory School in Suffolk, Croydon College and Sydenham High School, a Girls' Day School Trust school in south London.

Stretford High School was certainly my chance and it gave me and my friends, many of whom have kept in touch all my life, a very good grounding as the future secretaries of Manchester's businessmen. Commerce was to be our future and when I was ready to go out into the world at sixteen I had a shorthand speed of 140 words a minute and a touch-typing speed of 60, and I had passed all my RSA Proficiency exams. I knew about writing letters, their layout and the correct way to fold them; I could type at speed for hours and my telephone manner was praised.

While we received a very good commercial training maybe it would have been helpful to have had a fuller education in English literature, history and science – I have not really found my schooling in the Roman period to be very much use at all. But over the years I have been very conscious of just how wrong it is to bracket children into one compartment which defines their future. I believe we all develop, change and mature depending on our experiences and when we have people like Mr Booth influencing our lives. The inferior education dished up to so many youngsters in the 1960s and 1970s is hard to defend and I was strongly behind Tony Blair's 'education, education, education' mantra when he successfully led us into the 1997 general election.

But what we had also been taught was that as girls we were destined only to

3

be reliable, conscientious assistants to men. Even then something inside me was rebelling against that doctrine and although I did not know it, I was going to play a small, but not insignificant, role in changing some of that – not just in the north-west but also at national level. But that was some years on – the big date on my immediate horizon was in August 1959, one week after leaving school, when I reported for my first day as 'secretary' to one of the managers of a major printing concern in the north-west. I was raring to go and expected to have letters to type, phone calls to make to fix my boss's appointments, reports to compile and plenty of files to complete: all that we had been taught at Stretford school.

What a let-down. At the end of the first day I had found my way round my little office, tidied up a bit here and there, but that was about all. I saw very little of my boss, or anyone else, come to that. But I presumed that my boss was having a very busy time somewhere else and couldn't spare the time to sort out what he wanted from me.

At the end of a few weeks doing precious little, however, I decided to take things into my own hands. The chatter amongst the other girls was that one of the secretaries at the other end of the office was very busy. I could tell from the speed and sound of the typewriter rattling away that although the fingers on that keyboard could fly along, they were very busy indeed.

'I wonder if she needs any help,' I suggested.

As it happened my neighbouring secretary, a more senior girl, gladly gave me some tasks and I went off happily to my desk. And that went on for a day or two until my own boss angrily confronted me and demanded to know what I thought I was playing at. Apparently there had been discussion at a board meeting that he had not enough to do himself and thus not much to give to me – confirming speculation in the works that he was underemployed.

'Why can't you bring your knitting like the other girls?' he stormed.

As I sat at my desk, eyes brimming, I tried to come to terms with what to me was a totally unreasonable and very disappointing start to my career and my new stage in life. Knitting? Me?

It was not long afterwards that my hero arrived in the shape of John Glass, the genial Father of the Chapel – the printing industry term for the chief shop steward – who asked me if I was interested in working for 'the union'. Was this something religious, I wondered. He was after all called Father . . . No – the union was the means by which the print workers' pay and hours were settled, it was explained, and a minute secretary was needed at the local branch office in Manchester.

I felt I had little to lose in making a change – even after such a short period – and agreed to my name going forward. What I did not find out until some time later was that the trade unionists at our works had decided that I needed a little protection. My often absent boss, it was being alleged, had a sideline of a dubious nature and the men in the works had agreed amongst themselves that the new young blonde secretary needed looking after. For the first time, but certainly not the last, I had good reason to be very grateful to trade unionism.

From that moment on the movement was to give me my real education: my training in negotiation, in chairing and conducting meetings, in public speaking, in human relationships, in politics and power. It would set me on the road to becoming the first woman elected in Britain to head a major national manufacturing trade union, to my own place on the Trades Union Congress, to sitting on major committees of inquiry and to a seat in the House of Lords. Even to vetting prospective knights and peers (and peeresses) of the realm.

But that was a long way ahead. On the bus that morning, going down to Manchester from the neat council flat in Peel Green in which my family now lived, I had no idea of the way the world for Brenda Dean was about to open up and change. Small wonder that, ever since, I have loved change all my life.

There was not a lot of change in fact at the Manchester branch office of the National Union of Printing, Bookbinding and Paper Workers in Roby Street, just off Piccadilly. Although the office was right in the middle of Manchester, not much seemed to have changed for a long time. But there was a comptometer and my colleague Jean, eight years my senior, was 'trained', much emphasis being placed on that word by the formidable Amy Knox, the assistant branch secretary, who showed me round.

The comptometer, a sophisticated calculating machine, was felt to be needed because each day shop stewards or branch members would come to the office and knock on a little hatch door. In the back office Jean or I would open up, take the members' subscriptions paid over in cash and issue a receipt. Then Jean would key the figure into the machine and that would have to tally with what had been paid into the bank for the union's central accounts.

Somehow I never managed to hit it off with Knox, who seemed to think that I was a flighty young thing and someone to be kept very firmly in her place. As a first intimidating step she doubted if my shorthand speed was going to be fast enough to take down the words of the branch committee members. I had no doubt that my speed of 140 words per minute would be up to the job. And I soon proved it.

However, a difficulty did arise from the fact that since I was at sixteen a minor, the law of the land forbade me from working late. 'No problem,' said the members of the branch committee; 'we'll meet earlier.' And they did – another example of the way it seemed the trade union movement was setting out to be my guardian angel. And my university.

Mind you, with Knox around, I needed some protection. She would find any fault with me that she could – a lingering whiff of perfume or a pinch of face powder left in the sink in the tiny loo were sufficient to engender a formal complaint to the boss. It all seemed so petty. But then she kept running into a formidable obstacle in the shape of Joe Sheridan, full-time secretary of the Manchester branch and very much his own boss.

Full-time was perhaps not the best way to put it – Sheridan never arrived until 11 a.m. because he first had his family's newsagent's business to deal with before turning to union matters. It was well known and none of the members seemed to mind this piece of pure private enterprise. But he put the hours in later, often working well into the night, and it gave me time in the morning to get things sorted out on his desk. Quite quickly he let me assume more and more of his routine work. At first I suggested changes to his dictated letters, which he amiably accepted. Eventually I wrote most of his letters myself and he signed them off. Then I suggested a change in layout for the style of his letters. We had been taught well at Stretford and all my life I have been very fussy about what letters go out in my name and how they look; if humanly possible, they should also be signed personally by me.

Sheridan was about fifty, dark haired, well built and really quite good looking. He was always well turned out, I particularly recall, and I suppose this made an impact on me because even then I noted how first impressions do indeed count. At first I was Brenda or Bren to him but gradually as we came to work more and more together he started calling me by the nickname Brandy, although I'd never touched a drop!

Upstairs on the first floor Amy Knox fumed and complained about me to the other assistant secretary, Fred McWhirter. But so far as I could tell they seldom made much of a contribution to helping to share the burden of Sheridan's workload. Neither of them ever went out on the branch's real work of negotiation of pay and conditions. That was how I came to go with Sheridan sometimes to negotiations to take a note of what had been said. When I had typed up the minutes I suggested we should sign off the note with the employers – which most readily agreed. We usually turned out anyway to have a better note than them. It was in this way that I got to know many of the print, paper and newspaper distribution employers in the north-west and without realising had my first foot on the promotion ladder. Quite a few of them became friends and kept touch with me over many years.

Again Sheridan willingly allowed me to have my say with him after a meeting to ask why he had taken a certain line in negotiation. Then I got to discussing tactics with him before the meeting with the employers and revelled in knowing what our bottom line would be but seeing if we could edge it higher for our members.

To me there is nothing quite like that thrill. Ever since then I have loved negotiation and quite deliberately avoided at least two major political opportunities to keep with it. It all goes back to those early days at Sheridan's side in Manchester.

Although I liked and admired Sheridan, I found him to be a man of amazing contradictions and prejudices. For a start he was an active Freemason – a taboo for most in the Labour field – and I well remember staying late at the office taking him through his responses to the incantations of the ceremonies. The fact that this was a secret society and no woman – let alone a young girl – was supposed to get a whiff of what went on behind the solid oak doors of the masonic lodge was of no concern to him whatsoever.

And despite my emerging special relationship with Sheridan he was not really in favour of equality. He believed a woman's place was in the home and was really an old chauvinist – though he was quite willing to make exceptions if I could make light of his work for him. That was how I persuaded him that the office needed to buy an electric IBM typewriter, which to me represented the white heat of new technology – as it did indeed to the whole office. I explained I could get out his letters faster, make special displays for branch announcements and indeed have top-rate copy out in a flash.

'OK,' said Sheridan. 'Order one.'

I did and I still remember it cost over £350. Big money in those days. But Sheridan happily picked up the idea and introduced it as a further branch improvement he had decided to put in hand!

Having the IBM machine on my desk was of course a new kind of enabling power. I did not realise at the time, but my arrival and such minor changes as I had brought along represented a further challenge to Amy Knox and an explosion could not be prevented for much longer. She saw the IBM as a further encroachment on her role as office manager but it washed over Sheridan.

Still I had to be very careful with my suggestion that if I could have some practice time on the comptometer I did not see why it could not be mastered. So Sheridan carried it out to his car at the weekend so that I could have a try with the machine at home on the kitchen table. And it was just as I thought – there wasn't a lot to it. In fact, it didn't take long before I was almost as fast as the trained Jean in making the calculations, and I started to suggest ways in which the money collection and cash-handling system could be speeded up and made more efficient.

Each month 1,200 cheques had to be drawn up to pay pensioners – some in pounds and some for quite small sums of money. I suggested that the bank printed a facsimile signature on the cheques, which would save hours for the branch office, but that was ruled out instantly. (Years later, when I became branch secretary, we did this alright!) So I turned it into a game, which is a way I have always approached boring, repetitive tasks. Timing myself, I worked out a system so that I could manage 300 cheques an hour even if it was among the most mind-numbing tasks that greeted me each month.

I had already cut my organisational teeth on arranging visits from London officials, who found for the first time that they were booked into hotels, they had their itinerary and rail tickets sent to them and, yes, it all worked. That was quite new. I had also quietly started to upgrade my job description and insert the word 'administrative' in front of 'secretary'. I thought it sounded better and in any case was a truer reflection of my job description by now.

Then came the moment when I won the task of organising a branch dinner to bid farewell to the union general secretary, Bill Morrison, up from the south. It was to be a really big do at the Co-op Hall in Downing Street, Manchester.

To take on the task of organising the major event was a natural development for me and I revelled in it. It was to be a formal affair – something which I had never attended in my life. But I was determined that I was going to enjoy it and spent the previous Saturday afternoon at Estelle Modes in Market Street choosing my first ever ballroom-length dress. I still remember it – strapless black velvet with swathes of white satin at the bust and the hemline. Looking back, maybe – just maybe – as a youngster of eighteen I went over the top. But that evening for the first time the penny dropped. I learned quickly that if I looked too good, and the menfolk cast their eye over me, their wives would very quickly notice. A single girl, in a strapless ballgown and with hair professionally coiffured, was a threat. Wow!

And of course Knox was incensed that I dared to change in the tiny loo rather than rush home to Peel Green and try to get back on the bus in the rush hour. She pounced and – oh dear – another speck of powder in the basin. As Sheridan said, when he congratulated me on the smooth way in which the event had been carried off, if I could just remember to wipe round the basin afterwards it would help. I promised to try.

But Amy Knox was not going to stop me now.

Chapter 2

My life wasn't all work, although sometimes to my family and friends it probably looked like it. But if you love what you are doing and getting a real thrill of job satisfaction, time flies and I certainly had little to spare for much social life.

But it was in that period of my life, while working at the Manchester branch office, that I hit on a personal philosophy which I have adopted ever since. I call it 'Brenda's time'. Somehow in the midst of all that is going on around me each day, if possible, I carve out half an hour or maybe just fifteen minutes to do what I want for myself.

In those days I could pop out to the shops, get some nail polish, a lipstick or a birthday card. I might make a phone call to my mother when she was alive. I found that unless I made a deliberate effort to grab a moment for myself at the end of the day I would remember, sometimes with a tinge of regret, that I had forgotten something personal I had wanted to do, or something I wanted to say. Busy career women sometimes become overwhelmed, exhausted even, often trying to square the pressures of a top job with trying to run a home and bring up children. A few minutes of Brenda's time, they might find, can be a useful tonic.

Certainly I found a little piece of Brenda's time helped me keep things in perspective even during the Wapping dispute. I remember once going out and blowing a large sum on a suite of plastic garden furniture. It is advice I have occasionally offered schoolgirls when they question me about the pressures of a busy career.

When I started at the branch my pay was £4 17*s*. 6*d*. a week, which rose after six months to £5 7*s*. 6*d*. It compared quite favourably to the £3 17*s*. 6*d*. on which I had started my first job at Brands Packaging. By the time I was eighteen and had begun to demonstrate I was a useful pair of hands the union branch had given me a couple of rises and for the first time in my life I had a little to spare in my purse. So by saving up I got my first car at twenty-one.

Every young man remembers getting his first car but back in those days it was quite unusual for a young woman to be behind the wheel, especially in her own car. My parents gave me £150 towards it as my birthday present but I had to find the rest. Such was the new-found confidence that my trade union mentors had helped to nurture in me that with little hesitation I signed a hire purchase agreement and the car was mine.

By that time I was playing a bigger role in the activities of the wider union movement in Manchester and the north-west. These were the beginnings of a power base that was to lead me to the top of the union, although I little realised it at the time.

In those days there was a proliferation of no fewer than seven print unions, which came together seeking a united view in a loose grouping called the Printing and Kindred Trades Federation (PKTF); even the journalists, usually loners, were involved. They met at our office and so I would usually take on the paperwork, book the meeting time and take the minutes. I particularly remember the booming voice of Bert Stone, the National Union of Journalists activist in Manchester, who took a dominant role. He frightened some people but I got on with him well. But he was adamant one day that I could not attend a meeting and became very mysterious about its purpose.

At first all I knew was that this grave matter concerned the high-quality local printing firm C. Nicholls – but then I discovered that they were printing *Lady Chatterley's Lover* by D. H. Lawrence. And during the production some of the lads had 'borrowed' a copy, which had suddenly become very hot property. A judge in London was considering whether the book should be published and every copy was impounded. Bringing the illicit copy into the branch office was akin to dynamite, according to Stone.

Today, with the explicit society which we have fashioned, it is perhaps hard to imagine that Stone and the other members of the PKTF were concerned about the effect on me of even coming within earshot of Lady C. In fact, though, I was a lot closer because I easily overheard the hushed discussion through the flimsy partition wall which separated my small room from the secretary's office. Silly men! And then to compound matters I discovered a print from the actual book left in the photocopier in the office next to mine. In those days copiers were giant machines, quite complicated to master, and it did not surprise me that a man had not only failed to grasp its workings but had left behind the evidence.

Not for the first time a photocopier had offered up its secrets – although to tell the truth I did not find the sample of Lawrence's literature totally compelling . . .

The more I came to know Joe Sheridan and came under his influence, so I begun to understand more the stresses and tensions beneath the surface of the Manchester branch. Outwardly all was brotherly and fraternal – just below the surface there was always the chance of a knife flashing. Especially if a back was turned.

Sheridan rather revelled in it and perhaps some of his members thought he was too close to some employers but that is a risk we all run. He was not particularly sophisticated but he liked to eat and drink well and he knew his way round some of the best watering holes and restaurants in the north-west. He liked a drink but I never saw him drunk. From Sheridan I did not need to learn my table manners but from him I acquired the confidence to hold my own in a restaurant, to order for myself and never to be overawed by bossy head waiters. Useful learning for a young woman in those days.

I also learned more and more about negotiation, which is the lifeblood of a trade union activist. Sheridan seldom entered a room to negotiate without a pretty shrewd idea of what would come on to the bargaining table and where the line would be drawn. That was usually because the night before he had taken it upon himself to talk to his opposite number on the employer's side and that line had been worked out and agreed.

Where I came to disagree with Sheridan was that he rarely bothered to tell the chapel or workshop representatives what he was about or to involve them. It was a lesson I drew on and when I came to do the job I always brought the shop stewards into the picture. Before I signed off a deal with the employers I insisted they allow me time to meet all the workers – in working time – to take them fully through the deal and to give them a vote on it. In that way I seldom lost a deal or had the humiliation of going back to the employers to confess I could not deliver on one.

Sheridan liked power, always sensed where it lay, and he liked to use it. He was often brusque, though, with his members and had a tendency to make enemies. And once he had an enemy no quarter was given by Joe Sheridan. That may have been the reason that a member brought a charge against him and sent it to Tom Smith, the general secretary, based in London. It was the first time I had come across this arcane system of 'justice' in the union and I found it quite shocking. It meant an allegation could be made against an individual and for weeks, often months, while the investigation into the charge was being conducted, nothing could be done. So while rumours could swirl around about an individual, some mud would inevitably stick but that person could not answer or make a rebuttal.

With hindsight I realise now that if Smith had had any guts or true leadership in him he would have promptly demanded that the person making the charge against one of the union's senior officers must either 'put up or shut up'. But he allowed it to drag on and this probably began to affect Sheridan's health, although I did not realise it at the time. But what I did learn about the union's justice system served me well, because those who tried to pull Sheridan down tried it later against me when I eventually took over the reins from him.

Meanwhile I had begun to become involved in the first stirrings of what became known as the North West Group in the union. Traditionally one of the regions of the union would host the biennial delegate conference and our area's turn had come round to organise it. Sheridan, as leader of the Manchester branch, the biggest in the area, was asked by London to take over the organisation of the whole group of union branches in the north-west, which included Merseyside, Burnley, Oldham, Blackburn and parts of north Wales, and to pull it all together. So not so surprisingly he gave me the task of sorting out the administration – right up my street.

Our management of the conference was so successful – indeed acclaimed – that we started to act as a group on policy. We realised we had fifty-two votes between us and that together we could have an influence and act as a brake on the over-dominant, left-inclined London branches, whose officers tended to think they *were* the union. The attitude was that we could pay our subscriptions and conduct our local negotiations but anything serious or political – well, that was Man's Work and it was done in London.

As our regional activities became more cohesive, better briefed and better disciplined we began to have an impact on the union's decision-making and we found to our satisfaction that we were causing some concern at the union headquarters in Nightingale Lane, Balham. I was also making some impact myself. Several of my supporters in the branch and the group urged me to stand as a delegate to the union conference in my own right and I was successful in winning a place at the 1968 event, which was held at the Floral Hall in Scarborough. Vietnam was the big issue but that was – of course – Man's Work, so items covering matters such as training and education tended to get crowded off the agenda or swept up in a ragbag towards the end of the conference week.

One from our branch argued pressing for higher funding for further education, which was a particular interest of a very decent branch member, Ernie Shepley, but he was not elected to go to the conference. So I was told quite suddenly: 'You're a delegate now – earn your bread. You put it.'

I had not expected to speak at my first conference as a delegate and indeed I had never addressed a conference, but I had been speaking at branch and group gatherings and it was now or never to show what I could do. Yes, I would put it, I would speak, I said. By the time Thursday came around I felt I was as prepared as possible. I had worked on my speech, timed it carefully and although I had it all written out I knew most of it – it was in my head, a method I have used throughout my professional life.

I had chosen my clothes carefully too – an orange woollen A-line coat dress, as they were called then, with full-length sleeves, beige shoes and my fair hair piled up high. So I was ready for anything – except the sneering reaction from the men of the London Central branch at an adjacent table to ours. I could hear their mocking remarks as I walked to the rostrum and then there was total silence. Apart from the knocking of my knees!

And just then I saw one of the London Central branch members put his tongue out at me.

For a moment I panicked and right then I could have ruined it all. But deep inside I realised that what they were trying to do to me, men had been doing to women in industry for years – intimidate us. And I was not going to have it. Indeed it helped to make me feel quite bolshie. Then I remembered the advice from three of my more senior, elder colleagues who tended to take me under their wing. 'Settle yourself in,' they had told me. 'Take your time, take a couple of deep breaths and don't look at the delegates near you – throw your voice over them.' It was good advice then and it is still sound. It helped me keep my nerve and I put across my speech, firmly, and reached my peroration safely within the time limit; to over-run is even worse for a woman because that plays to the male argument that we always use two or three words where one would do. Not this time!

Surprise, surprise – it was all over. And as I stepped down from the rostrum there was applause – it had gone over well. Not only that; quite a few delegates were pleased to find that young, articulate people like me were willing to play a role in the union's affairs.

When I regained the safety of my own delegation there were hand clasps and hugs – 'You're blooded now!' someone summed up. And quite the best moment was when the London Central delegates came over to apologise, not realising that it was their attempt to throw me that had steeled my determination and given me the self-confidence I needed. It would not be the last time the London Central members tried to destabilise me. But I never forgot that by holding firm and saying clearly, deliberately, what I wanted to say, I could get my message across, and that a woman's voice can usually be heard very clearly over the clamour. It was a good lesson learned.

Meetings, minutes, negotiation, hourly rates, time and a half – all those industrial relations terms swirled around me in the months ahead as more and more the thrill of being an active trade unionist consumed my daily life. I just loved it – to the cynic it may look or sound boring but to emerge from a meeting knowing that ordinary people's lives are to improve because of your efforts is exhilarating. It really is truly satisfying to complete a successful negotiation – any real bargainer will confess it.

So it was that by the time I was twenty-eight my first opportunity to place my foot on the ladder arose when a vacancy came up in the branch for the post of assistant secretary. 'Go for it,' said Sheridan. 'You can do it.' I felt I could but when the boss put it that way there was no hesitation on my part. Looking back I have little doubt that Sheridan had shrewdly calculated it was in his best interests too to have Bren or Brandy at his side – and to protect his back – rather than have to break in a new assistant secretary. And perhaps to nurture a future challenger.

One such undoubtedly was Harry Conroy, a member of the branch committee, who clearly had his eye on the officer vacancy. I did not trust him a bit and neither did Sheridan. That instinct turned out to be correct because some years later Conroy would seek to bring me down as the new branch secretary of Manchester. I won the election for assistant secretary fairly convincingly, in an honest contest against Conroy and some others – I was the only woman standing in the election – but I little knew it was the start of a bitterness which went deep. Eventually it probably consumed him.

As the result was declared, however, I had no knowledge of it and generally the branch reacted well. Wherever I went amongst the major print, paper and packing companies in the north-west there was a warm reception. We had many women members at firms such as Kellogg's, the huge US-owned cereals company in Trafford Park, and the important plant of Her Majesty's Stationery Office at Chadderton, near Oldham, where the members had perhaps not followed union activities very closely. But they went out of their way to tell me they had voted this time!

And when I started to turn up outside the factories in my new blue MG sports car, paid for with a three-year loan from the branch deducted monthly from my equally new salary, members indicated their approval. Suddenly they quite liked the idea of being represented by a young blonde woman with some style. And the bosses seemed to approve too. Many years later some of them actually told me they had seen me as a 'breath of fresh air' – as they themselves put it – and they decided I was the person who would be able to embrace the changes that were urgently needed if the industry was to remain competitive in the north-west.

My salary was good for a young woman and I was being paid far more than most of my friends. I had independence, a job I loved, responsibility and a foot on a career ladder. Looking back my family must have been rather surprised but they took it in their stride and I certainly tried to make up for my absences and long hours, maybe buying them dinner or taking my mother out for an occasional Saturday spending spree. She loved climbing into the MG and taking off for the boutiques in Lytham – and so did our Angus, the family's white terrier, who sat in the back, nose in the air, barking at the other dogs as we passed. Perhaps he thought they were owned by employers . . .

Chapter 3

The year 1971 will go down as an important one in the history of the trade union movement. And in mine, I suppose, because the clash with the Heath government over the introduction of the Industrial Relations Act presented me with an unexpected opportunity, though not one I had sought.

The movement's campaign against what it saw as an oppressive piece of law-making by the new Conservative government brought to Manchester Bill Keys, the union's newly elected general president, effectively the No. 2. Keys was quite refreshing as a leader of our union compared to people such as Tom Smith, who hated leaving London and kept his head down. But there had been change at the top of SOGAT, the new name of the union, and Keys clearly represented it. A left-winger, he perhaps saw in the new legislation a chance to stamp his authority on the union and set out on a nationwide tour of the branches.

As one of the biggest outside London, our branch came early on his hitlist and we arranged a well-attended meeting for him to address. It went well and there were several supporting speeches from the platform, but I noticed that no woman had put a point of view so I asked if I could speak. Keys generously waved me to the rostrum and I seized my chance to explain what the onerous new Tory Act would mean to the lives of ordinary working women.

This was not about whether union power should be cut back by government, I argued; it was more about the right of ordinary men and women to combine and to protect their working environment. It affected equal pay and sex discrimination, and it would prevent the union representing its members properly. As I spoke women members in the audience started to nod their heads in agreement, and I realised I was touching nerves.

Keys saw it too and gave Joe Sheridan a nudge. 'She's good – who is she?' he whispered.

'She's my new assistant secretary – her name's Brenda Dean. Good speaker,' confided my boss.

A few days later the phone went and it was Keys calling from London. He explained he wanted me to join him on his campaign round the rest of the branches in the north-west – to put across the woman trade unionist's point of view, just as he had seen me do in Manchester. Would I do it?

'If you think I can be of help and can do it, of course I will be delighted to help you on the campaign, Mr Keys.'

'Call me Bill,' he said. 'That's settled, then.'

So we toured the branches around the region, which stretched from Burnley and Oldham in the east to Liverpool and across to Flint in north Wales. It was a great learning experience because it gave me an opportunity to study the way Keys handled the meetings, played an audience and clearly drew on it, to hammer his theme. As I watched I polished my speech and improved my speaking technique. SOGAT was arguing against registration and defying the government and it was heady stuff.

I did not appreciate it at the time but it was also a chance to show myself to a wider audience of the union than just my own branch. The union had no woman officer at national level and though 30 per cent of its membership were women it had hardly bothered to cultivate their interests. They received differential pay to the male members and seldom had their individual needs given special attention.

Our big campaign culminated in a rally in Trafalgar Square, traditionally the venue for major protest. As we stood at the base of Nelson's Column, a lion at either side of us and the speakers' voices echoing back from the National Gallery, I little thought that within a few months I would be there, speaking from the rostrum. I watched the technique of those who went before me, including that of Vic Feather, then the No. 2 at the TUC, and in my book a very big gun indeed. Others too spoke to wind up the crowd.

When the campaign ended I realised again I had learned a lot, and made my name much better known in the north-west, particularly with the women members. That was one of the reasons I later saw scope in the International Women's Year of 1975 to try to alert women workers to its significance. I was now much more aware of the way that women were treated as second class and I was always on the lookout to combat it. The Year looked like a golden opportunity.

But when I asked what Manchester was going to do to celebrate the Year I found that nothing – absolutely nothing – was planned by the city, nor by enterprise and certainly not by the trade unions. It seemed that in the north-west, the cradle of the suffragette movement (the Pankhursts lived in Manchester) and a pioneer in the employment of women in the textile mills, in wartime engineering such as building the Lancaster bomber at A.V. Roe at Trafford Park and in the beginnings of the computer industry, our region's role in International Women's Year was going to slip by unmarked.

Not if I had anything to do with it, I decided.

I started with my own branch and soon got the approval of the branch committee, which agreed without much discussion to spend some money. I do not know that the delegates had any idea how it would turn out but perhaps they knew enough by now to realise that I had some sense of organisation and that the money would not be wasted. I then contacted other unions with big memberships and offices in the north-west, such as the Amalgamated Engineering Union, the Transport and General Workers' Union and the Union of Shop, Distributive and Allied Workers. They all had significant numbers of women workers and could not afford to be left behind by a print union. And when they heard that SOGAT was willing to contribute they too put their hands in their pockets to boost our funds.

But I decided not to limit contact to the trade union movement – to me it seemed right that the Year's celebration went across the traditional boundaries. The Year was about women – not just some women. And so I made contact with all the political parties – not just Labour but the Conservatives, the Liberals and the Communists too; also contacted were the government office in the north-west, the local branch of the Fawcett Society, which campaigns for equality between men and women, and any other women's organisations I could find. I wrote to schools, hospitals, the police, local authorities – indeed anywhere women might be involved.

I invited them all to send a representative to a social evening in our large upstairs club room above our branch office. It was big but even so I could see that the numbers coming meant there would not be room enough for everyone to bring their partner. That went down badly with Colin Barnet, the regional secretary of the TUC, who grumbled about his wife being excluded from what he felt should just be a trade union affair. This was a gift to the *Manchester Evening News* – a row in the union ranks – and at first it shook me. But I thought about it and decided Barnet was wrong and I responded to his attack, for which he never forgave me. Looking back he probably felt that the TUC ought to have been leading the event. But neither Barnet nor the regional TUC had done anything.

Suddenly it all snowballed and Barnet's quibbles were soon forgotten. The organising committee which I had formed found itself at the head of one of the biggest events ever held in Manchester, attracting the attention of the local newspapers, local radio and regional television. It was another learning experience for me. Suddenly we were news. I found myself giving interviews and getting to know and feel comfortable with local media people.

The *Manchester Evening News* really rose to the occasion. I persuaded the management to let me have their front office showroom, centrally located on Deansgate, one of the best thoroughfares in the city, for an exhibition on the contribution of women in so many different spheres through the ages. Shirley Conran, the author, and then a very big name in the growing field of women's journalism, came to Manchester specially to open the show.

The crowning moment to the campaign came when I approached the Chief Constable of Greater Manchester Police and asked if he could arrange to have our parade through the city centre to be led by a woman police constable on horseback rather than a man. I was told that no commitment could be made. But on the morning of 9 May 1975, as we started our march, there astride a magnificent grey horse – I'm sure it was a mare – was a very smartly uniformed woman constable. She was the cherry on our cake. (I learned subsequently that she was the first woman to be recruited into the mounted unit in the city.) And when we started off behind her were the men of the quite superb Manchester police band.

The parade itself was stupendous and with fifty-one floats was one of the biggest ever held in our city. The police had even arranged for all the floats and transport to be accommodated in the car park in front of Strangeways Prison.

The whole day went off without a hitch and the festive mood was magical. The parade ended at Platt Fields, the site of many historic events in Manchester, and the keynote speaker was the formidable Nancy Sear, once in personnel work and later an academic at the London School of Economics – and later still a colleague of mine in the House of Lords. Sear was always in the forefront of the campaign for women's rights.

The unions were very prominent at the parade. Once they got the message they pulled out all the stops and were very supportive – including a contingent from London printers which included some of those delegates who had tried to send me up on my maiden speech at Scarborough.

A number of schools, particularly those which had only girl pupils, also really seized the chance to bring out the significance of International Women's Year. We invited all schools to take part in an essay competition on the theme 'Equality, Development and Peace'. That presented me with my first opportunity to make the acquaintance of the late Brian Redhead, later to become the doyen of the BBC *Today* programme, but at that time editor of the *Manchester Evening News*. Apart from giving enthusiastic support in the news columns, Redhead agreed to be the judge of the schools essay competition, which turned out to be a daunting task since we had several hundred entries.

I found Redhead to be a great supporter – and great fun – and he became a good friend whose early death, quite suddenly, really affected me. We kept touch over the years as our careers progressed in parallel – though he never gave up his home in Macclesfield. He had a flat in one of the tower blocks in London's Barbican where we had dinner. And we often met up at the big TUC and party conferences. His flat looked down on the floodlit St Paul's Cathedral and the outlook over London was magical. If he could not get back at night to his home in Macclesfield his flat was not a bad substitute. Redhead's neighbours included the late John Smith and his wife Elizabeth. Another at the time was Arthur Scargill, the mine workers' leader – 'He keeps his coal in the bath, you know,' said the mischievous Redhead. He was never short of a laugh or a piece of good gossip.

Another spin off from International Women's Year, which perhaps I did not fully appreciate at the time, was that the event had not done my own profile any harm. Not only had I come across in the media as someone with wider interests at heart than simply union-related issues, but my members, particularly the women, were quite proud to see SOGAT leading. And I had made contact with a wide cross-section of the city I loved, Manchester – where I always say God's Own Country begins.

I also felt I wanted something else to come out of Women's Year, something of significance to women in particular. Then I had an idea about cancer screening, which in those days was in its infancy and the disease itself an unspoken subject. I talked to the cancer screening programme in Manchester and together we worked out a schedule for them to visit each printing establishment in our region and to screen for cervical and breast cancer. The branch committee backed the idea and agreed to give £2,000 for the production of a short film to teach women self-examination for detecting the early signs of breast cancer.

After a little prod one or two employers came on board and accepted that this campaign was worthwhile. It was the old story – once the more enlightened agreed to give time to their women workers, the rest of the bosses fell into line. We told them that apart from giving women workers time off to be screened they would need to pay three pounds a head for the screening but that was all they would need to do. We undertook to arrange the visiting schedule, fix the appointments and be responsible for all the administration.

I learned a lot from this initiative – certainly that once you have determined something is going to happen, then you can make it happen.

Oddly I had more difficulty with the SOGAT women members than from anywhere else. For a start cancer was then unmentionable and most women did not want to know about it. They were fatalistic about their chances and felt that if cancer struck, that was that. But a good supporter of mine, who was Mother of the Chapel at her plant, was found through the screening to be suffering from the early stages of cervical cancer. Fortunately, it had been diagnosed in good time and could be treated. The word not only went round her members but also quickly spread to other women workers in neighbouring factories and soon we were having no difficulty in persuading them to put their names down for a check-up.

There was still one hurdle – such was the chauvinism existing then that the women were too intimidated to stop their job and walk through the factory to the screening unit. 'As soon as we walk to the door there will be wolf whistles and all kinds of remarks from the chaps,' explained one young woman member. So we arranged with the screening unit that they would set up at Factory A and see women from nearby Factory B. Then a couple of days later they would switch to the second factory location and the women would slip quietly away there one by one.

It worked a treat and looking back I think this was the singular best outcome to the International Year in my city.

And then out of the blue I was invited to speak in Trafalgar Square, when the TUC asked me to take part in the rally they were organising at the culmination of International Women's Year. By now I was confident I could speak in public and could generally get across my point, but speaking in the square still presented me with a major challenge. There were 50,000 people in the parade to Nelson's Column and the speakers were headed by Marie Paterson, that year's TUC president, and my personal heroine, Barbara Castle. On the plinth at the foot of Nelson's Column were many other well-known faces but at thirty-two I was the youngest to be addressing the rally.

Adding to the challenge was a group of noisy young women, so-called feminists, dressed in jeans and anoraks, who seemed determined for some reason on disruption. And they were having some success, though it was hard to fathom their objective. I decided to take them on and as one of them shouted I stopped and looked straight at her. It suddenly went quiet. 'Yes, you have a point; we will have to look at that,' I said. It seemed to surprise the group that someone was seriously considering what they had to say and they quietened down to give me a relatively clear run.

The Trafalgar Square rally was the culmination of an idea I had had all those months ago which I had put forward rather tentatively at the branch committee. But it had been well worth it and incidentally not a bad mark for Brenda Dean either, although that had never been my intention. As for Nelson, I did not know then that it would not be all that long before I spoke again in that historic location, when I would once more have to conquer the butterflies and speak under the watchful eye of England's national hero and his four lions.

Chapter 4

The year of 1976 brought me trauma – and quite unexpectedly an unheralded opportunity.

At the office in Salford we were again heavily involved in planning the delegate conference for the whole union, which was to take place in the Mecca Ballroom in Blackpool. The union's conference was held every second year and was a big affair lasting a week with about 800 delegates. Joe Sheridan had been asked to preside over the planning by the north-west region. By now our branch had acquired a reputation for organisation but Sheridan soon handed the job to me. It was meat and drink to me – even today there is nothing I enjoy more than pulling together all the strands and seeing an event coming together 'on the night'. This event, however, was to be very different.

Sheridan had not been at all well and was on a kind of light-duty regime. He suffered from a heart condition and what was called fluid retention so that increasingly he had been leaving me to get on with the day-to-day duties of running the branch. Adding in the task of preparing for the Blackpool conference was to me just one more for my worklist. I really did not mind it at all – in fact I revelled in the challenge.

Although I say it myself, the conference did go off well and there were quite a few complimentary tributes given to the north-west region at the conclusion of the last session and a warm vote of thanks, to which Sheridan was naturally asked to respond. He had been a bit quiet all week and clearly was not his normal self but he was a good speaker and he brought his peroration neatly to a conclusion.

But as he stepped down off the stage, from the back of the room I saw him stagger and then collapse. Several delegates ran to him before I could get there but I could tell it was serious and told someone to call for an ambulance. The medical team arrived very quickly and put Sheridan into a wheelchair to take him rapidly off to Blackpool's Victoria Hospital. Without hesitating I insisted on going with him in the ambulance even though the conference needed winding up, delegates were streaming off to their hotels and to the railway station and there were a thousand and one tasks to tie up.

But in my heart I felt it was going to be too late – I saw the look the ambulance men exchanged as they carried Sheridan out. And on arrival at the hospital a doctor quickly pronounced him dead.

Quite suddenly I realised I had lost my mentor, my sponsor and the friend who had guided and taught me most of what I knew since I was sixteen. It was quite shattering.

Somewhat dazed I oversaw the wind-down at the ballroom and watched the crates off to the Salford office, and then my father arrived to take me to my home. By now I was the proud owner of my own first home, a modern bungalow in Thornton, on the Fylde peninsula between Blackpool and Fleetwood, an area from which many years later I would select my title of residence in the House of Lords. As my dad drove me there I was lost in thought.

But he wasn't. 'What you need now, my girl, is to go to bed and get some rest.' For once I was not in charge and did not argue. Dad made me have something to eat and then, although I didn't realise it at the time, gave me a sleeping pill. Or maybe two. He would never have got away with that if I had been on top of things.

Dad was right, though, and for a number of hours I was out completely and so it was not until the next day that I began to collect my thoughts. I realised that the branch had a crisis and needed to make some decisions so I started to get in touch with the committee members. I called a Branch Committee meeting for the following Monday morning.

Maybe it was naïveté or maybe it was shock at Sheridan's death but the thought of succession had not really entered my head. My first thought was to ensure that the branch affairs were properly conducted. But I learned that weekend a lesson about the Labour movement which never left me – that a death of leader may be sad to those around the personality concerned but to others it is an opportunity. And there can be some very unseemly scrambles almost over the coffin. One only has to think back to the deaths of Hugh Gaitskell, or more recently John Smith, to realise that in the Labour and trade union movement, if you leave a vacuum someone moves in to fill it very quickly indeed.

As I discovered by the Saturday evening, the telephone lines around the branch area had been very busy indeed. It was a branch committee member named Ken Heseltine who alerted me. He was Father of the Chapel at the *Manchester Evening News* and clearly fancied putting his hat in the ring but he had the decency to call me. I could not say that for some of the other aspirants.

'Who's going to go for the job? We need someone to take over the branch,' people said as I rang around to fix the committee meeting. I did not respond directly but it became increasingly clear the prospect of my standing was not even being contemplated. I thought it over. The men seemed to be saying that it was alright for a woman to do the No. 2 job – to organise, to negotiate, to speak publicly, to raise the branch profile – but the top job was clearly Man's Work, and that was that. So, as I saw it, I could stay on for years as the No. 2 or get out of the movement and seek a future elsewhere. Why? I asked myself.

Quite suddenly I had come up against what many women have experienced – the so-called glass ceiling. It was that perhaps more than anything else which persuaded me I was not going to give up without a fight. I was going to give it my best shot. Joe Sheridan had trained me for this task, he had always urged me to go for a challenge and, looking back, although he probably had not thought it through fully himself, I realised he had been grooming me as his successor.

But I clearly needed to have a plan. Events were moving fast over the weekend and somehow I had to pre-empt them.

When the branch committee assembled on the Monday morning I spelt out calmly what was to happen. I did not ask for views; I just laid it all out. In deference to Sheridan, I declared, the branch now had to conduct itself with dignity. We had our respects to pay to our late branch secretary and the branch would organise and pay for his funeral in full co-operation with his family. There would be many in Manchester and elsewhere in the country who would wish to attend. All that had to be organised. In the meantime the branch would be in official mourning for a week and not until that had been concluded would it turn to the matter of filling the vacancy. An election would then be announced and nominations called for in full accordance with established practice. In the meantime the branch would be run by me as acting branch secretary.

In case anyone was in any doubt, I added that I was aware that 'worms were coming out of the woodwork and I had a bloody big hammer to knock them back in!' – a broad hint against electioneering. This was a very important time for the Manchester branch of the union and it must be united in ensuring that everything was done properly.

I then produced a circular I had already written setting this all out, which I asked the committee to approve for circulation to all our chapels. This was so clearly the right way to proceed that there was no discussion or argument. If someone had tried to raise the question of the succession – and I have no doubt some wanted to do so – it would have been felt so out of keeping with the mood. Even the most ambitious around the committee table could judge that to be a wrong step. So the circular was approved and the meeting adjourned.

I then got on with organising Joe Sheridan's funeral, with the help of his son, Billy. His family were content to agree to this. They probably had not realised just what an important figure he had been in the union movement in the north-west and in SOGAT. I threw myself into ensuring all the arrangements went well and although I did not see it at the time, that demonstrated to the branch and the chapels that their assistant branch secretary was now running the show and all was going smoothly.

The funeral service was held at Manchester Cathedral. It was a major city occasion and there were fifty black cars parked in line outside. The traffic had to be stopped by the police for the event. Anybody who was active in Manchester and the north-west at that time attended – MPs, employers, civic leaders, trade unionists – they were all at the cathedral that day. After the ceremony there was a lunch at the Imperial Hotel in Blackpool. I know now that the wake is where many important events in history have been clinched but I was still on a learning curve. It soon became clear to me though that many of the key movers and shakers in SOGAT were present and watching developments closely.

Before that, however, there had been an unexpected visit at the branch office by two national officers from London. Without a prior phone call Bill Miles, a national officer, and Michael Upcroft, a member of the union's national executive, came to the office. I was furious and for a moment or two lost my cool. To me it seemed to be a sudden call to check up on me. Miles, who became my closest adviser later in the Wapping dispute, had a beautiful smile – I had little doubt that in the past he had been quite a ladies' man – and said simply, 'We just came to take you for lunch and see if there was anything we could do to help.' It was quite disarming and I chastised myself for thinking ill of them, but events had started to move at such a pace that I was no longer shocked to discover the lengths that people would go in the run-up to an election.

When the contest was called I found I was up against several other candidates, all men. One of the most prominent was Harry Conroy, who quite clearly believed the job was his by right. What right I never discovered, although I was well aware that Sheridan had considered him not only a lightweight, but very untrustworthy too. Conroy worked at the Co-operative Wholesale Society plant at Reddish and so he had quite a big chapel and a seat on the branch committee. But he was not as popular as he imagined and in the results was poorly placed.

His failure, however, unleashed a malevolence which even after all these years I still find shocking to think about. He was behind a 'newsletter' which mysteriously began to appear around the branch pointing at my 'sports car' – which I was buying myself, admittedly with the help of a branch loan – and claiming that I supposedly owned a house in the wealthy area of St Anne's, way outside my price range, and that my parents also had a big house in the area. In truth my home in Thornton was quite modest, and my dad, bless him, had sunk his moderate railwayman's life savings as the deposit on another bungalow not far away in Cleveleys.

I did not realise it at the time but this vendetta by a smearing newsletter technique was to be used by Conroy again, later in my career when I had developed a thicker skin, but the first time it was quite unsettling. I resolved to take the issue head on and sent the material to Albert Powell, the union's president and No. 2 officer, responsible for upholding the SOGAT rule book and maintaining discipline. A formal charge was laid against Conroy and under the rules I was then supposed to say absolutely nothing and not to discuss the matter with anyone. But the scurrilous newsletters continued, giving the impression to ordinary rank-and-file members that if I was not denying the material then maybe there was something in it.

I decided to ignore the rules and fight fire with fire. It is a policy I later adopted on several occasions in my career. I answered the charges in a circular printing the checkable facts side by side against Conroy's anonymous lies. Each time a smear came out I immediately counter-attacked. I made no accusations but simply told the truth about my personal circumstances. I was not to know, but quite a number of inactive members, particularly women, started to read my replies and to identify with me. Overall it was doing Conroy and his clique more harm than me and gradually his attacks petered out. In the meantime, though, he had helped me to raise my own profile amongst the membership, which was to be very helpful in the ballot ahead. The clash also helped to raise my name locally and I was becoming better known in the industrial field of the north-west, which in those days had a major manufacturing workforce.

I found I quite liked media events, meat and drink today to trade unionists and MPs, but rarer in those days. I remember a call from the BBC in the north-west asking if I would appear on an anniversary of the wartime programme *Workers' Playtime*, which was to be broadcast from McVitie and Price, the biscuit people. That was when I met and became friendly with Sandra Chalmers, sister of the better-known Judith, who was to interview me. The compère was Nicholas Parsons, who rather patronisingly asked me a daft question on whether it was fair that women had to spend a penny to go to the toilet and men did not. I brushed that aside politely but contemptuously and received a huge roar of approval from the women workers in the plant. They seemed to like what they could see – a woman trade unionist smartly turned out, not scared to say what she thought and not willing to be put down by smart alecs.

Once the branch election results were declared it was back to business. I had easily beaten all the other contenders, some probably better known in the branch than me. Conroy retired to lick his wounds but certainly not to accept the result, and for some years to come he was going to be fairly close to my back and with a knife to hand if he got the chance. But the vast majority were with me, I felt, and accepted the election result. In the office, in particular, there was not all that much change, as for some time I had in effect been acting branch secretary because of Joe Sheridan's ill health.

My place as No. 2 was won in an election by Gerry Foley, who worked successfully in harness with me for several years even though we differed strongly on politics. Foley was a committed, honest member of the Communist Party and thought politically. I was a member of the Labour Party but had no dogmatic political philosophy – indeed I tended to see myself as an industrial animal and wanted little to do with party politics intruding in the workplace. Come to think of it, I was moving in the direction of what was one day to become New Labour.

Certainly I was keen to develop good relations with the employers in Manchester and the north-west and they seemed to welcome me. I had already shown my negotiating ability in recent months and most of them took the change in their stride. There were humorous moments, though, as some macho management found it hard to come to terms with having for the first time to bargain with a woman across the negotiating table.

The Newspaper Proprietors Association (NPA) in the north-west had a tradition of hard bargaining but when the negotiations were over everyone always had a drink together before parting – even if there had been a failure to agree. Jack Collins, who managed the *Daily Mail*, chaired the employers' side and when we had concluded asked me what I would drink. I had already thought about it and realised it would set tongues wagging if I simply asked for a tonic water.

'Dry sherry, please, Jack.'

'If you're doing a man's job you'll have a bloody man's drink,' he blurted out.

'In that case I'll have a tonic water,' I replied, and added, 'If that's going to be the way you negotiate you're going to be dead easy, Jack.'

A little later it was time for the annual NPA Christmas reception, which had always been an all-male affair. I don't think there was anything dubious about the event, such as what they nowadays euphemistically call 'lap dancing' – no more than the odd blue joke. It was probably more of a hard-drinking, all-boys-together situation. But certainly no invitation from the NPA arrived for me although I saw them come in for Foley and others.

I gave it careful thought and decided I could not allow this situation to pass or another would simply confront me later. Instead I sent a message through that my invitation had not arrived but that I had checked my diary and would be able to attend.

I thought carefully about what I would wear on the evening of the event and arrived smartly turned out but wearing nothing too flashy or frivolous. I walked into the room, spotted Jack Collins, the tallest man there, and made a direct approach to him, hand outstretched. 'Hello, Jack,' I said. 'How nice to see you – how are you?'

He gulped, I think, but that was all. He greeted me in return and we were soon into conversation and that was it – the era of the NPA all-male event was over.

But though newspaper production and distribution was important in the north-west it would be a mistake to think that it provided the majority of our membership, an impression confirmed by Wapping. In my region the majority of my members were in general printing, packaging, box-making, paper-making, bookbinding and a variety of inter-related skills which never ceased to fascinate me.

One of our biggest groups of members worked at Kellogg's, packaging Corn Flakes, Frosties, Rice Krispies and a myriad of other brands. But though on the surface it looked efficient, the truth was that our plant was nothing like as productive as sister plants in the United States. And that was not because our members were particularly indolent but because they were using outdated machinery installed, years earlier, deep in the basement of the factory. The equipment needed replacing but the management were unwilling to reinvest unless they could get assurances that the new equipment would be used efficiently and that the staffing levels would fall.

For the first time we were able to put into action an idea suggested initially by Sheridan, that members should see the new equipment in use and witness for themselves the obvious savings and efficiencies which would not only make their plant better but probably ensure its future; in other words continue to provide their jobs.

I always had got on well with the management and when we put these thoughts to them they were quick to respond. A few weeks later a group made up of chapel officials at Kellogg's, some branch officers including me, together with representatives of the rival so-called craft union, the National Graphical Association, set off from Manchester by train for Germany. The Kellogg's management had done their homework and we saw everything we wanted and were able to talk with the German workers and the officers from their print union. And each evening when we had done our work, Kellogg's saw to it that there was a good meal, with wine and beer for those who wanted it – and most did. We went on to Switzerland to see where the new equipment was made and had detailed talks with the manufacturers about the technical changes they had made and what was planned. And then we flew to Chicago to visit a number of machinery manufacturing plants and see the latest technical developments in actual use.

Over a time span of about eight months we negotiated with the company, which of course had to satisfy itself that spending many millions of pounds was going to be fully justifiable to its board. But it was not long before our members were talking amongst themselves not about if the new machinery might come but when it would arrive and how soon it would be fully operational.

When we had negotiated the deal, including quantifying the savings, and the report I had prepared for the branch executive had been discussed it was virtually all over – the Kellogg's chapel representatives made it crystal clear that there was no question of any veto coming from that direction. And they accepted what became known as Brenda's Rule – in any deal in which big savings were to be made there should be a third for the company, a third for the employees and a third for the customer.

It was an important lesson not only for me but also for other managers in the north-west, and word of it quickly spread. Just like the trade unions, the employers were in frequent touch with one another, often changing jobs or meeting socially or on the golf course, and it was soon known how successful the Kellogg's mission had been. So the visit that we made was the first of several; over the years we went to see new machinery in the USA, Germany, France and Switzerland. We even saw papermaking in the forests of Karelia, on the Finnish–Russian border.

A few years later I used the same technique to try to introduce change faster into Fleet Street ahead of the Wapping confrontation. I took a group from the London newspaper branches to the United States to see the so-called new technology – it may have been new to Fleet Street but not to regions such as the north-west and Yorkshire, where such methods had been introduced progressively for years (see Chapter 7).

Another idea that came to me about that time was what I have since thought of as my Fledgling Policy. Every now and again in my career I have come upon young women with potential but who are quite often lacking in confidence. They have the ability, but their conditioning, upbringing or just the men around them never permit them to spread their wings. Yet Joe Sheridan had given me a chance – a kid so shy that her parents had worried about her lack of confidence. So I resolved that if I had the chance I would try to help develop some of the young women I would meet over my career.

I suppose it began back in the branch office at Salford, where I could now run the office with my methods. I had four young women working in my team and from the beginning it was fun. June Swinbourne became my personal assistant, whereas previously she had been trying to look after Sheridan. It included a number of young women, one of the youngest being Diane Russell, who years later was to become my personal assistant when I went into the House of Lords.

Swinbourne watched and learned; following in my footsteps after I won election to the national office and moved to London, she stood for election as assistant branch secretary and won. Until the demise of the last printing union (which subsumed SOGAT) with the takeover by the engineers' union Amicus, Swinbourne enjoyed a successful career as a union official though, like me, she had never been in printing herself. I like to think that some of the grounding working for me helped in her career. Later in my career at ICSTIS, the premium rate telephone services watchdog, I found several young women worth encouraging. It was the same at the Housing Corporation and indeed at several government departments where I had contact. More recently I find young women are more determined and less inhibited than they were – than I was – and no longer shy to admit they are seeking a role model. I hope my Fledgling Policy helped a little.

But back to the eventful year of 1976. I had two approaches then, which would, as it turned out, have quite an impact on my future.

The first started with a phone call from Whitehall to sound me out on whether I would be interested in joining the staff of Harold Wilson's Cabinet Policy Unit. This was heady stuff for a young woman from the north-west; the bright lights of London beckoned. I listened carefully to the person on the other end and decided to play along without commitment, agreeing to travel down to London for a formal interview.

How I had come to the attention of those in Whitehall was a mystery and I never did find out who had put my name forward, although several people later laid claim to it. But after agreeing to go for the interview I felt I had better tell the union general secretary, now Bill Keys, before he heard it from elsewhere. His reaction, predictably, was hostile, but he did not instruct me to abandon the interview and I duly presented myself to the Cabinet Office at 70 Whitehall. As I waited to be shown into an interview room I little thought that years later I would have a permanent pass to the premises.

I then met two people from the policy team, who seemed to be assessing me as they outlined the kind of work on which I would be involved. It would be a two-year temporary post though it might be extended. But as I listened it quickly became apparent to me just how transient could be the life of a political adviser even in the days of Harold Wilson.

Back on the train from Euston it did not take me long to make a decision. Here was I, my own boss, with a good salary, a pension and my own car – and I enjoyed working in the trade union movement with its members. I would be mad to abandon that for the heady wine of illusory power. I went straight to Blackpool, where our union conference was about to start, and saw Keys at his hotel on South Shore. When I told him about the interview and my decision he completely changed tack and told me I was mad to turn it down. If it had been him, said Keys, he would have grabbed at the opportunity. It may have been the truth because there is little doubt that Keys had ability but that he had achieved it by his own efforts with very little education or training. And his aphrodisiac was power – and plenty of it.

Another consideration was that I had not mentioned the approach to the TUC, which rather liked to keep a handle on this kind of appointment and ensure that anyone getting a public job had their 'seal of approval'. So they would not have liked it when a few weeks later I had the second approach to which I decided to give serious consideration. It was to become a part-time member of the Supplementary Benefits Commission, which at the time was chaired by a wonderful man named Professor David Donnison.

The commission provided the safety net for those who fell outside welfare benefits and was trying to make sense of the arcane system of payments being made to the unemployed, the disabled, the homeless and people in real need. I found the work very absorbing and worthwhile, and this time I was to be on the commission itself, not just a researcher. It was my first experience of social work but it started an interest and of course crossed over into my work as a trade unionist. It probably laid the foundations for my position years later as the first woman to chair the Housing Corporation – certainly I found that the lack of a home is usually the beginning of the downward slide which leads people to become totally dependent on benefits and even to begging on the streets.

Before I could take up the job, though, I realised I had to be very careful about the people who were paying me as their branch secretary. At the time the formal offer came through to join the commission I was leading a branch delegation to the biggest print exhibition in Europe, known as DRUPA, at Dusseldorf. I had taken the decision that instead of farming out our people to guest houses and small hotels around the crowded city, I would try to keep the team together by taking a block booking aboard a large barge moored on the river bank in the city centre. Each delegate had their own comfortable cabin. We ate well for breakfast and many good restaurants were within walking distance. Each evening before we set off for an evening meal we would have a drink together on deck while comparing notes on what we had seen and learned during the day, and all in all the floating accommodation was judged to be a great success. It was in that atmosphere that I called them to order and announced I had a problem and sought the branch committee's advice.

I explained about the commission and why I thought it would be good for me and for the branch if I was to accept. I gave an assurance that I would not allow it to interfere with my branch duties in any way and that I would hand over my commission fees, less tax, to the branch. In fact they subsequently went into a charity, the Retired Members' Fund.

It only took a few minutes. The committee members were unanimous that I should take the commission post – not one query was raised and in fact they wished me good luck. It was a reaction typical of the generous, warm-hearted branch which had given me my chance in life and once again I vowed never to let them down. Hopefully, in that glorious warm sunny evening, they knew it.

Of course, once again I had bypassed the TUC on the appointment but although nothing was said I realised I had probably taken a slot that Congress House would happily have filled. I suspect that Donnison was never likely to take kindly to a Buggins' Turn nominee, however. He told me later that he had sought from Barbara Castle, then the social services secretary, an undertaking that she would only appoint to the commission people Donnison believed he could work with and would make a contribution. It was a useful lesson again for me and one that one day I would employ. An added bonus for me was a letter of appointment personally signed by Castle, my heroine.

These moves, coupled with a nasty period within SOGAT, probably contributed to an interesting development at the union. Keys tried to carry the union with him on what was in effect a challenge by the London Central branch on who ran the union and where the power lay. But for once he had over-reached himself and his old London colleagues would have none of it. Keys probably should have known better since, as the former branch secretary of London Central, he had practised the very same bloody-mindedness and strong-arm tactics for which the London print workers were infamous. Indeed it was the first of a number of opportunities which, if picked up, might have avoided the ultimate disaster of Wapping.

The showdown came at the union's national conference, at which the Yorkshire branch secretary, Dennis Hill, and I opposed the London mob. 'You're not on,' I told them as they got up and walked out of the conference hall. With the combined votes of the north-west and Yorkshire, Keys carried the conference but there was very bad blood indeed between London and the rest of us. I had forged an alliance with Hill and the pair of us were ultimately to contend the future leadership of the union, but we remained friends and I would have very much liked to have him at my side in later years. Sadly it was not to be, as I will explain in the next chapter.

I knew I had made some new enemies in London but thought little of it at the time. And later that evening I was in trouble for going along to the London reception – I was supping with the enemy, I was told. To me that was rubbish. Yes, there had been a very strong disagreement but we were all in the same union, were all colleagues and soon would have to work together again.

Keys had been thinking. It had dawned on him that the power base that had been built up in the north-west by combining our individual branch votes and working as a team was ultimately a threat to the union leadership. Some weeks later I had a call from him to tell me of a new post that was being created which was ideal for me. There was to be a national women's officer of SOGAT and it was a 'perfect' slot-in for Brenda Dean! There was just one snag – it was an appointment and not an elected post and therefore the incumbent was dependent on the orders of the general secretary. There was no seat on the National Executive and no vote; the job was simply to be women's officer, just for women members.

I would not wish to be unkind to Keys, but I think it had just begun to dawn on him that, horror of horrors, his successor would not be his choice. And worse, it could be a woman!

Once again I decided I was staying in the north-west. And once again I had noted the difference between the illusion of influence and the fact of real power that a ballot bestows upon the elected. It did not take me long to decline Keys's kind offer.

Some months later a new offer emerged which did sound quite attractive and challenging. It was not that I was bored or without challenge in the branch but

I had fairly quickly got on top of the task and worked out a system which is one which I have used many times in my career.

June Swinbourne had become my secretary and there were three other young women working with her. (I don't go out of my way to recruit women to work for me personally but it has seemed to work out that way.) This small team worked together and indeed played together and they were on top of the job. My diary was managed centrally and I never took on an engagement unless the back room knew what was going on. They learned to juggle my time and to decide which engagements should have priority – although I of course always had the final say-so. They prepared letters for me, which I always insisted on signing personally, and the system quickly developed and became very efficient. You had to be up very early in the morning to wrong-foot us.

But it also meant that by efficient use of my time I could consider a new offer that came my way – to join the Price Commission, set up by the Labour government to monitor price movements, while another body, the Prices and Incomes Board, tried desperately to influence wages. Roy Hattersley was the Secretary of State for Prices and Consumer Protection at the time and to the best of my knowledge I had never met him. He was from Sheffield and had a seat in the West Midlands and so I never associated him with my neck of the woods. But somehow my name had been suggested. I received a telephone call asking me to travel to London for an interview with the then permanent secretary, John Burgh, former private secretary to George Brown at the Department of Economic Affairs and later to be head of Trinity College, Oxford.

I was getting to realise the influence and importance of civil servants and to tell which branch they adhered to – to the four-fifths who say firmly 'we can't' or the crucial one-fifth who adhere to the view 'why can't we?' and are determined to move events along. Burgh seemed to belong more to the latter school of thought, despite his clearly classical approach and I was attracted to the offer that I should accept a two-year term as a full member of the commission.

It did not take me too long to make up my mind and a few weeks later I found myself sharing an office one day a week in a tower block at New Covent

Garden overlooking the Thames. My two companions were Ian Hay Davidson and Tony Colman. Davidson was a chartered accountant who was to become the chief executive of Lloyd's of London and Sadler's Wells, and managing partner of Arthur Andersen. Colman, who was with the Burton Group at the time, eventually became Labour MP for Putney.

The three of us hit it off and had plenty of laughs but on the way I learned a lot from both of them, particularly how the world of business and private enterprise looks at an issue. And maybe I opened their eyes a little about the way working people think about such matters.

They were fascinating days – not least when I was given my first task as chairman of a small group to conduct an inquiry into beds. Joking aside, there is a lot more to bed construction – the quality, the springing, the material – and marketing than many would believe. Ever since then I have become quite determined that a bed should be replaced regularly – far too many people hang onto old worn-out sleeping berths and wonder why they are always tired, or why visitors never want to stay. After ten years chuck it out!

At the time the suspicion was that the manufacturers had quietly come together to work out a case for a mutual price increase and our job was either to accept the argument and allow yet another price increase to be passed on to the pay-pegged consumer – or to force the bed makers to find their savings from improved productivity.

It was an important learning curve for me, because as a trade unionist I had to carry the panel with me and they were drawn from many differing backgrounds. But yet again my trade union experience and training paid off. If there is one field in which the movement is superb it is in organisation and the running of meetings, both to time and to reach a clear-cut decision. It goes back to the days of the late Walter Citrine, a former TUC general secretary, who wrote a simple bestseller for the TUC called *The ABC of Chairmanship*. Anyone given the task of running a meeting – big or small, never mind its status – should read the book and be confident in their judgements, in the knowledge that Citrine is not only in their pocket but right behind them.

The casework was quite heavy and the weight of the documents thudding through the letter box at my home in Thornton was daunting. And a lockable metal safe was delivered by Her Majesty's Stationery Office in which to keep it all. I think I left it in the garage.

My work with the Price Commission was a serious benefit to my members and to other trade unionists. We were on the inside taking part and influencing pricing decisions and it meant I was far better informed to discuss with my members what was going on around us all. But of course the sands were running out as Jim Callaghan, who had by now replaced Harold Wilson as Prime Minister, and his team struggled to restrain wages and prices and it was not all that long before they were to lose the battle – and leave the door open for a much better-known blonde woman than me to make her mark.

Chapter 5

SOGAT had its headquarters at Hadleigh in Essex, quite near Southend, hardly a natural location but handy for the general secretary, who lived locally. For the lay delegates it meant a difficult journey, changing trains in London. The executive met every other month, often for two days at a time, so that it usually meant an overnight stay. For those who liked a drink – and most of my male colleagues definitely did – a convivial evening in the bar with overnight expenses to meet the bill was quite acceptable. I found it a useful time to catch up with paperwork, but I would occasionally have a good meal, although Essex was not at that time high on the list of gourmet locations.

But there was also time for some gossip and a chance to build relationships. Dennis Hill, secretary of the Leeds branch, and I often chatted and on one occasion he raised the question at the back of both our minds – and the forefront of quite a few others on the SOGAT executive: the succession. Neither Bill Keys nor Albert Powell, the union's president and second in the hierarchy, were getting any younger. Hill explained that he wanted the No. 2 role as union president, in which he felt he would be much more comfortable than as general secretary. I listened as he outlined his thoughts and why he wanted to have responsibility for upholding the union's constitution and its rule book, to preside at the biennial conference and at the regular executive meetings.

Both of us had well-run, efficient branches but mine was by now much bigger than Yorkshire, financially in good shape and recruiting well. But if we ran against each other we both knew we would split the vote and a Londoner would get the job again. If, however, I would not contest the presidential vacancy and support him, Hill promised, looking me full in the eye, that he would then not stand for the general secretary post and would swing Yorkshire behind me. It was a good offer – though not without its risks. But it did not take me long to accept the deal and Hill and I shook hands on it.

Three months later Hill asked for another private talk with me when we were at Hadleigh again. He was clearly somewhat embarrassed. To my surprise he said his supporters had told him in forthright Yorkshire terms that he may have made a deal but they wanted none of it. Supposing the general secretary vacancy came up first – what then, they demanded? If he did not put his hat in the ring for the first post that came up he was unlikely to get a second chance. By blinking, in effect, it meant London would probably get not just one of the top jobs but both of them.

'You know what that means, Dennis,' I said. 'You have released me from the deal and that means I will be free to run in whatever election I wish.'

Hill said he knew what it meant and he accepted it. We shook hands. All bets were off. This was just as well, because a few months later Powell shook the union to its core by announcing to the executive that he was in ill health and after ten years in the post would be seeking early retirement.

Powell was one of the nicer people in the trade union movement, almost Pickwickian in appearance, perhaps not surprisingly, because he was an expert on Charles Dickens's works and everything Dickensian. His coloured waist-coats, silver fob chain to the fore, were often commented upon by the activists. He was a Freemason and became a justice of the peace later in life, enjoying dispensing justice with Dickensian wisdom.

Powell was also extremely laid back and never stretched himself too energetically. The backlog in disciplinary cases, unresolved rule issues and a number of other complex internal matters piling up in his filing tray was proof of it. But he simply lit up his pipe, content to allow a little more dust to settle. As an Irish Dickens would perhaps have put it, 'God made time – and plenty of it.'

I gave the prospect of the post at the top of the union some thought but, although I had my inner doubts, I saw no reason why I should not compete. By now I had taken part in *Any Questions* on radio, was regularly being interviewed on television and, though still a regional figure, was quite well known nationally. I had spoken at the TUC and Labour Party conferences and in Trafalgar Square, and I had often been featured when the media were looking for a woman's angle – though I never majored on that aspect. As far as I was concerned I was a trade unionist who just happened to be a woman and I was interested in their issues but only as part of my interest in all working issues. Even so, when I came to put forward my own nomination I put my name down as Brenda Dean, rather than just B. Dean, and in the hundred or so words allowed each candidate I made full use of the chance I had to point out that I was different to the twelve men standing for the job.

The only betting that ever crossed my mind was an occasional flutter on the Grand National or the Derby – usually when someone arranged an office sweep. So I never really considered the odds of my name coming out on top in a ballot against twelve men, but quite a few of my executive colleagues seemed to fancy my chances, notably Bill Miles, who without my encouragement promoted himself to be my 'campaign manager'. Had I known then how good he was at choosing the winners in each day's horse-racing I might have taken more notice; I found this out later, when several of us would give Miles a float during a major conference such as the TUC or the Labour Party and he seldom failed to produce a good dividend for us at the end of the week. He was a very good student of form indeed!

I suppose it was also a recognition that events were moving fast that Miles himself did not toss his hat into the ring, because he would have made an excellent president. Throughout the year-long Battle of Wapping he seldom left my side.

The result of the ballot for president was due on 16 August, while most people were on holiday. I certainly was. By this time in my life I had a steady partner and we were aboard his yacht sailing in the Isle of Wight area. Nick, another sailing friend, was with us and we decided to spend the night in Yarmouth harbour. Rather than cook on board we agreed to go to the Bugle Inn, nestling in that pretty little town, and I was constantly being urged by my companions to get on the phone and find out the results. I refused to be rushed and preferred to get the meal under way but when I slipped away to the toilet I did make a call.

It took some time to sink in. Not only had I beaten the field of twelve men but I was nearly 7,000 votes ahead of Dennis Hill – I had 17,398 and he was second with 10,982. In third place was the London Central branch secretary, George Willoughby, with 8,899, so at last the London dominance of the union had been broken. In all 78,353 votes were cast out of 193,520 ballot forms issued so it was a respectable result and quite a rebuff for Norman Tebbit, then Margaret Thatcher's employment secretary, who continually harped on about poor voting results that showed how unrepresentative union leadership in Britain had become. It was a good demonstration of true union democracy at work.

But what sank in even deeper, as far as we were concerned, was the strong message to Londoners that the regions were no longer content to play second fiddle. George Willoughby had already announced that if he failed he would stand down and soon afterwards he said he was indeed taking early retirement. Willoughby was an oddball and quite unpredictable. At one point when he was at loggerheads with his branch committee he locked himself in a cupboard and refused for hours to come out and face up to the problem.

But back at the Bugle that evening my two dining companions continued to urge me to go to the phone – it was long before the widespread use of mobile phones. Finally I put them in the picture – though rather quietly, because a room full of sailing types was unlikely to produce a majority of paid-up Labour activists. Even so a bottle of champagne was ordered and I savoured a victory the significance of which was beginning to sink in.

I then telephoned Bill Keys from the hotel lobby callbox and was warmly congratulated but he assured me there was really no need to break my holiday and travel to the offices at Hadleigh. As he continued, though, it emerged there was to be a meeting with the TUC about a problem caused by the Fleet Street branch of the Electrical, Electronic, Telecommunications & Plumbing Union, whose members had been led to believe that they could walk out of their own union and join ours.

The rationale of their branch secretary, Sean Geraghty, was that his members' work in newspapers made them much more akin to print workers and their pay scales than to other fields such as electrical contracting and power station supply. It was a nice argument, lubricated by frequent sessions in Fleet Street pubs by members of the London Machine Branch, often attended by officers such as Keys, who saw himself in the vanguard of the left wing. But it totally overlooked the fact that the EETPU was led by Frank Chapple and Eric Hammond, who followed policies well to the right and would not take kindly to the loss of a significant number of paying members – quite apart from the politics.

I had already made my views very clear at a meeting of the union executive when I had strongly argued against poaching the electricians, because it was completely in conflict with TUC rules and it was unlikely that the EETPU would take it lying down. But I spoke alone – not even Hill came out in support.

My point was that the print unions were not invincible and not every union enjoyed the power and privilege they had through a rigid closed shop. I reasoned that under Chapple's leadership his members had been prepared to cross picket lines and sign single-union deals behind the backs of other unions. So they were unlikely to back away from a fight with us. The testosterone amongst London print workers, who loved a fight, convinced them that they would win it, however.

I was again a lone voice at the executive meeting – although I saw a strong supportive nod from John O'Leary, the national officer responsible for paper making, who was safely out of the line of sight of the general secretary. But though I lost that day nothing had happened that changed my views. So when that election night Keys rather casually mentioned there was to be a further meeting I made it clear I was coming back to London. It was also pretty clear I was not welcome.

The president's role in SOGAT, apart from being deputy to the general secretary, was as custodian of the union's rules and constitution and above all to look after the wider interests of the union's members. As events at Wapping were later to prove – when the electricians crossed the picket lines to do our members' work – it was very much in the interests of the members that someone should try to blow a warning whistle. I would not be taking over immediately and the presidency – and the chair of the SOGAT executive –

would still be in the hands of Albert Powell until the formal handover. Nevertheless I determined to be present.

Next morning I took the ferry over to Lymington from Yarmouth for the London train; sailing was over and I was back in working mode.

The meeting with the Fleet Street branch of the electricians had been arranged in a committee room at Congress House, the TUC headquarters in Great Russell Street, and when I arrived there were plenty of congratulatory handshakes – and a few hugs – although I was under no illusion but that my election had ruffled a few feathers. But business went on, in normal trade union practice, and as it continued I realised that events had moved on considerably. I discovered that the electricians had even had their own branch notepaper printed as SOGAT members and it became clear that the executive had not been told the whole picture.

Apart from Keys the driving force for picking up the EETPU members was John Mitchell, the rather scholarly but macho secretary of the London Machine branch, who until now I had not really trusted. (Later, however, he did become a supporter.) His argument for bringing in the 'sparks' to our ranks was that they played a central role in the new technology that was rapidly overrunning print and existing demarcation lines were no longer tenable. That was a nice argument but one that still completely overlooked the situation as it existed in national newspaper production. It sounded good but did not really stand up to examination amid the deep rivalries of the competitive unions involved.

The meeting lasted for several hours and it was obvious to me and to others round the table that we were likely to be in big trouble with the TUC, under pressure from Chapple and Hammond to enforce the long-established 'no poaching' rules. Indeed it soon emerged, not surprisingly, that the TUC was not content to sit back and see a membership wrangle break out between the printers and the electricians. They are great believers in 'jaw-jaw' rather than 'war-war' at Congress House and it was not long before the issue was put into 'procedure', which meant arbitration by officials and senior TUC General Council members. As I saw it there could be only one outcome but Keys and some of his London friends were confident they would pull it off and get permission to take in the Fleet Street electricians. 'Some hopes,' I thought.

The first step on the ruinous Road to Wapping had been taken . . .

It soon became clear that my lifestyle was destined for a very big change. The union headquarters were at Hadleigh, which was not exactly the centre of the universe, but my branch was based in Salford, near Manchester. So while in the south I was living in Islington in north London, which was conveniently close to Euston, with a good train service to the north-west, but also quite well placed to get to head office. And I still had my bungalow in Thornton-Cleveleys, near my parents and my brother and his family. Now I had to turn that all around and very quickly. I was determined, come what may, not to leave my branch in the lurch and to find a successor efficiently, but I had to be aware that I was now at the beck and call of the whole union across all the UK.

Keys wrote me a four-page letter of welcome setting out how he saw our working together following a talk we had after the meeting at Congress House. In it he admitted that there was a considerable backlog of work left behind due to Powell's sickness, which he wanted cleared up as soon as I could do it. 'Quite frankly I have been running the show single-handed almost since the amalgamation [with NATSOPA, the print assistants' union] and I believe it is beginning to show,' he declared.

With Keys it was always as well to read the fine print and in his letter he wrote: 'As soon as possible I would like you to play a full part with me on trade issues. In most cases these will be where a crisis has arisen. Sometimes we will have to work together, and other times separately, but I can assure you that I will at all times be prepared to assist.'

How soon would be 'possible', I asked myself. And did that include issues posed by the Fleet Street electricians, which I intended to monitor very closely indeed? Still, his letter was very welcoming and he set out my working conditions and salary. I would have a new Rover, which meant, sadly, my lovely scarlet Triumph TR7 would have to go. And my salary would be £22,184.56, which was not bad at that time for a working girl from Salford.

Keys also said he wanted me to take over on 6 October, the day he went off on his annual holiday. The earliest I could vacate the north-west, following an election for my successor as branch secretary, would be 17 October but Keys said in his letter that he wanted me 'to look after the shop' from a distance if necessary. So I needed to hit the ground running. He summed up: 'I believe you will find the task before you very challenging, possibly frustrating, and at times rewarding. It is my firm belief that you are more than capable of meeting the challenge and the members' expectations. For my part I am delighted to be afforded the opportunity of working with you, be it only for a short time.'

Although I did not realise it at the time, that last sentence was quite significant but for the moment taking over as No. 2 in a major union was a big enough challenge.

Moving very fast I got out a circular in the Manchester branch on 25 August announcing the election for my successor and calling for nominations by Monday 12 September. The King – or Queen – was dead. Who would fill her shoes?

So at forty the whole scope of my working life was in for a major shake-up. I chose Barbara Danby, on the Head Office staff, as my PA and we hit it off from the start. Bill Miles had recommended her and together we set out to sort the backlog of paper bequeathed us by the departing president. I soon began to understand why my own disciplinary case involving Harry Conroy had taken so long. Little had been done about the case, as was the situation with most of the disciplinary files I found awaiting me. Danby and I got stuck into them and after about a couple of months we were able to come up for air. I had closed a number of outstanding cases and ruled in several of the most controversial.

The president's word in all these cases was final in the union and what mattered was that members felt that they had been treated fairly. Often the cases could be dealt with by correspondence but in some cases a hearing was necessary. On one occasion I had to go up to Liverpool to hear a wrangle that typified the intransigence and stubborn nature of the area. Some of the branch officials were not doing their job, it had been claimed, and branch members complained that others were in cahoots with employers. All this had tended to paralyse the Liverpool branch. But steadily we got through the work.

Technically I was still general president-elect, as Powell was working through his farewells at branches up and down the country and he had yet to receive a final farewell from the SOGAT executive and Head Office. So he was in the chair at the September meeting when Bill Keys dropped his bombshell. He too was to retire!

I was still a member of the executive and was equally as astonished as everyone else when Powell disclosed that he had received a formal letter from the general secretary in which he argued that the union was facing a long period of instability because so many of its senior officers – including Keys himself – were due to retire within a short time of one another. He listed the officers and wrote: 'If we proceed in the order defined above we are going to be in a constant state of elections for the next five to six years and to make matters worse if the President decided to apply for the General Secretary's job and got it, the length of the balloting would be further extended by at least a year.'

Keys went on to argue that he was not thinking of going soon but if a general secretary-elect was in place the continuity would ensure the leadership of the union. It was an interesting argument but was there another reason?

'I must say,' Keys's letter continued, 'the thought of retiring early has occurred to me on many occasions recently. I say this because of the extreme pressures I have been under for the last two or three years which unquestionably is affecting my health and family life.' He added: 'In thinking this issue through I am of the opinion that it may be of value to the union to have a new leadership, hopefully bringing with it new ideas that can meet the challenges of the future.'

Copies of Keys's letter were circulated round SOGAT's executive chamber and there were not exactly whistles of surprise, but a bombshell had undoubtedly been tossed in. What was most interesting was that his letter to Powell was dated 8 August – three weeks before my election as president! And he had not said a word.

It could hardly decline but the National Executive voted in favour of the president's recommendation to accept Keys's letter and formally consented to the election process beginning. The last date for nominations to be received would be Friday 2 December 1983 and the result of the ballot would be known by the following March.

The executive usually met for two days and never was there such a night for speculation, gossip and intrigue. The delegates were taking bets on who would succeed Keys – and whether, only just elected as president, I would, or could, stand. Maybe those clever fellows had boxed in Brenda Dean. Surely she could not put her name forward so soon? And surely the members would not accept it anyway?

It was quite a calculation to make. Had I missed a trick? Maybe others had organised it so that I won the No. 2 job only to leave the way clear for a man – Dennis Hill of Yorkshire perhaps – to emerge as the union's leader.

Bill Miles had no doubt that I should stand and that I would win. Furthermore he intended to be my campaign manager. And that was a comfort. But intriguingly, Keys and Powell came to see me and both urged me to put my hat in the ring. They argued I was on a roll, my profile had never been higher in the union and now was the time to clinch things. Maybe they had a point.

Although I did not show eagerness I was actually under no illusions myself. I had to contend the top job, not because I particularly sought it but because I owed it to all the women in the union who had so clearly backed me for president. Also it was time that women showed they could compete at the top and were no longer willing to play second fiddle in a permanently male-dominated situation. I could not blink now.

An aspect that was interesting was to know Keys's actual personal timetable. Once someone in the trade union movement indicates they are in the mood for retirement their power and influence immediately begins to ebb away. New alliances are struck as people manoeuvre. But working for a long period as his understudy, in the difficult days that so clearly lay ahead of us, was not going to be easy. Another aspect which Keys later disclosed was his concern about rumours that the Treasury was considering ending the tax-free lump sums that were then permitted to be drawn down on pensions. The SOGAT officers' pension was well endowed and lump sum arrangements were generous. But would that be allowed to continue? Not according to regular speculation that kept appearing in the better-informed financial newspapers. It might even figure in the Budget in the coming April.

There was clearly going to be no shortage of would-be successors and several of the national officers would put their hats in the ring – not least Ted O'Brien, the brother of Owen O'Brien, who had been the general secretary of

NATSOPA before their amalgamation into the new SOGAT. But while the election build-up began there was plenty to be done. At my old branch Jim Crowther, a Father of the Chapel at the paper manufacturers Bowater, was elected as my successor and June, my former PA, now married to Jim, had beaten six rivals to be elected as deputy branch secretary. So I was content to leave the branch in safe hands and concentrate on my new duties.

Meanwhile the focus of many in the union was who would take the keys of the castle. At the next executive meeting at Hadleigh I thought I detected clear indications that some tactical discussions had been taking place – certainly amongst the Londoners. Whereas in the ballot for president the candidates had all had their full names on the ballot paper, it was now argued that the candidates should simply have their initials and surname and be limited to a short summary of their experience. Someone had apparently worked out that because my name was Brenda it had given me an unfair advantage over the twelve men who stood against me.

I pointed out fairly calmly that my name was actually Brenda, but it was clear the idea of initials and surname had been tossed around in the bar and had support so I saw no point in showing it caused me any concern. Which it didn't! I just thought back on some of the specialist appointments I had held such as being a member of the National Women's Commission and could see that such a reference would give a pretty clear clue as to my gender – if it mattered.

But actually I had more immediate priorities – it was part of my new job to be responsible for running the most important body of the union, which was the biennial delegate conference, due to take place in Bournemouth in April. As president I would be in the chair and something like 600 delegates representing every branch in the union would be present. In most cases these were the movers and shakers in the union, usually either branch secretaries or chairmen (or women), and back at the branch or workplace their report was a first-hand account of how their union was being run. So their personal assessment of the new broom was important.

SOGAT prided itself on the efficiency with which it was run and I had no intention of falling down on the job. I knew also that my keynote address was going to set the seal on everything and it had to be good.

As I have explained, the trade union movement teaches its rank and file how to run meetings, how people should conduct themselves, the importance of the rule book and how to manage a major conference. Chairing a meeting presented no frighteners for me but this was certainly going to be one of the biggest at which I had presided and it lasted a whole week. I also knew that among the delegates, while I had many dear friends, I also had a few enemies who would not be averse to seeing me trip if anything could be arranged.

The key, as always, was preparation. I have never attended a meeting at which I had not read and really digested the papers beforehand and understood them. I have stayed up late for many hours to get it done and, as I have told my 'fledglings' since, it has always paid off.

Just as it is important never to be late to a meeting, it is even more vital to understand what a meeting is about, to know the issues and what you want to come out of a meeting. I regret to say that I have been to far too many meetings when people present clearly have not read their papers – and that includes the chairmen. All too frequently people get over-confident and think they can 'wing it' – in other words, speak without adequate preparation – but to others the inadequacies are often only too obvious.

So on this occasion I was already working hard on my preparations. It helped that I had to see the resolutions off to the printers and sign off each page of the agenda. While at Hadleigh we had Doris Moss, who had always been responsible for running the conference, I made it clear I was not prepared to hand over my authority until I was completely satisfied.

But as the clock ticked inexorably towards the kick-off for the most important union conference in my career, so another schedule was moving on – the ballot for the successor to Bill Keys. I was not out electioneering but as part of my job I was racing around the country – to see our members in the myriad of places in which they worked. In paper-making, one of the most interesting and oldest skills in the country, to bookbinding, to gravure and to newspapers, the range of the work of our members was truly fascinating.

There was one trip off the beaten track that I particularly recall. I had an invitation to visit the training headquarters in Surrey of the Salvation Army. I felt I had to fit it in. When I was young, my brother and I would go off to

Sunday school with the Army. Once, when I was confined to the isolation of my bedroom due to scarlet fever, they came round with their band and played outside my bedroom window. I never forgot it. The hymn was 'Jesus wants me for a sunbeam'. So naturally I was delighted when I joined them for lunch and everyone stood up and burst into song – 'Jesus wants me for a sunbeam'.

But back to work. Suddenly the ballot for general secretary was due, barely six months after I had broken the mould to become No. 2 in the union and rub shoulders with my peers.

On 21 March 1984 the Electoral Reform Society contacted Hadleigh and disclosed that I had been chosen by our members to be the first ever woman elected to lead a major industrial trade union. The results were: Brenda Dean 25,454 votes, Danny Sergeant (general officer) 13,935, Dennis Hill (Yorkshire branch) 13,872, Ted O'Brien (general officer) 13,706, John O'Leary (general officer) 9,980, Maurice Suckling (London area organiser) 9,317 and Alan Shaw (lay member) 3,142. There was a 48.8 per cent return – so it was another rebuff to Norman Tebbit.

Apart from the implications of the decisive support for me, which was exceedingly gratifying and meant I had a real mandate, there were several surprises. I was disappointed that Hill had not made it to second place, although he was pipped by only sixty-three votes. But it meant the chances of him being elected to succeed me as president were slim. The other interesting feature was to see how evenly spread the votes were for my rivals. If the men had been able to get their act together and to settle on one candidate I might not have had such an outcome.

We held a press conference at Congress House and the turnout by the industrial correspondents and general press was impressive – they clearly thought they were on to a real news story. Keys was generous in his introduction of the ballot result and said he was proud to be able to make the announcement. In its 200-year history SOGAT had 'broken many barriers and pioneered many causes'. Now it was pioneering another breakthrough in electing a woman to the senior position in the union 'on sheer ability'. 'Brenda is young in years but brings to the job a wealth of experience,' he added generously. Keys also forecast a difficult task ahead – too true – but he said I had the ability to meet the challenge. 'There is no greater tribute or calling than to be able to serve your own people. There will be millions in this country who will applaud the sense of SOGAT in electing Brenda to lead this old and very proud union.'

That was quite a build-up but I had had time to think what I was going to say and I took a deep breath and looked around the Congress House room. 'This is a tremendous vote of confidence by the membership of the union, be they men or women,' I said. 'I am delighted but also feel very humble. I have no illusions at all about the difficulties we face but I intend to devote all my energies to meeting those challenges.'

Almost on cue came the first question – would I have difficulties because I was a woman? It was not a new question to me. 'I have never sought any favours or special consideration on that basis and I don't intend to start now,' I replied. I said I had been in the union for twenty-four years and my gender had never been a problem. 'Some men may have inhibitions about negotiating with me but that's their problem, not mine. The hostility I sometimes run into is because I'm a trade unionist, not because I'm a woman.'

What was going to present problems were the technological changes sweeping through the industry and we would have to have our wits about us. 'I'm all for change, providing it really benefits our members,' I declared. I wanted to make a mark in the sand and this seemed a good moment to do it.

Keys told the journalists no date had yet been decided for the takeover and the plan was that we would work in harness for the immediate future.

Then followed hours of one-to-one interviews, firstly with national television, then radio, not only from Britain but also from countless overseas nations – electing a woman to a major trade union post seemed to be news for those countries too. Then there were the interviews with journalists from all the national dailies – papers such as the *Daily Telegraph* wanted just as close a look for their readers as the *Daily Mirror*. The *Daily Express's* Barrie Devney reported a platinum blonde became Big Sister to 225,000 trade union members – and were they pleased. Well, I was not so sure about that. Devney added that I turned up in a demure black dress and pearls.

And the journalists were not only labour correspondents – their editors had sent along feature writers, too, for a close-up on this wind of change blowing, it seemed to them, through Congress House. One interview I particularly recall a day or so later was when I was urged to find time to meet a writer from the *New York Times* named R. W. Apple – Johnny Apple, as he was universally known. He came to Hadleigh to see me and I found him meticulous and delightful. Years later I would buy his travel books while holidaying in the United States. Apple wrote: 'An industrial relations executive said after a nightlong struggle with her, "I knew I'd been hit but I never felt the bullet."' I never found who said that but it was a nice, helpful piece and a cutting of it was thoughtfully posted to me by a kind stranger living in Amsterdam, New York. Sadly, Apple died as I was completing this book.

Meanwhile I had to get on with preparation for the conference, which was to be in Bournemouth, a place for which I have always had some regard. While it was not open to the press or the public the executive were kind enough to allow my parents to be guests at the headquarters hotel, the Palace, and to come into the Pavilion to hear my opening address. A nice event for them and quite a moment for me.

The speech went well, as did the conference overall, but of course there was a constant background of speculation about the future policy of the new general secretary, to which I did my best to turn a deaf ear. So far as I was concerned I already had a pretty good job with plenty of responsibility and I did not intend to allow ambition to consume me. I had seen it around plenty of times in the movement – and the bitterness that engulfs so many when they do not achieve a place they covet. And worsens when their rival does.

But more importantly, the pace of change was quickening and I knew I had to be ready. What I did not realise right then – although I had some inkling – was just how fast that pace would be and just how major the challenge was going to be.

One indication of the speed at which events in Fleet Street were moving was an approach shortly after the conference from Albert Powell to say that Rupert Murdoch wanted to meet me. Bruce Matthews, who was then the unflappable, genial chief executive for Murdoch in the UK and who maintained a good relationship with Powell, had approached him and said his boss wanted a face-to-face with me. 'What about dinner?' he suggested.

Powell made it clear this was to be an event that 'never took place', strictly confidential and not one that Keys was to know was taking place. I was not unaccustomed to such arrangements. The British public would be quite amazed to know how many have littered industrial history and to find that quite often, when harsh words are being hurled across the headlines, remarkable trust and complete confidentiality can co-exist between the two sides.

A quiet rendezvous was set up in a private room at the Waldorf Hotel in Aldwych with just the four of us present. I knew that as Murdoch's business was so highly geared it depended on an uninterrupted cash flow from his effective cash machine on Bouverie Street, the *Sun*. The trouble was that the flow was anything but uninterrupted: stoppages, flare-ups and rows —certainly not all the making of the print workers — were bringing production to a standstill night after night.

While Matthews engaged Powell in some knockabout, Rupert Murdoch did not waste much time in small talk. What he wanted to know was whether I could assert my new authority over the London members of SOGAT, who had not been averse to ignoring orders from Keys. Rupert made it pretty clear he doubted it. I looked him straight in the eye and told him I did not know but I was going to have a good shot at it. I said I would give it two or three months to find out and then I would come back and tell him, in all honesty, the truth. Murdoch indicated he accepted this but afterwards told Matthews that although he liked the look of me, he didn't think I could deliver.

Maybe if I had been around twelve months earlier things might have been different. By then, possibly, I might have been able to exert some authority over the London branches. But Murdoch's new printing house had been set up in the tax-free Enterprise Zone of Wapping, and new machinery was secretly being installed and tested. On top of that Murdoch himself was applying for US citizenship and would not be back in London for many months. When we next met the situation would look very different indeed.

Chapter 6

As the storm clouds gathered over Wapping there was another big problem – larger than life too, it sometimes seemed. I refer to Robert Maxwell.

He had first shaped up to Rupert Murdoch when the Australian's name was mooted as the 'white knight' to save the *News of the World* from Maxwell's clutches. In 1969 the Carr family saw the *News of the World* slipping from their grip and at the urging of many journalists sought help from Down Under, and Murdoch's arrival at the time appeared to have saved the day. It meant Murdoch had his first foothold in Fleet Street, acquiring a printing operation which was clearly under-used. Once it had been needed to run off eight million copies but as the *News of the World's* sales had fallen, for several days a week the presses deep down in the bowels of Bouverie Street lay idle.

Murdoch had quickly identified the opportunity given him to publish a new tabloid. Hugh Cudlipp, chairman of IPC, which then published the famous Labour-supporting paper the *Daily Mirror*, foolishly in my view let Murdoch have the title of the *Sun* for a song and placed a dagger at the *Mirror's* heart. Not long afterwards the *Daily Mirror* was in trouble and by 1984 the Reed Group, as IPC had become, wanted to get out. They made Maxwell produce cash but with the backing of National Westminster Bank he was able to do so and suddenly he owned Mirror Group Newspapers, which included a prestigious headquarters and press at Holborn Circus, other printing works in Southwark and Watford, and various other assets such as the *Sporting Life*, which I was told the Queen read each day.

As usual Maxwell had driven a good bargain and was about to make his assets sweat. I don't think he deliberately exploited the problems with the *Sun* and the prospects of a showdown with News International, but Maxwell always tried to take advantage of any situation. His line was that he wanted to show that one could achieve changes through negotiation but there was a head of steam building up among our members at the *Mirror*. He had been behaving abominably towards them – tossing out established agreements and breaching understandings – and it was clear to me there was going to have to be a showdown.

There was a stoppage on a Sunday night when Maxwell declared massive redundancies in the Mirror Group. I took a gamble and let it run, hoping I would be able to contain it to one night and reasoning that if there was to be a stoppage, Monday morning's reduced sales would suffer the least impact. Then the phones started and the upshot was that a meeting was arranged to take place that Sunday night at the offices of one of our branches in Lambeth, to which Maxwell turned up accompanied, amazingly, by Joe Haines, once Harold Wilson's press adviser at No. 10 and then the *Mirror*'s political editor. But right now he was Maxwell's poodle – and knew it.

By the small hours we had reached agreement. To his credit Maxwell had achieved savings of about 30 per cent, which, with the way events were moving at the *Sun*, were worth having. But I didn't trust mercurial Maxwell and he shocked me when he said, 'Brenda, this is a new beginning – you write tomorrow's leader in the *Daily Mirror*. And you write the press release.'

'No way,' I said. It was quite humiliating for Haines, who after all represented senior management, but I would have nothing to do with it. It was Maxwell's method to humiliate everyone, though he realised he knew he could not do that to me. He did not employ me – thank goodness – even if it worked with Haines.

That was just one episode with Maxwell, but almost every week he would be in trouble with our people. I would get reports of the chaotic way in which he was running what once had been so proud a newspaper as the *Daily Mirror*. He would send letters of dismissal to all our members; frequently, he would reach a deal and then he would rat on it. I reached a stage that I would not accept any deal with him unless it was in writing and what he put in writing I showed to all our members and would accept nothing else. He was totally dishonourable in the way he negotiated and was really quite impossible.

My first exposure to Maxwell was when I was general president of the union and there was a dispute running at a fine old company called Bradbury Wilkinson, which Maxwell had snapped up in the lean years of the depression early in the Thatcher era. They had an office block just near Liverpool Street station, which he promptly called Maxwell House – clearly oblivious to the brand of instant coffee! That was where Maxwell's computers were and our members decided to have a sit-in and one night actually took control of the building.

The situation gradually escalated to the point one night that Bill Keys decided all the national officers had to be present to negotiate. I personally thought this was over the top and only bolstering Maxwell's vanity, but Keys was then the general secretary and so we all turned up, ready to make a night of it.

The first thing one had to do was to stop the drinking in the meeting. People were there all night and the drink, lavishly provided by Maxwell, was flowing. Maxwell himself was not partaking, even though I knew he liked to. But every so often he would disappear and leave the union side to drink on – I suspect he was getting some sleep to recharge while our people slipped more and more under the influence. He had a group of Filipina women at Maxwell House who would supply hot food such as pizzas and top up the drinks while the boss was fast asleep, confident that gradually his opponents would be the worse for wear and less able to bring their brains to bear on the issue. It was a very smart tactic indeed.

On this occasion, though, it did not work and so Maxwell, always inclined to be litigious, took our union to court. Not surprisingly, because we were in breach of the law, the courts upheld Maxwell and applied a fine of £75,000 on ourselves and a similar amount on the National Graphical Association, whose members were with us in the dispute. Keys said we were not going to pay and so the dispute dragged on, inevitably, to Easter – Maxwell always seemed to have one eye on the calendar and knew when people wanted to get away. Like others, I had to come back early from my break because there was a meeting on Easter Monday, a Bank Holiday, fixed at Headington Hill Hall, the stately home in Oxford that Maxwell rented from the local authorities for a song and where he liked to hold court.

Keys and I drove up to Oxford determined that Maxwell was not going to run rings around us again. The NGA were also there. The talks started and I believed we were going to get an agreement. But we didn't, and Maxwell used a considerable amount of bad language; I have to say I had heard worse but it was surprising.

The following day Keys and I were at one of our London branches and a call came through to say Mr Maxwell wanted to speak to me. Why was he asking for me, and not Keys? We looked at each other but Keys intimated I should take the call. Maxwell boomed down the phone: 'Brenda, I am sorry about yesterday and that I used that language in front of you. It should never have happened and I apologise.'

I said something to the effect that I had never heard anything. I did not want to get into a situation of it becoming a personal issue. I went on: 'The important thing now, Mr Maxwell, is to get this dispute ended and you are aware that our union is not going to pay the fine and I don't know where that gets us.' I think I put the *Mirror* owner on the spot.

We then had to go off to Scotland for a meeting but the phone calls kept coming and going, in which Keys revelled. This was the kind of lifestyle he loved but it only made me more determined that if ever I took over I was going to do things differently, particularly when negotiating with Maxwell.

Eventually Maxwell said he would pay the fine for both unions. I remember Keys and I were in a little bedroom in a plastic hotel, a tiny box, and suddenly the dispute was forgotten and it was all about the fine. I urged him not to accept a Maxwell cheque. 'Tell him we want a banker's draft and that we will only call off the dispute when that money is in the union's bank. He'll bounce the cheque. Only when we have the draft will the dispute be over.'

Keys relayed this to Maxwell and we got the draft. So the dispute was settled but what was it all for, I wondered. What a way to conduct ourselves. It was no way to do business but that was Maxwell. Subsequently when I became general secretary I told Maxwell clearly that Keys's way of doing business was not going to be mine. I said very firmly that we had procedures and now that I had taken over I was determined to keep to them. I wanted to get some logic into the situation.

'Yes, yes, Brenda,' said Maxwell, 'I quite agree,' but the glint in his eye told me he was not listening. He asked me to call him Bob. I said no – he was Mr Maxwell and that was how I would address him.

'Why? Everybody else calls me Bob.'

'Well,' I said, 'I don't feel I can trust you and sometimes you do things to people who I represent which I find absolutely awful.'

A few days later he rang my home in Islington and asked to speak to Miss Brenda Dean.

Maxwell was renowned for his contact book and thought nothing of ringing straight through to the Prime Minister, Mikhail Gorbachev, Boris Yeltsin or any other political leaders or industrialists around the world. Probably even the US President if it suited him. But in this case the number was ex-directory and did not belong to me, so someone had clearly passed it on. Mr Maxwell was told firmly he had the wrong number. He never tried it again and got the message. If nothing else he was a quick learner.

But what really did get his goat was my attack on him at the Labour Party conference of 1984, when Neil Kinnock was party leader and preparing for the forthcoming election following his defeat the previous year. I had not taken into account just how thick quite a number of the so-called left-wingers in our movement were with Maxwell and how deeply they were in his pocket. For example, the communist leader of TASS, Ken Gill, got his equally left-wing deputy, Barbara Switzer, to demand of me what I was doing seeking the expulsion of one of their members! The late Ray Buckton, the footplatemen's leader, who would go to Headington Hill Hall and take Maxwell's hospitality, let me know he was not happy, as did a number of others suggesting that my criticism of Maxwell was causing them problems. Tough, I thought. There he is abusing our members and I am supposed just to sit on my hands?

One of Maxwell's practices was to take over a printing company and tell the workers the place was in a mess. They were not the problem, it was the management. But have faith – he, Maxwell, would sort it out. A few weeks later he would return to say he had now seen the books and the company was indeed in serious difficulties and there would have to be redundancy and indeed some equipment would have to be sold off. 'But not to worry! I, Maxwell, intend to invest in this company and its future is assured. A new four-colour litho press will be installed and all will be well.'

I had heard this story so many times I asked Maxwell one day if he had a low-loader with a four-colour litho on it which he ran up and down the country each day to various different printing works he had down for his 'new investment'! He was livid with me. Of course it later transpired that he had done very well selling off surplus printing machinery he had snapped up as, one by one, British printing companies went to the wall in the Thatcher era.

Because of his antics in a series of disputes around this time, I wrote to the Labour Party in my official union capacity asking that they should carry out an inquiry into his activities, which I hoped would lead to his expulsion from the party. I spoke in the industrial relations debate at the conference and quite calmly revealed that Maxwell might well be a Labour supporter but he was a very bad employer. When I told the conference I would not be attending the annual *Daily Mirror* reception, the Wednesday night highlight, for which people vied to obtain an invitation, quite a few delegates – if they followed their political consciences – could see their evening going down the drain. I did not name the event but just said they knew what party I was talking about and I would not be attending. So few attended that the *Mirror* party was a flop.

Charles Clarke, the future Home Secretary, at that time ran Kinnock's office and sidled up to me at the end of the session. 'Brenda,' he said, 'we know you've got awful problems with Maxwell and we don't want to make life difficult for you. Neil Kinnock won't attend the *Mirror* party if you don't want him to go.'

I said, 'No, I am not asking you to do that. Neil Kinnock is the leader of the Labour Party and I hope he is going to be Prime Minister. He has to do what is right for the Labour Party. You will not find me being critical. If he has accepted he should go.' Apparently Kinnock did go briefly but did not stay and Maxwell was angry. After all, it was the biggest reception at the conference and Maxwell had flown down specially by helicopter to attend.

Several of our members wanted to picket the event but I told them not to do it. Anyway it was not necessary because hardly anybody attended.

Later in the week, somewhere at the side of the Brighton Conference Centre,

Maxwell buttonholed me and asked, 'Can't we bury the hatchet, Brenda?' He wanted to know why I was being so tough with him.

'Well, Mr Maxwell,' I said very politely, 'it is because you are bullying my members and I don't like that. You had a very tough upbringing and you know what it is to be bullied. But that is what you are doing to my members.'

Maxwell replied that they were two entirely different situations and he did not believe they could be compared. He was furious with me.

He was right, of course – they were not the same. Still, he was bullying and I felt it was wrong. I told him he could not go on harassing my officers and running them into the ground.

He asked me once why I declined his invitations to Headington Hill Hall, which were social occasions, but I did not elaborate. Of course my officers were not pleased and regarded me as a bit of a killjoy since it meant they could not go. But I was much more at ease with Maxwell by keeping the relationship at arm's length and on a very businesslike basis.

At one point during Wapping he stopped me and said, 'I saw you on television this morning, Brenda, and you were superb. Your mother must be very proud of you. You did very well.' I replied that I didn't know about that but it was my job to put my members' views across and that was what I was trying to do. He was very complimentary and he introduced me to his wife, Elizabeth, a very nice lady. Funny how these tycoons seem to find themselves such nice wives!

Eventually of course I did reach a kind of relationship with him but it was very much on my terms. I never trusted him. I would only agree to see him, by firm appointment, at his office. And there would have to be a clear agenda.

In 1987 Maxwell sent me two tickets for the men's final at Wimbledon, which I refused to use. Maxwell was furious – and my partner was not all that enthusiastic either.

At the 1985 Labour Party conference the *Daily Mirror* party was held again but it never seemed quite to regain its zing. I went along and some of my members turned up to give me moral support! As usual Maxwell was in a dispute with us and this time it was about the future of the *Sporting Life*, whose print operation he intended to move out of London, which meant quite a number of jobs lost. Our London members stopped the *Daily Mirror* and so the Maxwell merry-go-round was on again. At one point in the negotiations there was a plan to print the *Sporting Life* at the offices of the *Morning Star*, which pleased our communist members but had the journalists falling over themselves to get out the story that the Queen was 'seeing red' about the future of her favourite paper.

The week he fell or was pushed from his yacht in November 1991 we were due to see him in court over the Mirror pension fund, which was the issue of course that brought the company down in the end. One of our Scottish members, Harry Templeton, who worked on the *Daily Record*, was a pension trustee and had taken the trouble to learn all about his responsibilities. He felt that there was something wrong with the investment policy and started asking questions. And he started being a difficult trustee. Now Maxwell did not like that. He was used to having his own way and telling people what to do, including pension fund trustees.

I was alerted to the pensions situation because I had seen what had happened at Thomson Withy Grove in Manchester, which produced the *Daily Mirror* and the *News of the World*. We could not understand why Maxwell should be interested in that plant but its pension fund, which had been very long established, had a surplus of, I think, about £200 million. That was why he bought it. Again and again he bought companies which might be in difficulty but had pension surpluses. Maxwell used them to fund the redundancy costs. There was nothing stopping him doing that at the time. But he never revealed how much he had left over from the various pension funds he raided.

Maxwell made Templeton redundant, SOGAT believed, because our member was onto him. We tried very hard to get Templeton reinstated but Maxwell was more determined to have him out than anything else I had ever seen him do. He was determined that Templeton would not be reinstated and he wasn't.

My friend, the distinguished journalist Geoffrey Goodman, speculates in his book *From Bevan to Blair* that Maxwell may have been murdered aboard his yacht by special agents. That's one scenario. But I certainly don't think he committed suicide. Maxwell did not lack personal courage. There is no doubt about that in my view. I gather he had been pretty depressed and had been drinking a lot. I think he had also been taking pills for a cold, and the result of this combination was that he fell overboard off the back of the ship. That's my view but no one will ever know.

Chapter 7

Robert Maxwell was not the only issue on my mind, although I have no doubt he would have liked it that way. I was looking at the wider picture and wondering how I could break the logjam of the Fleet Street workers' attitude – and to some extent those in Manchester and Scotland too – that change, like it or not, was coming fast.

I hit on the idea of copying the technique I had used to speed up the acceptance of new machinery and new methods when I was branch secretary in Manchester. Taking my members to see the plant in use by other workers abroad had several times helped to prepare the way for change and for new investment in my region. Would that work in newspaper production, I asked myself. I had only just taken over as general secretary but I felt it worth a try.

The union executive agreed with my suggestion of a study tour to the United States and Canada. There had been reports in the newspapers of several struggles across the Atlantic, of widespread deunionisation and a major clash at the *Washington Post* when helicopters had been used to fly materials in and out to maintain production while the newspaper plant had been surrounded by picketing printers.

In May 1985, just about twelve months after I had taken over the top job in the union, I led a study team of nine drawn widely from the union to look at new technology in the newspaper industry in the USA and Canada. We reported back a month later. Apart from Bill Miles, of course, there were several Londoners – Ted O'Brien, Ted Chard, George Holmes and David Hutchins. From Glasgow came Allan Watson, Cyril Brown represented Manchester and John Fellows spoke for Birmingham, which has always had vigorous news-papers. I was not the only woman because the party included Eve Norwood, the union's full-time health and safety adviser and something of an expert on equipment that was then quite new for most of us – VDUs or visual display units.

The outcome was a bound 42-page report which was written deliberately as a wake-up call, entitled *The American Experience*. We were unanimous that time was running out fast. And we said so in the very first words of the summary of conclusions: 'Opposing technological change is not an option for trade unions in printing – it is simply a road to rapid de-unionisation.' There had been a 50 per cent job loss in newspaper production in the USA and the Typographical Union's membership had declined from 110,000 to 40,000 in a very short time. We set out the case clearly and succinctly in a twelve-point conclusion which was crisply written and not too difficult to absorb. And we did not pull our punches.

I wrote an even tougher introduction: 'So, like it or not, the era of "New Technology" in Britain's newspaper industry has arrived,' I told people. 'We are fast approaching now the eye of the storm and the forces that involves will affect all who work in newspapers.' I pointed out that British newspapers had relied always on casual labour, paying no pensions and little attention to sickness, health and welfare. To conclude the introduction I wrote: 'We believe that a trade unionist's proper reaction should be at the table – not under it but sitting around it. And the sooner the better. We hope that when colleagues have read this report they will agree. And understand the pressures upon us.'

We put a great effort into publicising the report and it received good coverage in the more serious newspapers and the trade press. But the fact that we were being sensible and offering constructive suggestions did not catch the media's attention in the way that a threat to strike always seems to.

I sent copies personally to Bruce Matthews at the *Sun* and other managers in Fleet Street so I have little doubt that Rupert Murdoch had the chance to scan it. If he had wanted he could have seized that chance to challenge us to prove we meant what we had set down in our report – to call our bluff.

By then, of course, the secret computer printsetting equipment Murdoch had bought had arrived in unmarked crates at London's docks and was being installed at a secret location in Woolwich. Charles Wilson, later to become editor of *The Times*, was in charge of preparing them to operate on a British newspaper system and commencing a training system behind the backs of those whose jobs were about to be undermined. We were to find out that we were too late.

As I glanced through the report twenty years later, a greetings card dropped out with a picture of a large thumbs-up on the cover. It had been signed by all the delegation under the words 'You're a Winner' and declared, 'To our General Secretary and Delegation Leader – Brenda, you've won all our respect and affection for the way you've represented the union and taken care of us.'

That was very kind. Looking back, I just wish I had managed it for a lot more of my London members. In that way perhaps the brutal months ahead might have been avoided.

*

It seems to be the general impression that Rupert Murdoch's papers had the worst labour relations in Fleet Street and sometimes that was the case but not always. Really there was a state of anarchy everywhere – trouble could break out suddenly at any newspaper office, often over a trivial incident, and production of one of the most perishable goods in existence would just be stopped. The cost to the publishers was enormous and today one has to marvel that it went on unchallenged for so long.

There was of course a long history to it. It is said that Lord Beaverbrook's *Daily Express*, with the biggest sale for many years in the 1960s, was not averse to paying production workers generously to push up other papers' costs.

For years managers in charge of production in most Fleet Street newspaper plants carried large wads of notes and seldom sought receipts. And when the workers had to sign a chit for the money they put down false names such as Prince Monolulu, Charlie Chaplin and even Mickey Mouse. The employers looked the other way and so did the Inland Revenue. The other ingredient was of course alcohol. The river Fleet still ran under the road but drinks flowed above it from the hundred or so pubs which graced just the Fleet Street area.

I am not saying that no print workers were keen to do a fair day's work for a fair day's pay but they had learned to obey orders from the Father of their

Chapel, and they had learned that generally if they stood united, money would flow in surprisingly large quantities into their pockets. Many owned nice well-furnished houses in such London suburbs as St Mary Cray, Orpington and Bromley, where the all-night train services took them from Blackfriars station. That is if they did not drive to work in their smart cars which were parked all around the newspaper offices, making it extremely difficult sometimes to get the delivery vans into the loading bays. A crisis could happen anytime, anyplace and at any newspaper.

The journalists found it very frustrating indeed. Sir Harold Evans, former editor of the *Sunday Times*, has described how months of work cracking open the thalidomide scandal was endangered by a stoppage caused at the last minute by the printers, and there were many other examples. It was small wonder that when journalists were asked to move to Wapping, which meant crossing the printers' picket lines, quite a few – though not all – did so with alacrity. Even if some of them were also in tears.

I had worked in Manchester, where we had gradually overcome this kind of knee-jerk problem. We had procedures and we persuaded the men to keep to them. And the men saw that in the long term they benefited. The *Daily Mail* transport chapel, for example, presented me with a solid silver tray and a full range of cut glasses for every occasion, engraved with the words 'To Brenda Dean for the agreement she negotiated for us May 1979'. It is one of my proudest possessions.

But take the *Daily Telegraph* in London, which was in poor financial shape and saddled with mediocre management, wildcat strikes occurring there quite frequently. One evening I was changing to go out to the theatre – which I love – with friends, on a date that had been arranged for a long time. The phone went in my bathroom, where one is not supposed to have one but which I had found essential, and it was our union rep at the *Telegraph*, a woman, to tell me the job there was going to stop that night.

I had previously resolved that I was not going to go on like Bill Keys and live a life revolving round this madhouse. Keys loved it but to me it was getting nowhere. The union could have everything it wanted from me but I was not going to be at the beck and call of Fleet Street chapels. There was the rest of the union membership to think of, the majority of whom were outside London.

The union rep was the sister of a senior woman journalist on a Sunday paper, a Murdoch loyalist. The rep demanded I should drop everything and go there immediately. So I asked, 'Who has called the men out? Who's told them to stop?'

'Well, we have.'

'Well then,' I said, 'you'd better get them back again, because I'm not coming down there.'

My refusal to go almost caused a riot. The management did not like it either. But gradually things started to calm down a little, although I am not saying it was because of my attitude, and we started to get a bit of logic into them.

Then when I was at one of the major conferences, in the first year I was general secretary in 1984, my fellow Mancunian, the late and lovable Brian Redhead, was interviewing me on the BBC *Today* programme. At the end of it he slipped in a question about a stoppage the previous night at the *Daily Telegraph*. 'What was all that about?' he asked.

I simply said, 'I don't know what it was about. There is a procedure in place which should not allow those sorts of things to happen, and I will be dealing with it today.'

As soon as I got out of the studio the phones were red hot. 'Who's she to say we should not stop work?'

It was absolute anarchy – 'we stop the job and she can sort it out' was the attitude. And I was not going to have it. If there is a real crisis then of course you have got to drop everything and tackle it, and I have worked many times through the night. But Fleet Street's madhouse was often totally unnecessary – sometimes due to managerial ineptitude, sometimes to sheer cussedness on the part of the workers. In a way they deserved each other.

Robert Maxwell was the same as Keys. He knew he could pick the phone up on a Sunday afternoon and say to him, 'We need to negotiate immediately.' And it would happen. Keys would drive up to London, probably be up all night, and get to his desk on Monday morning exhausted. A 'glamorous' Fleet Street incident had sucked him in yet again and the rest of the union's needs were on the back burner. But he loved it. Maxwell said to me at one time in a dispute, 'I have abandoned Christmas this year, Brenda.' And I replied, 'Well, Mr Maxwell, you may have done for you, but not for me and not for my members.'

Chapter 8

When I became general secretary the Wapping problem was fairly obvious. After all, the empty plant, a massive building in an enterprise zone, was just standing there down by the river Thames and apparently not being used. So here was a wealthy entrepreneur with a global business operating with some considerable tax breaks yet not producing. It did not need much imagination to grasp that the situation could not continue. I knew Rupert Murdoch was highly geared financially and his bankers were not going to allow him much more time to put the printing plant to use.

It reminded me of the meeting I had had with Murdoch at the Waldorf Hotel when he asked if I could deliver. I was soon going to find out. I had told him that I did not know. I had only held the job a few weeks. But if he gave me three months I would try to find out. There was an onus on me now, I felt, to go back and tell him because my credibility was on the line and we had parted on the understanding that we would meet again in a few months' time.

About that time I was arranging the farewell dinner for Bill Keys at the Stationers' Hall, just off Ludgate Hill near St Paul's Cathedral. Once again he had surprised us all by suddenly deciding to go as soon as he could, rather than stick to his earlier plans for an extended handover period. What had happened to engender this change of heart were rumours that the Chancellor of the Exchequer, Nigel Lawson, was intending to stop the practice of allowing a tax-free lump sum to be drawn immediately from a pension when a person retired. It was always a sizeable concession, highly prized, and meant, for example, that on retirement one could pay off a mortgage or sail away on a round-the-world trip while still in good health. On the other hand it seemed very doubtful if Lawson could face down the wrath of

74

people who had been planning on these lines. A real vote loser, when you think about it.

A lot of work went into the arrangements for the retirement dinner and the Stationers' Hall was an absolutely stunning location. The event was moving along well and the wine was flowing when news came through, as they say in my part of the country, of 'trouble at t' mill'. All production had halted at the *Sun* in nearby Bouverie Street and it was not the work of the men but the management. Murdoch's managers had literally halted production as the presses were about to turn.

I was in a black ballgown but there was no time to change. With Bill Miles I immediately went to Bouverie Street, where once the weekly *News of the World* had been published in a leisurely manner. But now its presses were operating seven days a week. Inevitably the strain on the very old equipment was beginning to show and a lead stereotype plate had shattered, showering deadly splinters of metal around the machinery hall like wartime shrapnel. Fortunately no one so far had been hit. But the breakdown certainly lent some support to the printers' arguments that management had been pressing them too hard.

On the other hand, the men were unwilling to lose a night's work and wanted to continue even though the *Sun*'s management had inexplicably stopped the job. What were they up to? Was it all to help make the case for switching production to Wapping?

The reaction from our members finding their new general secretary in a black off-the-shoulder evening dress down in the hot, stuffy bowels of the earth was quite amusing but it demonstrated very effectively that I was not going to be aloof and absent.

I had several discussions after that incident with Miles and, whichever way I looked at things, they just appeared a complete mess. Our people's aspirations were way over what was deliverable. Worse, the NGA members were being totally intransigent not only on wages but on inter-union relations. They wanted to gain complete control in the machine room. Our people would not let them do that because they had quite a strong position in Bouverie Street which they were not going to give up.

Still I worked at the situation and started to get closer to our people, and I began to get some thoughts on what we could do. But that was only in our union. And I was not certain if I could deliver all our branches in London. Maybe I could get agreement with one but then another branch would not accept it.

It was about then that we started to be told by some of our people in the London Rirma (Revisers, Ink Rollers & Manufacturers' Assistants) branch, run by a lovely fellow called Dave Hutchison, that Wapping was preparing to run whether we went in there or not. There were meetings, admittedly not at very high level, and desultory talks were taking place. Our relations with the NGA were not very good, though, and our members felt that nothing much was going to change.

I also knew that Murdoch was very bitter about the NGA in particular because he personally held Tony Dubbins, the NGA general secretary, to account for his members' lack of discipline and intransigence. He had done two deals with Dubbins and on each occasion felt he had been let down. One of these dated back to a lunch Murdoch had had in his flat at Stafford Street, in St James's, with Dubbins to try to sort out a long-standing dispute affecting NGA pay at Bouverie Street. The newspaper tycoon thought it had been resolved but Dubbins and the NGA had walked away from it. That had happened not once but twice to Murdoch and he later told me he had not forgotten it. So he was feeling pretty sensitive and he also doubted the willingness of union officials to take the long road and commit themselves to deliver. That was really the situation when I came on the scene.

The summer dragged on, time slipped by and we made little progress towards getting a deal at Wapping. And all the time I was getting reports on the work being done on the installation and preparations for the plant to run. We were told there were all kinds of trials and there was talk of a new newspaper, the *London Post* as it was to be called, which would be an evening. Murdoch would not agree that the unions could have recognition at Wapping, which it could be argued was a greenfield site. Some green fields!

So our people were tending to focus on that, but not on the real issue.

Matters really started to come to a head in September while we were attending the TUC conference. We were told suddenly that Wapping had had a full test production run. This was quite clearly the real thing – trials were over. My gut reaction was that we needed to deal with this immediately and we could not let it go. Each day that passed now meant that News International was better and better prepared.

In a corridor at the Winter Garden in Blackpool we held what I suppose could be described as a council of war. Dubbins was there with his president, Bryn Griffiths, and most of his Fleet Street branch officials, who were also attending the conference. Miles and most of our Fleet Street branch secretaries were with me.

I was quite clear. I said my view was that they should just stop the *Sun* that night – which was Murdoch's cash cow – and force the issue to a head. The NGA and our people were good at stopping jobs whenever it suited them but for once this was the time to take unofficial action. We could not tell them to walk out because of the legal situation under Thatcher's legislation but it was now or never.

The NGA people were clearly not as much in favour of a walkout as me but they obviously did not want to appear less militant. The general feeling was to call a meeting. So one was fixed for the Saturday after we got back from Blackpool. It was arranged in Bouverie Street at the *News of the World* office. Bruce Matthews, Murdoch's No. 1 in the UK, was there; Miles led for us and Alf Parish for the NGA. It was agreed that general secretaries would not attend but I arranged to be in London and available at the end of a phone if and when I was needed.

I'll never forget as long as I live the phone call at the end of the meeting from Miles to report on the outcome. The general consensus of the meeting, he reported, was that they would not take industrial action. But of course they would if I instructed them! In the meantime they would commence negotiations with the company.

I remember my words. 'Bill,' I said, 'I don't believe what you are telling me. I can't instruct them to come out and if they want an instruction to stop the job I am not giving one. I am not prepared to put the whole union at risk. If that's what they need to react to this situation, which I believe is a crossroads, I am just amazed. But if that is their attitude – OK.' So they started negotiations, but it was quite obvious that management were just filibustering and spinning out time. One could tell the talks were not going to get anywhere.

I did not believe the management would move and if I had been in their position I don't think I would have done so. They now held all the cards and had been carefully planning events for a long time. All they needed was a little bit more . . .

They had done a deal with Eric Hammond, general secretary of the EETPU, which we knew nothing about. Hammond's union was going to supply all the labour Wapping needed. If necessary Hammond was prepared to bus these people through his own electricians' picket lines. But they needed time for training.

That was treachery of the highest order but that was the league we were in. It was payback time as far as Hammond was concerned – revenge for the stupid action of our people in recruiting the Fleet Street electricians from his union, the ploy I had found well advanced on my first day as president of SOGAT and which risked our union's expulsion from the TUC.

The talks dragged on and a new face emerged at the management table, Bill O'Neill. A tall good-looking Australian, he clearly knew printing backwards and was a tough negotiator. And he could do a deal. Instinctively we knew that he had Murdoch's confidence and was the troubleshooter. Some years later I became good friends with O'Neill and we have kept in touch. Though he is now retired and lives in San Antonio, Texas, when O'Neill passes through London we often meet up to recall these strained times.

Miles continued reporting back to me that he was convinced he was being given the runaround and that events were being dragged out. So I decided the time had come to call in a commitment Murdoch had given me back in April that we would meet again. I felt it was time now to confront him. I let him know that when he had wanted to meet me I had agreed and now I wanted to meet him. But circumstances had changed and there was no way that this could take place in private.

So a full-blown meeting was arranged, which I was expected to lead because I had called it. We had to come up from the Labour Party conference in

Brighton for the meeting, which was held on 3 September 1985 at the Inter-Continental Hotel in Park Lane. I was insistent that it could not just involve the print unions because I now knew that the electricians' union were in bed in some way with Murdoch, and of course there were also the engineers and the journalists to involve. So we needed to present a united front.

It was what I call a nothing meeting, really. I didn't feel it got anywhere. Murdoch had his full team – O'Neill, Matthews and several others. And we had five unions represented. The outcome was that formal negotiations would recommence. Yet really it was the same dance, going nowhere. Again and again in these negotiations Miles reported back failure and he was convinced that O'Neill was not budging. 'Well, that should tell us something, Bill,' I said. I was convinced News International was working to a plan and we were just being carried along with it.

The NGA then had the thought that a dispute should be engineered with one of the Murdoch titles, and that idea was initially quite attractive. It meant that while people were out at one newspaper others would be working and able to contribute to the loss of pay of those on strike. The danger was that it could easily escalate to violence, which on its own was bad enough, but was not an own goal we wished to present to the Thatcher government. There could be a picket line at one plant and not at another; elsewhere there could be trade unionists stopped when they had every right to work and many other kinds of inflammatory incidents. We could easily have branch against branch and even union executives being divided. It seemed a recipe for disaster.

During a Christmas and New Year break in Lanzarote, I spent a long time thinking about the situation and discussing with my partner our strategy. Whichever way I looked at it I could not see a way of resolving the situation without a dispute. And if our people were going to be in a fight about their jobs then I believed the union had to be in it with them – it could not be an unofficial dispute. If the *Sun*, *News of the World* and *Times* workers held any unofficial action I would have to tell them to go back to work. In any case, if I didn't I would be held to be in contempt of court and meanwhile would risk surrendering the leadership to unofficial manipulation by some of the left-wingers just itching for the chance. That could even break the union, because our people in the provinces would see what they regarded as greedy, over-paid Londoners swallowing up union funds and resources.

So a major confrontation was coming, which would be conducted under the Thatcher anti-strike legislation, and we would be fighting with one hand tied behind the back. I was determined not to fall into the trap which brought down Arthur Scargill in the miners' dispute by failing to hold a ballot. I also steeled myself to be ready to face sequestration and have the union's funds seized by lawyers acting on Murdoch's behalf because secondary action, for example by our members in the newspaper wholesale delivery houses, was quite predictable. We had members across the newspaper industry, unlike the NGA, which was only involved through its members in the actual pre-press and print operation. There was no point in fighting and ending up in prison, although I did joke publicly that, if I was sent to jail, I was going to demand to go to a men's jail.

When I got home from Lanzarote I was clear on the issues we now faced. I called an emergency meeting of the full executive on 14 January 1986 and presented a paper on the crisis. I still have a copy because it was the first real use to which I had put my new baby Apple Mac, the first graphics-based personal computer for home use, and it was a revelation.

I worked out the cost of the dispute to the union at £86,700 a week. The executive agreed that the time had come to ballot all our members in the dispute and to see if they were prepared to come out in what was to be the final showdown with Murdoch. I also warned, 'I believe it needs to be expected that we will have legal action taken against us, possibly on a scale we have not considered, such is the minefield of the legislation currently.' Perhaps not even I bargained for what the union would ultimately face.

We had more than 4,000 members potentially involved in the dispute and of course the union was financially not that strong. When I took over I found it was spending to the limit of its income and had very little in reserve. Nothing had been put on one side for a rainy day and the outlook was now decidedly stormy.

We called a big meeting to address the members involved at the Brixton Academy – a really huge affair. The Academy is where they used to put on what were then the new big rap concerts and I was told it ought to be able to hold everybody. It was just an empty black cavern. So when I got into my car to be driven to Brixton I was calmly aware that it was the first journey along the road to final confrontation with Murdoch.

The place was packed. We were on a small stage and everyone was standing – there was just no room to sit. We must have had well over 3,000 people there. I spoke to this huge crowd and knew I was getting my message across by the intent way the men and women were hanging on my words.

I said I wanted to separate the facts from the fiction at the beginning of this dispute so that they were all very clear about why we were going down this road. 'We were prepared to negotiate and we have tried very seriously to do so,' I told them. But there were four demands by the Murdoch management which I did not see that the union could ever accept: the so-called management rights, which would give Murdoch's managers carte blanche to make any decision affecting workers without consulting them; a ban on the closed shop; an undertaking that there would be no strikes under any circumstances whatsoever; and the whole agreement had to be legally binding.

I explained that on first sight some of the demands might sound reasonable until they were examined. For example, SOGAT had been prepared to try to get an agreement that would make unofficial strikes unnecessary. But that was not enough – we were asked to sign an agreement that there would be no strikes 'under any circumstances whatsoever'. 'Who could sign that?' I asked.

I told the crowd there was no way this could be an unofficial dispute. This was not going to be one of the usual Fleet Street affairs with an early capitulation by the employers. It could take a long time, I warned.

We knew that the Murdoch management had been planning this confrontation for many months and that they would in all likelihood go ahead and print at Wapping without our people being involved at all. They would just be bypassed. The same would happen to all the distribution channels – W. H. Smith, Surridge Dawson, John Menzies – in which we had many more members employed all over Britain. For that reason we would conduct a secret ballot, I said, and started to explain the procedure.

Then suddenly someone shouted out, 'There's a journo in here.' And there was young Mark Mardell, now the BBC's Europe editor but then a fairly new

IRN industrial reporter I rather liked, who had infiltrated the meeting with his tape recorder hidden. He had got into the meeting somehow, though everyone's union card was checked at the door. He was about to be manhandled and it looked rather ugly.

'Don't touch him,' I said. 'He's a friendly journalist – we're going to need people like him.'

So Mardell was politely asked to leave but it was quite a tense moment.

The members voted for a secret ballot to be conducted and that was that. But while it was being conducted a secret meeting was arranged between just four of us with Murdoch – Tony Dubbins and Bryn Griffiths, the NGA president, and from SOGAT Bill Miles and me. It took place in Gray's Inn Road, at the *Times* boardroom, and seemed to be in half darkness though I cannot recall why. Our union president, Danny Sergeant, as usual was nowhere to be seen. He wanted to stay out of the crisis it seemed. But I was quite happy to have Miles with me, who was much more familiar with the Fleet Street people anyway. He was an absolute gem, a diamond and someone I knew I could trust and rely upon implicitly.

We told Murdoch we were having the ballot, which we thought would be carried, but felt the way out was still through proper negotiation.

'We've been trying to have negotiations with you for months,' replied Murdoch.

Dubbins assured him this time it would be different.

Murdoch was not impressed. He looked at my colleague coldly and said, 'The music has changed, Mr Dubbins, but the dance remains the same.'

I knew exactly what he meant. And it also told me we could stay there for hours but we were not going to get anywhere. Murdoch had made his mind up. The die was cast, the deal had been done with Eric Hammond of the electricians and they were all lined up to go.

We got the ballot result on 21 January. It was spectacular and again a put-down for Margaret Thatcher's employment minister, Norman Tebbit, who had sneered that there was little democracy within the trade union movement. Well over 4,000 members had voted. Of these, 3,534 voted for industrial action with only 752 against so that there had been a 90 per cent turnout and of those

82 per cent were in favour. To these figures needed to be added those of the NGA, who had also decided to ballot.

Five days before the result News International successfully printed a 24-page section of the *Sunday Times* on the new presses at Wapping using Hammond's new 'printers' bussed in from Southampton. It was a provocative gesture but our members stood firm and continued working normally in Bouverie Street and Gray's Inn Road. The management probably hoped their action would provoke a walk-out which they could then use to justify sacking everyone and moving all production to Wapping.

So the lines were drawn for the last major industrial set-piece battle in Britain, one which would completely change the face of a long-established industry. No one knew that dark evening in January that the lights were about to go out in Fleet Street for ever, as the rest of the press lords followed Murdoch's lead.

There was, however, a strange last-minute development, which I have never previously disclosed. It happened when I was on my way to yet another of the strike preparation meetings in Borough Road, where one of our branches had an office. Just before I was to get out of the car, in which I was alone apart from my driver, Ken Tuppen, the car phone rang. It was one of the huge, old-fashioned early car phones, which often broke down but which was to prove a godsend during the dispute.

At the other end of the line was Bill O'Neill – I never thought to ask him how he got the number. He said, 'Brenda, we kind of feel for you in this situation. It is not that Murdoch wants to move against you; he would negotiate with you.' And what he was really saying is that they had found it impossible to negotiate with the NGA. He said, 'There is a deal that could be done with you but not the others.'

It was a tantalising eleventh-hour development and thoughts raced through my mind. But I just had to tell him. 'Bill, the die is cast now,' I said.

We knew then what the electricians' union had been doing and if I had accepted I would have been involved in the same kind of treachery. How could I negotiate a deal for my people behind the backs of the other unions? I imagine News International saw it as a way of pulling back from Hammond and swinging behind me as more of a known quantity and representing more of their workers. But it would have split the print workers and probably the whole trade union movement.

I must say the temptation was enormous. It would have been a way for me to sort out the issue. But I don't think I could have delivered all my branches in London, let alone my executive. Remember they were like boxers, all pumped up and ready to go. They were not going to have a dispute snatched away from them at the eleventh hour. It also meant that I would have represented the NGA in negotiations and I could never see them agreeing to that – they were far too proud.

So it was an interesting but an impossible offer. I had to say no.

I think in moral terms I did the right thing. But after almost 4,000 people had lost their jobs and after the suffering and hardship that they had to endure for a year, had they been asked then if a deal should have been struck, maybe there would have been a different answer.

I was fully aware of what I had just done. I could not tell anyone what I had heard. I just had to keep it to myself. History might judge me very harshly on that but it was one of those offers that had to be refused.

Chapter 9

Events started moving very fast after the ballot result, culminating in the ultimatum to all News International journalists that the editorial functions were being transferred to Wapping over the weekend of 25–26 January 1986. The bait was an immediate rise of £2,000 a year and free private health care; but to decline was not really an option – the NI management made it very clear that any journalist not moving to the new offices would be considered to have resigned.

The journalists were in crisis. Many had little time for the printers and it was difficult to condemn that. Only a year or so earlier the printers had walked through the picket lines when the journalists had staged, for them, a very rare official strike. As a result their strike had collapsed humiliatingly. But that was not the real concern of the reporters, sub-editors, photographers and artists who gathered on Gray's Inn Road outside the headquarters of the *Times* on the evening of Saturday 25 January to hear their general secretary, Harry Conroy, implore them to stand their ground. But he could not get it across that if the journalists closed ranks, refused to go immediately to Wapping but reported instead to their rightful place of employment, there was very little the management could do. Yes, there were executives who would get a skeleton paper out, but they could hardly keep it up for long.

People such as the bombastic Andrew Neil, then editor of the *Sunday Times* and glorying in his involvement with Rupert Murdoch (it couldn't last, I suppose) made a show, reeling off aggressive quotes to the television cameras. And Bernard Levin, once a stalwart NUJ member, later made much of lying on the floor of the bus that drove him through the picket lines.

Most journalists did not at all like the shotgun pointed at their heads. But on the other hand the tradition of getting a paper out on the streets is embedded deep inside the profession and for too long its members at News International had lost edition after edition. Too many NUJ members had seen their scoops lost, a picture dated or a column overtaken by events so that the siren call of management that things would now be different was appealing.

Several journalists did refuse to blackleg. I particularly recall Barrie Clement and David Felton, who were the labour team at the *Times*, opting for the sack rather than go to Wapping. Paul Routledge, a former labour reporter and then on the *Times*'s political team, also refused to go. And there was a very principled stand by Eric Butler, aged sixty-two, for sixteen years a sports sub-editor on the *Sun*, who continued to report for work at Bouverie Street until I suppose the lights were turned out.

Peter Wilby, later to become editor of the *New Statesman*, wrote a heart-searching article in the *New Socialist* revealing he had been with sixty *Sunday Times* journalists who had voted against moving but eventually felt forced to relocate. (In fact the vote was quite close – 68 to 60.) 'It is not a record of which I feel particularly proud,' he wrote. 'I behaved, in the end, just like any other mortgaged, middle-class suburbanite.' He had never had much time for the print unions, particularly the NGA and its interminable demands – the union had never shown the slightest regard, he wrote, for either trade union or socialist principles. But Murdoch had seemed hell-bent, not on forcing realistic negotiation on manning levels and new technology, but on sacking 5,000 people and starting afresh. 'We journalists, I suppose, had expected gentler treatment' – but they never received it.

Wilby, with thirty other *Sunday Times* staff, reported to the old offices on the Tuesday morning in a group which included two editorial executives, as well as two distinguished foreign correspondents – a revolt Wilby described as one by 'affronted middle-aged property owners – the sort of people who protest against the building of a new bypass'. But after a lonely few days they realised that their protest was pointless and that emotion was no substitute for a job or a pay packet. Reluctantly they reported to Wapping.

'Wapping' as a description of the location was strongly disapproved by the Murdoch management. Whenever we met I was asked to call the new site

'Tower Hamlets' but I refused. The word 'Wapping' had just the right ring about it and I was determined that that infamous location would go down in history with all the rest of the seedy memories of the old docks area.

Years later when I was fortunate enough to be offered a life peerage by the late and dear John Smith, I suggested in jest my title should be Dean of Wapping. But the Garter at Arms, who approves titles, as he explained to me, to spare the Queen any embarrassment, very quickly hit my suggestion firmly on the head!

The public probably has the impression that trade unions spend their time immersed in strikes and disputes and do little else. In fact much of the time we were dealing with bread-and-butter issues, but of great importance to members – pensions, health and safety, sickness benefit and attending meetings about all kinds of concerns to ordinary working folk. That is what we really got paid for. But as we rushed towards what became the final major industrial relations showdown in Britain we had to start preparing for the union to go onto what was virtually a war footing.

I have twice been privileged to dine in Lord Nelson's cabin aboard HMS *Victory* and was fascinated at the way in which it could be – and was – stripped for battle, its chairs folding away, the panelling taken off, the windows turned into ports for the guns to fire through. In the run-up to the fateful weekend crunch we were in much the same mood at Hadleigh. The adrenalin was running through our veins, of course, but it was not so much a macho atmosphere as a tense, heart-thumping feeling.

I was calm, though, because I had spent so much time thinking about the situation. I knew I was going to have to ask my members in wholesale distribution to give their support. These are the people who got the papers out night after night, working for a fraction of what the Fleet Street people were taking home, in cold dank warehouses, in trains that were not unlike cattle trucks, or driving alone over the moors in ice and fog. I knew more about these people than most at Hadleigh because in Manchester I had represented the largest group of them in the union.

I knew I could not expect all of these members to come out but I did think that those in the big cities such as London, Manchester, Glasgow, Birmingham,

Liverpool and Cardiff would back us. But equally I knew that this would be so-called secondary action, which was now banned by the Thatcher anti-union laws, and that our union would almost certainly be in the High Court within days.

Meanwhile, the Murdoch management was applying pressure on the wholesale management – the people running W. H. Smith, John Menzies and Surridge Dawson. They were being told bluntly that if they did not instruct their employees to work normally such weakness would go neither unnoticed nor forgotten. Those of our members who did strike lost pay but also were unable to claim any unemployment benefit and were threatened with the sack.

I must say that at the time I felt more for them than for some of the Fleet Street printers. Throughout the early stages of the dispute I knew that our biggest public relations problem was getting it across that this dispute was not solely about so-called greedy Fleet Street printers. I had to get the public to understand that there were others at Gray's Inn Road and Bouverie Street who were not on the printers' rates of pay and tended to be forgotten. This included the librarians at the *Times,* who lost their jobs and were heartbroken to see their historic files tossed aside. And the cleaners, the messengers, the clerks, the tele-ad girls, the secretaries, the copy takers, the computer operators, the catering staff, the telephonists, the circulation reps and the firefighters – their jobs went too when Murdoch accepted his lawyer's advice to quit the old offices and transfer the entire operation to Wapping. This meant that the new site could not be legally picketed under the new industrial relations law.

The total number of clerical branch members involved was approximately 820, 47 per cent of whom were women. The branch reported that the clerical staff had never been involved in any discussion over the move to Wapping, as Murdoch had always maintained that the move would simply involve production staff. For many, the first they knew about the move out of Gray's Inn Road and Bouverie Street was when they were told they had lost their jobs.

Another aspect that was going to be vital was, quite simply, money. The secondary action was going to get us into the courts and we would be on the way to sequestration, which would mean losing control of all our banking and finances. We had to think ahead about that very carefully.

I had taken legal advice from our lawyers, Thompsons, a famous name in the trade union world because the founder had voluntarily gone to jail in the 1920s with a score of London councillors, including the great Labour pacifist MP George Lansbury, rather than implement swingeing benefit cuts on hungry unemployed people. Thompsons were equally at our side throughout, in particular their John Harris, who was with me almost as much as Bill Miles in the year-long battle.

But I did not let Harris join us at the offices of the London Central branch when representatives of the NGA arrived with a bulky black case. Miles called me out of a discussion and we went along a corridor to what seemed like a cupboard or a cloakroom. The black case was opened to reveal a quarter of a million pounds in cash – quite a sight.

It was a loan from the NGA, offered because they too could see that SOGAT's funds were likely to be sequestrated. They had no members in distribution and so were unlikely to be involved in secondary action. In any case the NGA had experienced the process once in the earlier skirmish with Eddie Shah's newspaper plant. Come what may, they were not going to repeat that experience.

Those at the top of the NGA could also see that we were likely to bear the brunt of those difficulties and they were probably not too unhappy about that. Their reckoning was that SOGAT would end up bankrupt, weakened by the Wapping dispute, and would eventually topple into a shotgun amalgamation with the NGA.

I asked one of our branch officers, Terry Lord, secretary of the London Ruling and Manufacturing Stationery branch, which was unlikely to be involved in the Fleet Street dispute, to set up a special fund to handle all donations and help from other unions and the Labour movement. I could see that no money could come into the main union funds as it would immediately be frozen by the sequestrators. Lord, a member of the union executive, was highly regarded for his integrity and honesty. I asked him to open a separate bank account and to keep scrupulously accurate records – and a full list of all donations; I wanted no stories later, as happened in the miners' dispute, suggesting that money had been siphoned off and abused. Every penny, I told him, had to be accounted for.

The money the NGA were lending us was not going to the welfare fund but instead, as it was in cash, would be used to pay for meetings, taxis and subsistence in the weeks ahead – weeks which soon became months.

'Look, Bill, there's no way we can carry this around,' I told Miles. 'We've got to break it up quickly.'

Each of the national officers was told he was going to have £10,000 to look after, for which he would be taking full responsibility and had to know what happened to every penny. Miles took his sum and I put £10,000 in my handbag, which is quite a lump. Just imagine a handbag snatch in King's Cross – who would have believed me?

We had taken the precaution of opening a secret cash deposit box in the City, which my personal secretary, Margaret Tothill, fixed. (She later became the secretary of a judge touring the country for assizes and I often wondered whether she ever told him the story.) But the reaction of my No. 2, Danny Sergeant, the general president, was a real laugh. Miles and I explained to him that he was going to have to have £10,000 but that he would also have to be one of those responsible for accessing the safe deposit box, which would contain about £200,000.

Sergeant went white. He wanted nothing to do with it. I emphasised he had to be involved because as effectively No. 2 in the union he had to be ready to take over if something happened to me. And there needed to be a password chosen, which we wanted him to choose. It had to be something that could easily be remembered and one that came easily to him, we told Sergeant.

He squirmed. For a man who had stood for office and run against me for the general secretary job, it was hard to comprehend.

'Come on, Danny. Give us a word – one that means something to you. Whatever it is we will accept it,' I said.

After a long, long silence Sergeant suddenly blurted it out. 'Geronimo.'

It stopped my words flowing for a while . . .

The safe deposit account could only be accessed by Sergeant or me but only I ever went there when necessary, to top up our cash in hand. He did not want to know. By now I was becoming quite a well-known face and the sight of me coming from or going to a bank vault near Mansion House would make a news picture and lead to questions about what I was doing there. So I had to resort to a headscarf and dark glasses as I slipped in to open our box after writing down the magic word, Geronimo.

After the ballot the unions had to give New International seven days' notice of an official strike and I hoped this crucial period might lead to some serious negotiation. But in my heart I knew it was a forlorn hope. In any case Murdoch, in ordering the transfer to Wapping, made it quite clear he had no intention of backing off. Indeed he personally supervised the move and was to be seen about the offices in his shirtsleeves, happily giving television interviews and inspecting the output from his new printing presses.

We used the interval to get our house in order and to prepare for a long strike. Most of the SOGAT executive clung to the hope that as we had had a national ballot and had given strike notice, we would be covered under the Thatcher legislation, unlike Arthur Scargill. I told our executive that this was likely to be a long-drawn-out affair, not one of the quick overnight battles to which national newspapers had become accustomed, and that in all probability, like Scargill, we would see the union sequestrated.

It was obvious to me that Hadleigh, over an hour's drive from London, was hopeless as a strike headquarters. We had to be in central London, and as the branches owned their own offices they seemed unlikely to have them seized by a sequestrator, whereas it seemed quite possible we could be banned from Hadleigh. So we chose the offices of the London Central branch in Britannia Street, off Gray's Inn Road near King's Cross station and a stone's throw from the *Times* office, from where to run the strike. And handy for the media.

The branch turned over a complete floor to us, including a useful boardroom, but we needed to think about fast communication. Though it was only twenty years ago it seems strange to think that there was no email and no mobile phones apart from those in our cars. And even then numbers were not handed out too freely.

As a union we were quite well advanced in the installation of computers and each branch office had one so that we could gather in financial information each day and send out routine information from our mainframe. It was arranged that we would have the facility to send each branch a message each morning and afternoon 'without disturbing the system too much' but it was far too inflexible. So I decided we needed a good fax machine installed. This would allow us to talk quickly to the lawyers and the media, and maybe even hear from Murdoch himself.

Bob Finch, my personal assistant, investigated and on 20 January, four days before the transfer to Wapping, he reported he could get one cash on delivery for a mere £4,150 from a company in Ilford, east London, which could install it within forty-eight hours. Servicing was just £445 a year! (One could buy nine or ten machines for just the servicing charge these days and they would be very much faster – such is the way the technology has moved in only twenty years.) Finch made a number of other suggestions and summed up, 'As you have already said, the only way we can maintain and develop this particular dispute is by co-operation, dedication and communication.'

Another key decision was to set up what became known as the Union Jack Committee – a small group of executive members representing the whole union who would be at my side throughout the year-long dispute. We had five London branches, which could seldom all agree, but in any case the strike was going to involve the whole union, not just London. Our people in Manchester and Glasgow were heavily involved anyway but most of the other branches would be affected either through poorer service or by seeing the union's resources draining away.

I wanted to ensure that the provincial branches, whose members after all were the people who had voted me into office, were fully consulted and involved. I told the executive that we had to plan for the worst – not the best. It was going to be a long dispute. There was no way that the executive could meet every day but I needed a sounding board from amongst them.

I looked at the executive and first of all chose Roy Gunning from Belfast – trustworthy, very good sense of values, a straight guy who could not be fobbed off. Then from Edinburgh, which had our biggest branch in Scotland, I chose George Lamont. He was not part of the left-wing macho clique in Scotland. No pushover, he would tell it as it was. From Wales I had Tony Walsh from our big Cardiff branch. He was very commercially minded, with a business kind of approach – a bit hesitant sometimes, so I had to watch him. But he was pretty courageous and if one could swing him to a point of view, he would support it. I knew that was going to be important in the months ahead. Then, of course, I wanted the strategic thinker Dennis Hill from Leeds, who I had beaten in the general secretary election. I wished he had been the general president but it was not to be. Finally from London I chose Ted Chard, secretary of the biggest branch, London Central, who I knew would have to tread carefully with the militant left at his back but who I felt I could trust.

My loyal Union Jack Committee stood shoulder to shoulder with me throughout the difficult year of 1986. They spent weeks away from their offices to be at my side in London while still managing to keep their own branches ticking over. I will always value their sacrifice and contribution to the News International dispute.

As I feared, following the unofficial blacking of the wholesalers, we heard from our solicitors that our action in stopping their distribution was being challenged by News International in the High Court and we knew we had little in the way of defence. The judge thought so too, fined us £10,000 and ordered SOGAT to stop the illegal picketing. The fine represented a lot of ordinary workers' funds but we sent a cheque to court for £10,000, knowing it was money down the drain because, although we apologised to the court, we did nothing to desist. So that meant we were liable for contempt of court.

A week later we were back in court and the judge, Justice Michael Davies, turned up the pressure, ordering immediate sequestration of all our funds and assets and imposing a heavy fine. I sent a carefully drafted letter of apology to the court explaining why we felt unable to comply and issued it to the press but we were spitting in the wind.

In the press statement SOGAT emphasised it was an executive decision not to appear in court which had not been taken lightly but with 'great and genuine respect' for the court. Still there was little doubt we would be sequestrated.

I had rather hoped, though, that we would have some say about which firm of accountants would be called in to hold our funds but that was not the case. Instead the judge asked Murdoch's lawyers what firm he wanted and Ernst & Whinney were named. Arrangements had already been made with them, the judge was told.

In a handwritten letter addressed to 'Dear Miss Dean' I was told that Mr Justice Davies had found SOGAT in contempt and fined us £25,000. 'The fine should be paid by Banker's Order or cheque made payable to HM Paymaster General and sent to Room 277 at the court building in The Strand. Yours sincerely, Mrs B. A. Young.'

One lesson I had learned from the miners' dispute was that there was no point in playing hide and seek with professional accountants, who had shown Arthur Scargill they could find his union's funds wherever he hid them – even across the Irish Sea in the Republic – and charge the union a vast sum to do it.

So reluctantly our lawyers handed me Ernst & Whinney's address, Becket House (a martyr, rather appropriately, I thought) in Lambeth Palace Road, and their telephone number. I called up the partner responsible. He seemed surprised to get my call but sounded quite co-operative when I told him my attitude and asked to meet. I said I recognised he had a job to do and I hoped he would understand that I had one as well. An appointment was fixed for the early evening, that day.

My Union Jack Committee were anything but relaxed, though, when I told them they were all coming with me to meet a Mr Nigel Hamilton and a Mr William Roberts of Ernst & Whinney, who had been appointed Commissioners of the Sequestration by the High Court. This was to be their first exposure to the kind of pressures we would have to face and they were not at all pleased. Several refused at first to come and others made it clear they wanted to tell the accountants, very bluntly, what they thought of their role as sequestration administrators of our union.

I explained I knew how they felt but their attitude was not going to get us anywhere. We had to use our native negotiating skills to come out of the meeting having established a relationship and an understanding of how we would work. If we cut up rough, I told the Union Jack team, we could lose the use of our cars and be denied access to the Hadleigh office, and wages might not be paid. I also wanted the accountants to leave the welfare fund alone. Most importantly, I did not want the weekly cheques that some branches sent out to our pensioners frozen, because many poorer people depended on them to top up their state pension.

As we talked it through, trying to maintain a civilised dialogue, the tension at the accountants' offices was tangible and I could feel fury coursing through George Lamont of Edinburgh, who was sitting next to me. I thought he would leap across the boardroom table and grab the smartly suited accountant by the throat. But eventually we managed to reach an accommodation, as they say in such circles, and for the moment we were left with our office, use of our cars, and best of all, the staff and the pensioners would continue to be paid. Ernst & Whinney also agreed to release funds from our union bank account to pay the second fine which had been imposed on SOGAT by the judge – otherwise we would have been in contempt of court again, and the costs would have ratcheted further skywards.

To my surprise all but one of the main clearing banks co-operated and did not make life difficult. The exception, with great irony, was none other than the Co-operative Bank, which was supposed to be the friend of the working class and which had made many millions out of it. They refused immediately to cash our pensioners' cheques at Co-op stores, causing chaos and some hardship all across the country, which, at the time, I judged to be very unhelpful indeed.

A further nightmare was the arrival of a bill for £24,000 from British Telecom – needless to say the phones had been very busy indeed. Unless we settled it the union could be cut off and, without mobiles in those days, that would have caused a crisis in communication. We did not see how the sequestrators were going to free up funds for phones which were actively being used pursuing the dispute.

That was when our friends in Europe stepped in. There is much talk in the union movement about the international brotherhood but here it was in action – a cheque made out to British Telecom came through almost immediately. Trade unionists in countries including Germany, France, Sweden and Finland, particularly those who supplied the newsprint for Murdoch's papers, were concerned at our struggle and had found a way to help. It was truly a godsend.

Some of the louder mouths amongst the Fleet Street workers had been very critical of the Scandinavians for not stopping the newsprint delivery, oblivious to the fact that their workers also had agreements to honour and had no dispute. The lefties talked of 'principle' but it was hard to believe that they would have stopped work to help the Finns or the Swedes. Even so, it seemed as if some took matters into their own hands when a fire was started at a warehouse south of the Thames in an attempt to cut newsprint supply. Though we had our suspicions as to who was responsible, we kept our mouths shut but it did not surprise us all that much to learn that the fire raisers had picked on the wrong plant. Supply to Murdoch was not reduced by a single reel. Much later in the dispute, by contrast, some very determined fire raisers really did strike at the newsprint supply and started one of the biggest fires in London for many years at Convoys in Deptford.

From the outset it was clear that the media and its handling was going to be crucial in the dispute and on the face of it Murdoch held all the cards. But that was not how it worked out.

Murdoch had constructed, on the advice of Farrer & Co., his lawyers, a web of new companies obstructing us from interrupting News International's activities. Siting all production at Wapping, for a start, meant that we were acting illegally to picket because rightfully our places of dispute were Bouverie Street and Gray's Inn Road – within a few days just soulless empty shells. We knew we could stand there for years and nobody would care.

What of course we did not know at the time was the secret deal that News International had made with TNT, the big transport group, which originally – surprise, surprise – had had Australian investment on start-up. An entire fleet of unmarked lorries had been bought for the purpose and their drivers were trained but not told what their mission was to be. The TNT deal was a master stroke by Murdoch and it meant he could bypass completely the traditional distribution system by overnight train to sorting places where trucks took over – all of which were vulnerable to trade union interception. TNT was a totally new distribution company and so legally we were not supposed, under the Thatcher laws, to interfere with them either – even though they were taking our members' work away from them.

We had got an inkling of the plans a short time before the Wapping balloon went up, though. Bill Miles wrote on behalf of the union in November 1985 asking about the rumours that News International were planning to use TNT. Allan Fisher, News International's production director, wrote back on 12

December: 'So far as News International Newspapers is concerned I can assure you that we have no agreement with TNT for distribution of our titles and I suppose that any questions regarding what TNT and its representatives are alleged to be saying or replying to wholesalers are best addressed to TNT.' A straight lie.

Fisher said that Murdoch had mentioned TNT at a meeting to the unions on 30 September about the possibility of using their vehicles with the so-called new London evening newspaper – which later we discovered was a complete blind to obscure the covert plans to move to Wapping in January.

Miles wrote back on 19 December to say he just did not accept Fisher's story. 'There is irrefutable evidence that they [TNT] are carrying out a survey concerning distribution of the *Sun* and *News of the World*, and are making tentative arrangements to employ a number of people to carry out this function.'

We had already issued a press release to say that the first weekend of producing the *News of the World* and the *Sunday Times* with untrained labour at Wapping had been chaotic. From our own figures we found that of sixty main centres, forty-three – or 71 per cent – did not receive the *NoW* and 26 per cent of the *Sunday Times* failed to arrive. Where the titles did reach the provinces they had often arrived too late to be delivered. That was heartening, but for how long would it continue?

All this had to be explained to the media and as soon as the strike began we called a press conference at Congress House in Great Russell Street, the TUC headquarters.

I don't think I have ever seen such a big gathering of media people – something like a hundred journalists, writers, cameramen, radio and TV reporters, TV operators, sound technicians were all jostling around. The dispute had everything – a major showdown between a millionaire proprietor and print workers led by a young woman – as one headline put it very kindly, 'Beauty and the Beast'. I do not like exploiting my sex but I quickly grasped that this presented me with a major propaganda opportunity and I determined to take advantage of it fully.

I also remembered that I had to keep everything simple. I was determined not to fall into trade union jargon, which is a turn-off to viewers and listeners. Instead I pointed out that this dispute was not about fat cats but about ordinary workers such as tele-ad girls and librarians, with families and children to feed and mortgages to pay. People whose lives had been brutally shattered overnight and with not a penny in compensation – folk who just wanted their jobs and the right to work. Their readers and listeners could easily identify with them, I explained.

The journalists loved it – not least because for once here was a dispute about their own industry which they could really report. For too many years they had been warned by their owners and by the Fleet Street printers to 'keep off the grass', so that the industrial correspondents, while reporting the failures in many manufacturing industries, were forced to look away from the mess on their own doorsteps and had given up trying to cover the true story.

But not any more, Murdoch was to find out. I understand, though I do not know if it is true, that he told his colleagues that he had everything planned but had not bargained for the media battle he was confronted with by the young woman leading the main print union. Murdoch has a tough skin but one suspects that even he found it hurtful to be projected as a harsh and unfeeling grasping employer lampooned in cartoons, lashed in Parliament and lynched verbally in print.

The press conferences continued daily at Congress House for a while until events settled down and we were able to switch them to Britannia Street. Even so, the boardroom there, which could hold about forty, was always fairly full.

Each day we would start off with a morning session with the media and would always try to have a new angle ready for them. Sometimes as events sped along we might hold another press conference in the late afternoon for the daily papers and evening TV bulletins. So Wapping became a place name known in every household in the UK – and in many other places. In particular our struggle was being monitored in Australia, where Murdoch had his supporters (and plenty of enemies); in the United States, where printing had had its problems too and Murdoch was now a citizen; and in Canada and Scandinavia too.

Even in the early days, when in my heart I doubted if we could ever win, I realised that by mounting the public against Murdoch I might eventually be able to wring compensation out of him for my members and that became my bottom line. Of course the media were not satisfied to leave it there and almost every day someone like a woman columnist, a feature writer, a TV or a radio journalist wanted time with me. It all had to be built into my daily schedule, but I tried very hard not to let people down and to make myself available as soon as possible.

Virtually overnight I found I was becoming a household name, recognised in the street or doing my shopping. Taxi drivers in London are a special breed but they soon began to know my movements if I was not using my car and they would whisk me through the back streets of the city as they gave me their own views on Wapping or trade unions.

I still have a handwritten note of the interviews lined up for me on a day shortly after the press conference which was not untypical. It had been written out by my personal assistant, Margaret Tothill. They were with the *New Statesman, Marxism Today*, the *Australian National Times*, Japan's *Asahi Shimbun*, the *Washington Post, Time, Forbes, Libération* of France, the Australian Press Association, *Woman's Own*, the *Sunday Mirror* and United Newspapers, owners of provincial papers such as the *Sheffield Star*; LBC, Capital Radio, BBC World Service, the BBC *Today* programme and Swedish radio; Channel 7 television in Australia, Irish television, *Union World*, a weekly programme on Channel Four, BBC *Breakfast Time*, ITN, Belgian television, and the US current affairs TV programme *7 Days*.

And that was just one day.

Looking back through the cuttings of some of the interviews stirs up some wonderful memories of friends, for example Brian Hope, who was the industrial editor of the *Manchester Evening News*. He wrote, 'She's blonde, she's beautiful and she's got me into trouble more than once.' I am not sure what the instances were but he went on to justify his naughty sexist remarks because he recalled I had told him once, 'I love make-up and I spend a lot on my clothes.'

Hope went on to say that I was at the centre of the bitterest industrial dispute since the miners' strike but that there was never a hair out of place as I dashed from place to place. Which was good to know. 'The lady remains crisp and cool,' he added.

Ruth Wishart wrote a big feature in the *Scotsman* headed 'Sogat's Press war creates a media star'. She said, 'In fact the 42-year-old general secretary of SOGAT is, in anyone's terminology, an extremely attractive woman . . . not to acknowledge that at all would be to ignore the fact that she has chosen to use her appearance as one of the more potent weapons in a considerable armoury of talents.'

The *Daily Mirror* put it bluntly that the Thatcher employment laws had reduced the trade unions in Britain to near-impotence. 'No one has demonstrated this more effectively than Brenda Dean, general secretary of the print union SOGAT,' it declared. 'By her cool, reasonable style Ms Dean has suddenly become the pin-up of the trade unions.

'There is growing anxiety inside the Government that her reasoned approach is helping to sway public opinion away from Rupert Murdoch because of the way he sacked 5,500 printers. Still worse she seems to be persuading many that Mrs Thatcher's anti-union drive has gone too far.' I don't think the Whitehall spin doctors of the day would have liked that much.

Jill Armstrong wrote a major feature in the right-wing *Yorkshire Post* and gave me a very fair hearing. She noted that even to those totally opposed to trade unions I 'represented a far more acceptable face than that of the old-style trade union leader'. 'People do not quite know how to cope with this well-dressed, attractive woman, in the male-dominated world of printing. But many have learned to their cost that underneath that pleasant, open manner she is tough enough to make mincemeat of you should she choose.'

There were many more and I have only quoted a few to illustrate the point that in this uphill struggle to get our views across we were better organised and winning through, when all the betting would have predicted that we would be at the receiving end of an even harsher media than Arthur Scargill endured.

The other front on which we had to be extremely well organised was on the law. From the beginning I knew that the scales were tipped well against us but we could not be seen to lie down or capitulate while there was a chance of prevailing. Our lawyers, Thompsons, were so close to the trade union movement that they even had their offices in Congress House. True, they used a separate entrance but they were very close indeed to the trade union leaders and it was not uncommon for one of them to wander through the TUC corridors to the Thompson flat to join the solicitors over lunch or an evening drink. They had no employer or management clients – only the unions. Each of the various partners specialised in one of the major union accounts and our particular partner was gentle John Harris, who knew everything about the union, its personalities and its failings. He was almost part of the furniture.

Initially the firm's intention was to direct SOGAT to one of the barristers well disposed to the movement and who relied for their fees on a regular supply of briefs from Thompsons or one of the other solicitors' firms which specialised in the ever-growing field of employment law. I had given some thought to that while mulling everything over in Lanzarote and was determined that what we wanted was the best lawyer in this field – not necessarily a friendly face.

Eventually the solicitors came up with the name of Eldred Tabachnik QC, who shared chambers in King's Bench Walk, at the Temple, and the union agreed with this suggestion. From the very early stages Tabachnik was our prime source of legal advice. But each time I went to King's Bench Walk I found Harris already present before I was shown in to see Tabachnik.

After it happened a couple of times I spoke to Harris and asked him why. Somewhat embarrassed, he explained that this was the way legal etiquette worked – first the solicitor briefed the barrister and then the client came in to answer questions. 'Not any more,' I told Harris very firmly. 'Look – I am in charge of this union and the dispute. It is my name on the writ and if anyone goes to jail it will be me and neither of you. I want it clearly understood that in any briefing I will be doing it – in your presence of course but as I will be signing the cheques to pay the bill I expect to be totally and fully involved.' Perhaps a bit crestfallen but clearly judging which way the wind was blowing, Harris accepted.

I had studied the legal situation and understood it, but the clarity of the mind of a Queen's Counsel at the top of his profession was what I wanted and Tabachnik provided it. I do not know where he stood politically although I would be surprised if he was a Labour supporter. But his ability to go to the crux of an issue was impressive and what I wanted. He would brush away any irrelevancies and I got to like him over the year-long dispute.

Initially I gave him the paper I had presented to the union executive setting out the issues and the likely cost of confrontation with News International. We met at his chambers on the Sunday afternoon following the special executive meeting. Tabachnik thought it over the top. But later he admitted I was not far out.

I usually met him at his Temple Chambers early in the morning with Harris but on one occasion I even went to his home in Wimbledon in the evening.

There were other lawyers involved as well and I particularly remember James Goudie, whose wife Mary was later a colleague of mine in the House of Lords, and Nick Hinchcliffe, who I learned was a crack shot at Bisley. They all worked in the chambers headed by Derry Irvine QC, who later was a close colleague in the House of Lords and became Lord Chancellor. It was of course in those same chambers where a young Tony Blair met his future wife, Cherie.

Another key player in the developing crisis was the TUC. It is always there, in every major dispute, sometimes keeping itself informed, sometimes trying to resolve a dispute, or perhaps to get the employers or the government to intervene. The TUC's officials keep their ear to the ground, ready to mediate, and indeed pride themselves on their feel for a situation. But on this occasion, although they could see there was going to be a major and possibly violent confrontation, there was very little they could do. For once they were caught in the middle – not between employers and a union member, but between two very different unions. And although they possibly sided with the print union, the EETPU, which wanted the TUC to keep out, was a very big player – and payer – and could argue that it had right on its side. Had not its members been poached by SOGAT?

We lodged a formal complaint against the electricians' union for its blacklegging at Wapping and both Tony Dubbins and I appeared before the full TUC General Council to pursue it. But we knew it was extremely difficult territory for the TUC.

The TUC general secretary was Norman Willis, a lovely, jovial man but perhaps not the shrewdest ever to hold the post. He had been given a very rough time during the miners' dispute. At one time when he was addressing a noisy meeting in south Wales, a hangman's noose was lowered over his head from a rafter. I was determined that Willis was not going to be similarly humiliated in this dispute. My main contact, though, was John Monks, destined to be Willis's successor, who at that time was head of the TUC's organisation department. I had respect for him as he knew a lot about the complexities of the newspaper industry, having been heavily involved in the year-long dispute at the *Times* which preceded Rupert Murdoch's takeover of the oldest-established newspaper in the country and possibly the world. Monks knew Murdoch quite well from this period and the newspaper owner had some regard for him. At one time I believe he offered Monks a job, which did not surprise me because the TUC official was very able.

So although it could not really intervene, the TUC was doing all it could to help us behind the scenes. But we knew because of the poaching issue that we were really on the back foot. The EETPU were paying us back in spades, as the saying goes.

Another person involved was Neil Kinnock, then the leader of the opposition, struggling to pull the party together after its disastrous electoral failure in 1983. Kinnock hardly needed a punch-up in Fleet Street in the approach to the next General Election. Our London hotheads were demanding that he should intervene in all kinds of ways and should call for a boycott by the Labour movement of all Murdoch's papers. That was unlikely to be very helpful to achieving our ambition of a Labour government and an end to the restrictions of the Thatcher government. I was determined that we were not going to do anything to scupper Kinnock's chances.

However, Kinnock did refuse to have any contact with News International journalists; twenty years later this still seems to rankle with News Corporation journalists such as Michael Jones, formerly the *Sunday Times*'s political editor. They like to dish it out but journalists can get quite upset if they are on the receiving end, it seems.

Chapter 10

Once the dispute really began it was obvious that we needed to be extremely well organised at the actual Wapping site because News International certainly were and so were the Metropolitan Police.

There was an arrangement of nightly and all-day picketing outside the plant and major efforts each Saturday. Supporters would then come from all over the country to join in the effort to halt the TNT trucks leaving the printing works, to help to project the issue and emphasise that, whatever Rupert Murdoch might wish, it was not going to go away quietly. This demonstrated to News International, and to the people defying the pickets to go in and out each day, that the dispute was going to drag on. It also went a long way to help to keep up the morale of the thousands out of work with no income and very little prospect of ever finding a real job again. They wanted the right to demonstrate peacefully and although I was never happy about it they wanted to bring along their children too. It also often helped to involve a wider membership of the union and to counter fears that their union was being wrecked on a narrow issue.

Of course we suffered from the rent-a-mob crowd, too, who had scores to settle and were a major source of concern for us. There were people from the left who had grievances against the police from the miners' dispute and there were right-wing thugs seeking to knock hell out of left-wingers who had thrashed them in the past. I saw some of them walking along carrying lumps of paving stone and iron bars, telling people they had arrived to settle scores from the miners' dispute. Wapping to them was just an excuse for a punch-up. These were the last people we wanted anywhere near Wapping and it was a constant struggle – and a worry to me personally – that we had somehow to maintain control and discipline on the marches and particularly outside Fortress

Wapping's main gates. I knew we could so easily have lost our public support with a flare-up there.

From the beginning I went on record condemning violence and warning that I would walk away if our people indulged in it. At the same time, although increasingly it left a bitter taste, I said publicly that the police had a job to do and it was not our intention to take them on. Needless to say this did not go down too well with some of the hotheads.

Our left-wing activists such as Bill Freeman and Michael Hicks were good at organising this kind of demonstration and somehow acquired a double-decker bus, which was parked up in a side street across the Highway at Wapping, near some council flats. Both Freeman and Hicks were determined somehow to try to drive the dispute and needed watching closely. Freeman was more interested in the industrial aspects of the dispute. Hicks, though, wanted to be a martyr and did succeed in getting himself arrested and subsequently sent to jail. Although it had little impact on the dispute it appeared to make him feel very fulfilled. Actually it was a relief to me to know where Hicks was for a while and that he was beyond making mischief.

The London branches of course had plenty of money and they were not sequestrated so they had no trouble funding the bus and kitting it out. That became our operations room. Downstairs there was a small first-aid centre and a space where people could sit for a while and get tea or coffee. Upstairs was the office, and it was from those windows on Saturday 3 May 1986 that I was to watch, quite horrified, as Metropolitan Police officers with no identifying numbers on their collars beat up our people with a savagery which I had never before associated with British policemen.

Our people that night were pretty inoffensive in terms of a national dispute, and while they may have shouted insults they did nothing, so far as I could see, which deserved that treatment. It was pure thuggery, nodded through by the Thatcher government.

George Holmes, a level-headed Londoner, who was one of our branch secretaries and also a member of the union executive, took charge at the Wapping site and also liaised with the police. If I was not available I knew Holmes would always be there seeking to keep matters on an even keel. He got on extremely well with the City of London Police, through whose area we would march, starting off in Fleet Street. But it was much more difficult when we got into the Wapping area, which was in the control of the Metropolitan Police. Relations with the Met were bad almost from the beginning.

I tried very hard to achieve an understanding but the man in charge, Assistant Commissioner Wynn Jones, who was known as Rambo, did not want to have any contact. He liked to be seen in a jumper with epaulettes and conveyed a military presence – hardly the role of an unarmed civil force. I found out later that he had been in charge at Greenham Common, where the women protesters against US nuclear weapons had no time for him. They hated Jones. I was not all that surprised.

One could not help feeling that the Metropolitan Police were operating on some kind of amber light at government level, rather as they had during the miners' dispute. But should the police of Britain become more akin to the paramilitary force in Italy or in some of the Eastern European nations, rather than the civil police force of a democratic nation operating with public consent drawn through the ballot box?

The police would play games with our people – hiding in side streets, for example, knowing that some of our pickets would be unable to avoid the temptation to take advantage. They virtually invited the strikers to transgress. When they did the Met would suddenly emerge in full riot gear, batons flying, setting about our people, who had none of the protection their assailants possessed. Rambo liked to use the mounted police too, some of whom I later found were women, and the chance to gallop at pickets and scatter them was probably too much to resist. I suppose in a way it was an opportunity to try out riot control tactics in real-life situations.

When there were strong rumours and broad hints from the City Police that we were going to be given a thrashing I went to see Jones, who had his operational headquarters at Shoreditch police station, just off City Road.

I did not trust him. He was smooth and rather smarmy and denied any knowledge of such a plan. I quickly decided there was little point in trying to establish any kind of relationship and I was not all that surprised to see that his career faltered despite the impression given that he was destined for the top.

But while all attention focused on the News International dispute I could not allow myself to forget that I had a major trade union to run and that besides the 5,000 involved at Wapping there were almost 200,000 up and down the country who looked to us for leadership and attention to their pay and conditions. In particular I was in charge nationally of two sets of wage negotiations: one for the papermakers and the other for an even bigger group of workers, those who earned their bread and butter in daily print work up and down the country. There were more than 100,000 of them, producing the books, magazines, stationery, envelopes and account books on which the country runs each day. Fortunately George Beattie, our papermaking officer, was able to take charge of the paper agreement, which was due for review in February, but the general print agreement had to have my total concentration.

Luckily I have always been able to focus on one issue at a time and not to be distracted, so by March we were able to conclude a good deal giving our members a 6.4 per cent increase on their basic rates, which made me feel a good deal more comfortable about wider union events. And our 1,600 members producing printing ink won a good deal too; as I wrote in the union journal, 'after all, where would printers be without ink?'

All the time, though, I was conscious I was in the spotlight and was as careful as possible not to attract attention. One of the few places where I could get a little peace was at Geoff Wright's, my hairdresser in Baker Street, who would fit me in whenever my hair needed attention. With daily TV and press interviews, that was almost every day in the early stages of the Wapping dispute. Often he would come in early and open up the shop for me and the dispute was never raised – somehow Geoff and his team seemed to know to give me some space and time to think. Baker Street became an oasis for me.

With the demand on my time almost non-stop from the media it was tempting to forget that the real issue was with News International and that the propaganda battle was secondary to trying to resolve the dispute. On the other hand, unless we could keep the confrontation in the public eye it would slip off the front pages and off the screen, which would suit Murdoch admirably. That was where a young woman named Lyn Bryan was an absolute godsend.

In the early stages I was asked what help I needed by Rodney Bickerstaffe, the outspoken Yorkshire-bred secretary of the National Union of Public Employees, which was about to go into a three-union merger with the local government officers and the health service workers to form Unison. Over lunch he offered to lend me money but I said what I needed more was a vital resource – someone who could handle the media for me.

I had my eye on Bryan, who was known in the union world as a good operator who had had a key role in elevating Bickerstaffe's public image – though we all knew her raw material to be one hundred per cent!

Bickerstaffe very generously immediately arranged to second Bryan to SOGAT for as long as the battle lasted, though neither of us realised then that we were to be engaged in it for more than twelve months. Bryan knew all the industrial correspondents well and most of the political journalists too. She understood the subtleties of dealing with television, where background and sound are so important, as was then the time needed to get film or video back to the studio. No satellite transmission in 1986.

She moved in straightaway and immediately her calm competence was felt in the operation. It lifted an enormous burden from the shoulders of my own secretarial support and meant that one person was concentrating on the media issue. It took a great load off me because Bryan had my full confidence and I knew I did not have to worry about being wrongfooted or going into a press conference or media interview unprepared.

Bryan stayed the whole year and so close was our relationship at the end of it all that I rather wanted her to stay with SOGAT. I did not go behind Bickerstaffe's back but told him I wanted to make Bryan an offer. He raised no objection but sadly Bryan declined. Though I am sure she enjoyed working with my team, she knew the going was getting tougher inside the new Unison for Bickerstaffe and she returned there to help. But if I had ever thought of giving out campaign medals for the Wapping War – which, come to think about it, would have been a very good idea – then Bryan's name would have figured prominently.

In later years she worked in the Labour Party, where her knowledge must have been invaluable, and she was press officer for Margaret Beckett, the Secretary of State for Environment, Food and Rural Affairs before she became

Foreign Secretary. But Beckett made sure to take Bryan with her to the world of diplomacy.

But as the events and momentum of the dispute swirled around us the major hammer blow was undoubtedly the early sequestration of the union and the seizure of its funds. I cannot think of anything quite so debilitating for a trade union in a free democratic society. Indeed I hope that it is never allowed to happen in Britain again.

Our flow of funds was frozen, and bank accounts and assets worth £17 million seized; payment could not even be made for the oil to heat our convalescent home in Ayr; we were worried about paying staff salaries; would the phones be cut off? Above all, would we make some inadvertent mistake, quite genuinely, which would bring further High Court wrath down upon our heads and completely halt all our operations?

My attitude was to co-operate as fully as possible with the sequestrators because they could make life very difficult indeed. They wanted details of every account in each branch, not just in headquarters, and orders went out to the branches to co-operate. Not surprisingly several dragged their feet and I had to send a strongly worded instruction telling them to desist because otherwise it would bring things crashing down on all of us. We also asked every branch officer to provide their address and phone number because there was every likelihood that they were going to be barred from their offices.

A memo copied to me from Denis Bartlett, our finance officer, addressed to John Mitchell, the new organising secretary, rather summed up the atmosphere at head office. 'The representative of Ernst & Whinney who visits this office more or less each day, on the instructions he received, raised with me the fact that while their people were visiting branches in London, they discovered that on 11 February the sum of £5,000 was passed over to you. They wish to know about this money, where it is, and what has happened to it. Obviously I replied that I knew nothing about it but nevertheless they expect me to make enquiries.' I never heard what happened to that one but it was just part of the daily harassment on us all.

On 3 March we were back in court again even though I had persuaded the sequestrators to allow us to pay the £25,000 fine which had been imposed on

109

us two weeks previously. A new judge, Mr Justice Taylor, said the time had come to increase the pressure on SOGAT to make us purge our contempt. He had met the sequestrators and our lawyers in chambers but announced his decision in open court so that the media could report it. He ordered all the union's cars to be seized and warned that, unless we did purge our contempt quickly, the union headquarters at Hadleigh might be closed.

The judge agreed we had been co-operating and for that reason he would not order the offices closed yet, but added, 'I should make it clear that it is by no means axiomatic that that state of affairs will be allowed to continue indefinitely. It has to be said that behind the whole of this exercise there is contempt by the union and its officers.

'It seems to me', said the judge, 'that there is no good reason why the motor cars should not be taken into possession by the sequestrators with the other property of the union. It may be that if this step is taken the impact of the sequestration might be felt more acutely and the contempt brought to an end more quickly.'

The only good news was that the judge did allow us to pay £600 for the Ayr convalescent home's central heating and what he called other 'compassionate' payments so that we could continue to operate Ayr and our other home at Rottingdean, near Brighton. But he also made it clear that he did not consider that any of the union's ninety branches were legally independent of the headquarters and their assets should be seized.

On 10 March nearly all the union's cars had to be driven to locations identified by Ernst & Whinney. From then until the end of the dispute, nine months ahead, it would be bus, Tube, train and occasional taxi for most of us. In London the cars had to go, oddly enough, from our Hadleigh headquarters to Hadleigh Street Garage in Bethnal Green, a location under railway arches which did not meet with the drivers' approval at all. Nor did the scribbled receipts they were given go down well.

I have little doubt that some of our people were feeling frustrated and took it out on the 'attendant', who apparently gave as good as he received and told our officers their cars would be auctioned off if not reclaimed within ten days. And that he was employed by the auctioneers! But when the cars were covered in plastic sheeting it caused uproar with some of the car buffs amongst our ranks. They would be sweating under the plastic, I was warned by my colleagues.

The twenty-nine cars seized included my Rover 3500 and the president's Vauxhall Senator, with other Vauxhalls, Fords, a Datsun, an Austin and even our delivery vehicle, a Ford Escort van. Similar impounding took place in Bristol, Huddersfield, Stockport, Newcastle, Luton, Edinburgh, Glasgow, Nottingham, Birmingham, Norwich and Leicester.

I took the impounding in my stride because a loss of a car to me, while extremely inconvenient, did not strike at my pride in the way in which it seemed to affect my male colleagues. But their intense irritation forced me to write to the sequestrators to complain. Never mind the strike, this was serious!

I told Nigel Hamilton that my officers felt the vehicles' location was unsafe and that they would be damaged unless properly protected. I also sent a couple of the handwritten receipts on scrap paper to show that we did not feel the arrangements were up to scratch. I asked if it was true that Hamilton was planning to auction off all our cars.

He replied very quickly and struck a very conciliatory note. The site had been chosen because it was the cheapest inner-city location that could be found – which eventually SOGAT would have to finance – and it had 24-hour security. But he told me a better site was being sought. There was no intention to sell the cars, he added, and instructions had been given to the auctioneers not even to think about it. The plastic sheeting should not cause any short-term problems. 'We have spoken to our agents and reinforced our instruction that these vehicles were to be taken in without comment. However, it appears that some of the union staff who delivered the vehicles did so in an aggressive manner which may have prompted misunderstandings,' summed up the sequestrators.

I circulated the letter and that seemed to calm the issue. They say that if you want to annoy a woman, interfere with her hairdressing arrangements. If you want to do the same with a man, interfere with his car . . .

A few days later I was in fact mobile again because the National Graphical Association, which was also in the dispute but had not been sequestrated, said it could lend me a car 'for the duration'. My driver, Ken Tuppen, went by train to Bedford and borrowed a small automatic Ford Orion which was to serve us well in the days ahead.

*

In the course of the next few months an avalanche of mail arrived addressed to me containing helpful ideas, bitingly unfair criticism, useful information, tip-offs and pleas for help from members suffering the real impact of the shutdown.

One particular group of people I was very concerned to keep on board was the local residents living around the Wapping site. Suddenly, almost at a stroke, their home life had been shattered by busloads of helmeted police in riot gear; a swirling crowd of pickets, some disciplined and some not; articulated high-revving trucks, horns blaring, charging through the crowded streets; TV arc lights and photographers' flashbulbs; and above all virtually non-stop noise.

One of the members of our executive, Billy Osborne, a real Londoner, who was among those who had been fired by the *Times*, worked closely with George Holmes, liaising with the police, but he also concentrated on keeping in contact with the residents. He had a lot of assistance from the late Peter Shore, then the local MP, who was a great supporter and put Osborne in touch with the Association of Wapping Organisations.

At Osborne's suggestion I wrote to tell residents how much we valued their support and to say that I was aware of and apologised for the disruption to their lives. 'We know this must be very disturbing for residents and we are extremely sorry for the inconvenience this is causing.

'We have instructed all our pickets to behave towards residents with respect and courtesy. We hope you will understand the feelings of our sacked members – seeing people being bussed in from Southampton doesn't help our members, nor does it help local people who could be employed in the Wapping plant in the future.'

Patrick Hanshaw, the chairman of the association, wrote back to thank me for the letter and pledged continued support. 'It is not too many years since Wapping's docks were the hub of the universe regarding London's river trade. Our forefathers were always in the vanguard of the trade union movement's struggles for the working class of this country.

'As a dockland community we hope and pray for a successful conclusion in your fight for justice.'

But a sadder note was struck by Mr William Dennison, who lived at Tarbert Walk, Stepney, asking that the non-stop clash at the junction of Wapping Road and The Highway be kept to the minimum because a seventeen-year-old boy named Richard living nearby was dying of cancer. The letter was spotted by a member of the team which did little else but open and handle the daily mountain of post. Neither poor Richard nor his parents complained about the constant clash between the TNT truck drivers and our pickets but Mr Dennison appealed for this human tragedy to be remembered by those at this vital junction. Richard died on 10 April.

I wrote to Mr Dennison to tell him that I had been alerted to this crisis for Richard and we were trying hard to help. 'Immediately we knew we put in hand the necessary directives to comply with the wishes of the family and I do hope we were successful in achieving that,' I said in my letter. 'The local residents have been so patient, understanding and supportive in our current dispute. We are deeply grateful to them all.' It was the least I could do.

We had good support from the local authorities. At the outset of the dispute John Riley, the Labour leader of Tower Hamlets Borough Council, met with Osborne and some other London branch members to discuss the situation. Permission was given for our caravan and the council said it was stopping buying all Murdoch titles for the libraries, an act of solidarity copied up and down the country. Tower Hamlets stopped all advertising with News International and withdrew co-operation with any of its representatives. The council also passed a resolution pledging support and noting the lack of job opportunities for local people while News International was recruiting in Southampton and Australia. I don't suppose Murdoch actually noticed but it was a sincere gesture.

Riley also undertook to take up with the police why local residents were being stopped from walking near their homes and why so many roads in Wapping had been sealed off by the police. He explained that the police had powers to close roads but he doubted if they had permission to site infrared cameras for surveillance in council flats on the St George's estate in Cable

Street. He promised to investigate and also undertook to check out the validity of the rolls of razor-sharp barbed wire which had been used to surround Fortress Wapping.

Across the water, as they say in Docklands, Southwark Borough Council also wanted to register its protest; many of our members 'in the print', as it was known locally, lived in the borough. Southwark replicated many of the decisions taken by Tower Hamlets. But Southwark's leader, Tony Ritchie, added, 'the printers' fight is our fight. Once again the British Establishment watches as a foreign union breaker does their dirty work.'

From County Hall, Robert Carr, on the staff of the Greater London Council's controller of transportation weighed in too. On 25 February he wrote to Mr T. Bell, the divisional general manager of TNT, to express the concern of residents, supported by Peter Shore, at the use of lorries in the narrow streets around the printing plant. TNT had permission to bring vehicles into central London, said the GLC, and it was not concerned with the industrial dispute. But it was concerned at the reports it had received that vehicles were being used 'at night and weekends . . . and moreover driven at great speed to the annoyance and distress of residents. You will appreciate that the purpose of the lorry control scheme is to minimise the nuisance . . . this current state of affairs is completely unacceptable to the council.' The GLC threatened to revoke the licences which allowed TNT to operate at night within the inner London area.

'I must therefore ask you to reply by return of post (or by telephone) setting out your proposals to alleviate, at the earliest possible time, the problems being caused by your vehicles,' demanded Carr. I doubt if TNT shivered in its shoes but a ban on night transport could have been extremely inconvenient – and embarrassing. It was another piece of pressure mounted, but as we toiled outside Wapping, the presses inside continued to roll.

A really spirited effort came from the Rev. Walter Bailey in Rotherham, who wrote directly to Mr Justice Taylor to say he was appalled that a British judge could act in such a way. 'Surely morality comes into judgments? The printers have had 5,000 sacked by a wicked tyrant. As a Christian the union should defy you and as a Christian minister I am prepared to go to prison in support.'

In the midst of all that was going on there was pause amongst our letter

With my brother Bobby, taken in Blackpool by a self-operated photo machine.

THE NEW PHOTOMATON
Blackpool

My father (*left*) and Keith. They always got on well together.

Joe Sheridan's funeral at Manchester Cathedral. (*Manchester Evening News*)

With my brand new, bright red Triumph TR7. The members loved to see me arrive at their factories and park in the reserved management spaces! This was taken outside SOGAT's Manchester branch office in Salford. (*Daily Telegraph*)

The best part of being a trade union leader is going out and about all over the country, meeting the members and seeing what their daily work really involves. I found it not only useful feedback but a tremendous recharge. This was my experience visiting the *Birmingham Evening Mail* in May 1986. *Above* with the paper's management and two of our West Midlands branch officers, John Fellows (*extreme left*) and Roger Mann (*extreme right*); *below* talking to SOGAT members who accepted and keyed in classified advertising – using 'new technology' long before Fleet Street.
(Birmingham Post & Mail)

Visiting the *Yorkshire Post* accompanied by Dennis Hill, our Yorkshire branch secretary (on my right), who I hoped would become union president and my deputy. (*Yorkshire Post*)

A laugh on the shop floor in Bristol. (SWPA)

With Allan Watson, leader of the Glasgow branch, who later led his members to vote against me in the new union formed by the merger of SOGAT and the NGA. (Alan Wylie)

A SOGAT social occasion at Hadleigh. *Left to right* the president, Danny Sergeant; his wife, Kathy; me; Bill Miles; and the union's health and safety expert, Eve Horwood.

A SOGAT executive meeting at Hadleigh, when I had become general secretary-elect. Bill Keys, still then general secretary, is on my right, Danny Sergeant is on my left and next to him is Bill Miles. (Hugh Finlay)

SOGAT's biennial delegate conference was big, businesslike and not easy to address. Delegates took notes so that they could report in detail to their branches. This was at Bournemouth. (Sebastian Studios)

As SOGAT general secretary, in my office at Hadleigh.

sorters as they read one of the stranger letters that came in. It was from Dorothy Squires, the late singer, who told us she was suing News Group newspapers, the holding company for the *Sun* and the *News of the World,* and two of its writers in her real name, Edna May Moore. She was determined to bring down Rupert Murdoch.

Squires was in the Court of Appeal seeking a judgment for contempt of court; by her estimates Murdoch was guilty on no fewer than fourteen counts. 'I firmly believe that if the unions stand up to this Devil incarnate they will be able to write their own ticket,' she told us. 'I watched him on TV deliver his ultimatum. It strikes me he is in no position to make ultimatums. Hopefully for the sake of your members you'll succeed before I do but I want Murdoch put in a residence where he rightfully belongs. I may never achieve this but I have fought him for over fifteen years.'

I do not remember what happened to the late Dorothy Squires dispute but it was kind of her to give us her support and that was not untypical. There was widespread backing from many walks of life in British society and indeed internationally.

Typical was the determination of 83-year-old Ms Janet Begrie, who would not accept that she could not cash her £5 Christmas cheque from the local SOGAT branch provident fund because of a mere judicial act of sequestration. She had been ill so it was not until 26 February that she presented her cheque at the counter of the Royal Bank of Scotland in Bernard Street, Leith. She argued her case at the bank counter. The teller happened to be a member of the banking clerks' union and eventually he paid over the five pounds in cash, which Ms Begrie went off to spend as quickly as she could. Just as well because next day a member of the Banking, Insurance and Finance Union arrived at the SOGAT's Edinburgh branch office seeking Ms Begrie's address urgently so that the money could be reclaimed. Somehow the branch could not seem to find it.

In his letter to head office George Lamont, the branch secretary, pointed out that the High Court decision was not valid under Scottish law but he did wonder what Ernst & Whinney would decide to do about Ms Begrie's moment of triumph. We never heard.

The BBC news at five o'clock one evening reported that a young paperboy in Yorkshire had been sacked for refusing to deliver the *Sun*, losing about £5 a week. When asked why he got involved he explained that SOGAT had helped to feed him during the miners' strike so he felt he had to help us. That boy's action encapsulated the way in which society was being torn apart by the dispute, with not every person on the side which one might have predicted.

A number of letters came in warning us not to follow the line taken in the miners' dispute and quite a few of them were from miners who sent in money. They knew we had been one of the best unions for supplying their families with food and clothing during their big confrontation. One writer from Sheerness counselled against involving the Kent miners. 'Violence will lose your cause public support, which is almost certain if you use this so-called help.' Another writer from the same town held similar views about Kent miners, advising us to turn down any help from Arthur Scargill's members. 'You need them like a giraffe needs a sore throat.'

The bank clerks' union may have been more militant than we realised, because I received a letter from Noel Howell, one of their officials and formerly an industrial reporter with IRN, enclosing one of the clearing banks' instructions to staff to refuse to cash cheques and not to deal with anything involving SOGAT. 'This dropped off the back of a lorry,' wrote Howell. It was quite helpful. I wrote back to thank him and noted it was surprising how much did fall off lorries at that time.

On a more serious note came an anonymous letter from inside Fortress Wapping clearly written by a journalist unhappy at events. He told us that two Australian journalists had moved from Gray's Inn Road to Wapping in spite of the fact that they had over-stayed the permitted time for temporary immigrants. 'I find it quite reprehensible that these members should vote at our meetings to break with the union when other members who may, perhaps, have more principles, are out of work. I find it no coincidence that they, like Murdoch, are Australians who seem to have left any humanity behind.'

This writer copied his letter to the National Union of Journalists, to the NGA and to the Immigration Department at the Home Office, adding, 'You will notice that this letter is not signed but having been forced to transfer myself to Fortress Wapping I am not prepared to leave any openings from Murdoch for recriminations. Cowardice if you like but I am sick and tired of hearing phrases such as "Murdoch will win" or "It's a tough world and I must look after myself".' He named the journalists who probably had no work permits but I doubt if the Home Office moved. In the Thatcher era civil servants also knew when to keep their heads down.

And from America came a postcard telling us the names of people summoned to London from the *Chicago Sun-Times* – Marlene Rae, Dick Nardini and Gaby Labelle. 'Forewarned is to be forearmed,' wrote our friend. 'It must be the first time that strike-breakers have crossed the Atlantic.' Well, going that way, I suppose! He added that a page editor of the London *Sun* had been seen making up page dummies in the *Sun-Times* composing room the previous June.

A number of Labour MPs were active in this field of pressure, notably our own sponsored members, Ron Leighton and Bob Litherland, and I went to address several backbench groups in the House of Commons. At an early meeting I revealed that we knew of a number of Australians working at News International who we doubted had permission to work here. I listed five who had managerial positions and were probably a cadre of professionals to whom Murdoch had entrusted the operation of his audacious plan.

Ron took the matter up with the government and in my correspondence files there is an interesting letter signed by Ian Lang, then the parliamentary secretary for employment. He said that details of individuals' work permit arrangements were confidential but 'I can say that no applications have yet been received by my department in respect of any employment in the UK for the individuals you mention.' So that was unequivocal. Interestingly, the letter was copied to David Waddington, then Home Secretary, as immigration was a matter for the Home Office.

Further indication that we might be winning the battle for public opinion came when Kenneth Clarke, then employment secretary, let slip outside No. 10 a few words of criticism of Murdoch's intransigence. This apparent deviation was rapidly put down by Margaret Thatcher's press department at No. 10.

But the concern over immigration-busting also came up when I went to the House of Commons to meet the committee of backbench Conservative MPs interested in media matters. One person present was John Gorst, the right-wing Conservative MP for Hendon North, who had taken a leading opposition role in the Grunwick trade union battle for recognition by women working in a photographic print factory. I hardly expected his help but Gorst took up the issue, surprisingly, with the Home Office. He went out of his way to seek information on the number of Australians active within the environs of Wapping. And he kept me in touch by letter with the progress he was making, which was quite helpful. The Home Secretary was more likely to react to a Conservative MP than he was to listen to me.

Gorst wrote to me on 27 February to say, 'I have asked the Minister to investigate this matter and I will be in touch with you when I have a response.' Then he added a postscript by hand: 'I have dealt with this by letter but if there is any undue delay I am quite willing to table a Question to speed things up.'

There was further evidence of the way in which Wapping had divided British society in quite unexpected ways. Tim Brinton, Conservative MP for Gravesham, with whom later I came to be on friendly terms, wrote to thank me for going to see the committee. He wrote: 'While I cannot guarantee you support from our side of the House I think you ought to know that a number of colleagues and myself all agreed that you made an excellent presentation.'

Another Conservative MP, the late Sir Bernard Braine, who represented Castle Point in Essex, was shrewd enough to realise that he had a number of my members amongst his constituents. He wrote to a SOGAT member: 'I am not sure my party does support Mr Murdoch . . . I would not wish to take sides in a situation like this, although I know that quite a number of my constituents who have worked in Fleet Street for many years and who are good sound reliable people, are greatly disturbed by what is happening.' At first he felt that we had brought the issue down on our own heads but after some detailed briefing from our members he came around to agreeing that we might well have some right on our side.

There was support too from a member of the president's committee of the CBI, Sir John Harvey-Jones, chairman of ICI and probably the best-known employer in Britain at that time. He backed me quite strongly on BBC television's *Question Time* on 6 March 1986, arguing that the Murdoch method was not the most appropriate way of conducting labour relations in Britain. Quite an endorsement.

Chapter 11

We had never been able to prove it in the months of tortured negotiations over who did what at Wapping, but we had a very strong suspicion that people such as Bill O'Neill, the labour relations head, Bill Gillespie, managing director at the *Times*, and Bruce Matthews at the *Sun* were all working to a predetermined plan ordered by Rupert Murdoch.

Bill Miles reported by the end of 1985 that after five meetings with the management he was still no further forward – what he called 'roadblocks' kept being placed in the path. 'The company has not shifted its ground and is firmly stating its intention not to do so,' he said.

The News International management wanted a legally binding agreement banning a closed shop, an undertaking of no strikes and giving management a complete 'right to manage' without any discussion by workers' representatives. In other words they were insisting on an agreement that they knew from their own experience could never be acceptable to any group of workers belonging to a free trade union in Britain. But still they dug in their heels. We wondered why. Whenever it seemed we might be taking a step in the direction of reaching some kind of agreement all engines were reversed by the management, even at the price of embarrassment or loss of face.

Tony Isaacs, the leader of SOGAT's *News of the World* chapel, did in fact completely wrongfoot the management when his chapel voted overwhelmingly to accept the News International terms to transfer production to Wapping. Needless to say excuses were made and this amazing offer – exactly what was sought – was hastily declined.

Suddenly on 4 February 1986 everything became clear. Mick Costello, the industrial editor of the *Morning Star*, had one of the best scoops ever in the fiercely competitive field of labour journalism when he printed a letter signed by Geoffrey Richards, senior partner at Farrer & Co., Murdoch's London solicitors. It was dynamite.

The letter, dated 20 December 1985, set out in crystal-clear terms and in great detail how to engineer a situation in which it would be possible to dismiss the entire labour force without paying a penny in compensation for loss of jobs or redundancy. Which was exactly what had happened. It was addressed to Matthews and copied to Murdoch himself, and also to Gillespie, O'Neill, Robert Searby, QC, later to become deputy chairman of News International, Charles Wilson, editor of the *Times* (who had masterminded the importation from America of the computerised typesetting equipment in unmarked crates), and three other executives on the labour relations side.

Headed 'Strike Dismissals', Richards's blueprint set out the master plan in great detail – oblivious of the fact that his entire letter would appear in the communist newspaper and be picked up instantly by media all around the world, the solicitor wrote: 'Since the very first day I was involved in the *London Post* project I have advised that, if a moment came when it was necessary to dispense with the present workforce at TNL [Times Newspapers Ltd] and NGN [News Group Newspapers], the cheapest way of doing so would be to dismiss employees while participating in a strike or other industrial action.'

Then he went on: 'A strike would be better either because it is easier to identify a striker or because only one or two people may black a particular piece of equipment, and there may be a dispute as to whether others can be required to work it or not.' In that case, said Richards, the person would almost certainly be repudiating his contract and could be instantly dismissed; he would not be entitled to redundancy payment; he would have no claim for unfair dismissal, providing all the workers had been fired at the same time; and the employer was under no compulsion to prove a reason for dismissal.

'Given that we are now much nearer the date of a possible explosion – although I appreciate that a more 'evolutionist' approach may still (necessarily) be adopted – I thought it would be sensible, not least because some of these points came up only on Wednesday, if I reiterated the advice already given.

'It will be useful if the key people have the main principles of the law firmly in their heads at all times.'

Richards then went into more detail explaining that if workers were fired for being on strike they could not then bring a case for unfair dismissal before an industrial tribunal. He also dealt with the occasional case where perhaps a person was off sick and did not actually take part in a strike or an employee was too frightened to take part. These isolated incidents could be easily mopped up without difficulty; 'most judges have held that it is not practicable for an employer to enquire into the reasons or motives of employees for non-attendance at work.'

It was important, stressed Richards, that any worker dismissed was not re-engaged. If that happened the whole plan could founder. 'This may be a difficulty for us, not least because of the large numbers involved. However, in the context of the closed shops of Fleet Street, where chapel administrations hold such particular sway, it may be easier to persuade an industrial tribunal that action by a chapel is indeed action by each and every member.'

The actual dismissal notices were important and it was vital to see that they were distributed properly. Richards continued: 'Dismissal notices will need to be posted over the various buildings immediately the decision is taken to dismiss. Chapel administrations must be informed immediately and letters should be sent out to each employee as quickly as possible. There may be merit in having piles of dismissal letters at exit doors, even if that involves an element of duplication.

'We talked about this some months ago,' revealed Richards, 'and it may be desirable to talk about it again early in the New Year.'

After this coldly calculated way of deciding the lives and future of nearly 5,000 people Richards summed up: 'That brings me to the last point. Both NGN and TNL operate very complicated rota systems in many departments and both publish a weekday and Sunday newspaper. Many of the Sunday employees are different to the weekday employees. The idea is to catch as many employees in the net as possible, and it seems to me likely that that will be done best if the dismissals take place at the weekend rather than near the beginning of a week.'

To conclude, he added: 'Let me know if you would like me to expand on any of this in discussion. Yours sincerely, Geoffrey.'

At last we had the proof of a conspiracy we had long suspected and we could now defend our cause much more strongly before our critics. Even those who were firmly on the side of the Murdoch camp could see that he had been wrongfooted and there was a noticeable cooling of his support.

Our internal computer system really came into its own when the Farrer & Co. letter was leaked. The full text was distributed to every branch, pointing out to our members that at Christmas, Murdoch was being advised on 'the cheapest way . . . to dispense with the present workforce. This letter sums up the brutal calculation to dump everyone who has worked for News International in order to maximise profits. This letter shows clearly that far from pursuing a negotiated settlement NI was preparing to get rid of its workers on the cheap.'

I made sure that everyone of influence saw the letter and circulated copies widely to the TUC, Neil Kinnock and as many opinion formers as possible. And I was able to write a letter to MPs and demonstrate that our members were less the sinners than sinned against.

There was one more letter to write. It went to Mick Costello. He was, I knew, a hard-line communist, a well-educated diplomat's son who spoke fluent Russian. But he had done us a great service. 'Dear Mick,' I wrote, 'I am writing to congratulate you on the "scoop" you achieved in the damaging letter from Farrer & Co. to Bruce Matthews. I want not only to congratulate you but also to thank you for the service you have done for our members.' I added a postscript to say I had no objection if my letter was published. Our politics may have differed but I had no doubt that Costello had delivered into our hands a major strategic weapon.

How Costello obtained that letter no one ever discovered and labour correspondents were renowned for keeping confidences. It may have been found in one of the in-trays at Wapping. But it is intriguing to wonder if there was a communist mole inside the Lincoln's Inn Fields offices of Farrer & Co., who numbered then amongst their clients not only Murdoch but also HM the Queen.

The rather tawdry letter of actual dismissal was dated 27 January 1986 and not individually addressed but impersonally sent to Dear Sir/Madam. Signed in facsimile by Bill Gillespie it stated: 'On Friday 24th January 1986 NGA, SOGAT and the AUEW declared they were in official dispute with the Company and called on their members to withdraw their labour. Since then, despite a public invitation to perform your duties of employment you have shown that you are not willing to perform your contract of employment.

'In these circumstances we accept this repudiation by you of your contract of employment and hereby dismiss you with immediate effect.

'The Company is also accepting breaches of contract by all other employees who have also been or are participating in industrial action as terminating their employment.

'Your employment having ended, your Form P45 and any money due to you will follow shortly.

'Yours faithfully . . .'

Geoffrey Richards would no doubt have approved of the terse brevity of the note ending the years-long newspaper careers of Londoners such as Billy Osborne, from whose personal dismissal letter I have quoted. I doubt if Richards would have reacted with Osborne's equanimity, however, if he had received a similar letter of dismissal . . . left in the lobby of his office to pick up as he finished work.

*

While the battle for public opinion raged – and we were doing a lot better than Murdoch or his public relations advisers had ever envisaged – still the nightly confrontations continued. And at weekends, especially when the Sunday newspapers were going out, the crowds were growing. Our figures, gathered through the wholesale distribution members, showed production was still affected. But gradually News International were gaining ground. So we had continually to come up with new ideas and what these days are dismissed as 'photo opportunities' to give the press photographers and TV cameramen some action pictures.

One of the first ideas was to stage an all-women demonstration to bring out the point that the dispute was not solely about printers and their pay packets but that many other people had been affected too. This was particularly the case with women working inside the Gray's Inn Road and Bouverie Street offices, where advertisements were taken over the phone, offices cleaned and canteens staffed predominantly by women. It was the same in the offices dealing with accounts and administration and in the libraries. They had all lost their jobs at a stroke.

The police were informed that a large number of women trade unionists would be gathering on Tower Hill on the evening of Saturday 8 February at 6.30. Once the numbers had gathered all men were asked to stand on the pavements as the women marched past. We had women stewards shepherding us along and controlling the onlookers and six women were chosen as pickets. Two came from the *Times* chapel, two from the *Sun* and two represented the London (RIRMA) branch. It was a good-natured gathering as we marched along chatting, but quite tense nevertheless, as we tried to remind ourselves that this was a very serious occasion.

At Virginia Street I led the six pickets through a previously agreed gap in the police cordon – in the early days the police were more co-operative than was the case later – and we walked down to the News International main gate as the seven male pickets on duty withdrew to the top of the roadway entrance. It worked out well and the media turned out and interviewed me in front of the gates, festooned as they were in razor-edged barbed wire, helping to make the point of the brutality of the present confrontation, which we could now prove was not of our making.

With the truth of the News International plans out in the open it was now much easier to seek assistance and fresh letters went to trade unions in the UK and abroad enlisting help.

We were doing well overseas in our media battle too and sometimes events played into our hands. An invitation to our union for me to head a small group from SOGAT to attend the Congress of South African Trade Unionists, which had amongst its top brass the miners' leader, Cyril Ramaphosa. To my amazement the apartheid government let it be known that I could not have a visa and that if I arrived at a South African airport I would be turned back. It just demonstrated what a mess such a ridiculous rigidity of policy was achieving for the increasingly beleaguered South African government. We ensured my visa ban had maximum publicity and then announced the £10,000 which would have been spent by the union on air fares and subsistence would go as a donation to the South African NUM.

To the late Jim Slater, then the leader of the National Union of Seamen, I wrote asking if anything could be done to stop copies of the Murdoch titles being handled on the cross-Channel ferries. The suggestion actually came from seamen themselves but they wanted an instruction from their union.

We asked Alastair Graham, who led what was then the Civil and Public Services Association, what could be done about the job centre in Milton Keynes recruiting casual workers to handle magazines in London at £50 a day. Our branch secretary had spotted an advertisement which stated that those who took on the job 'must be prepared to cross picket lines'. He had made enquiries and been told that if the job applicants were successful for the first two Saturday nights in February they could then get a contract.

Nothing surprised me much now about the character of the dispute but I was nonplussed to find the Department of Employment offering that kind of work.

I also wrote to dear Jimmy Knapp, also sadly no longer with us, who was then general secretary of the National Union of Railwaymen. Again information had come into our office from some of his members who had seen the newsprint for News International being moved by rail. The reels were coming from Belgium and being moved by train from Tilbury to Stratford and the railwaymen wanted an instruction to stop the paper moving. I asked Knapp what he could do. I sent a similar letter to Ray Buckton, general secretary of the Associated Society of Locomotive Engineers and Firemen, the train drivers' union. Until Wapping, the newsprint reels had usually been moved by road to Fleet Street but this was a departure and obviously made them less vulnerable to interference.

Of course all the trade unions wanted to help but we had to understand that like us they were very vulnerable to the new Thatcher laws. So-called secondary action with the newspaper wholesalers was why we had been sequestrated and it was hard to ask other unions to run the same risk. Nonetheless most of them tried.

Another appeal was to the postmen to see if we could stop bingo cards going out in the mail. Commonplace now, but fairly new to Britain twenty years ago, bingo was one of the ways in which the *Sun* built up its sales and anything we could do to interrupt the cash flow to Murdoch was worth a try. A letter went to Tony Clarke, then deputy general secretary at the Union of Communication Workers, asking for help. Nothing was actually said but quite a few bingo cards never actually reached their destinations, apparently.

Many people wrote to us about the cards and we advised them to return the cards to Wapping in unstamped envelopes. And one postman, a Mr P. Erridge living in Dover, sent in a small sum of money to our welfare fund. 'I am a postman and this is money I earned delivering *Sun* bingo cards,' he told us. Good on him – it was grass roots support like that which helped enormously to keep up our morale.

We also tried to see what could be done to halt the *Sun*'s promotions on commercial television but hit a real roadblock. The late Alan Sapper, the well-disposed general secretary of the Association of Cinematograph, Television and Allied Technicians, explained that advertisements were contained in a long commercial tape automatically slotted in to the programme schedule. Any tinkering with this – and the cine technicians had tried it to support the South African boycott – and another of Mrs Thatcher's government-inspired writs would come winging their way, he explained.

Of all the unions with a difficult hand to play, foremost was the Transport and General Workers Union, to which the majority of the TNT drivers belonged. If any group were strike-busting, apart from the electricians who were being bussed straight through the picket lines twice a day, then the TNT drivers, who drove their big articulated trucks out each night, were at the top of our hitlist. But how to stop them?

The late and dear Ron Todd tried hard to persuade his members to help but he could not get them to agree. They were not the only ones. As workers up and down the country watched the way that the once-powerful printers at Wapping, and at Manchester and Kinning Park in Glasgow, were being neutralised under the new Thatcher anti-union laws, they decided to keep their heads down.

Early in the dispute we received a confidential phone call from one of the

TNT shop stewards, too frightened to give his name. He told us it was true that the majority of the TNT drivers were supporting us but early in January 500 new drivers had been recruited. They were not then union members although the management had asked for application forms so that they could be circulated. That made it look better, I suppose.

But more revealing was his news that from 30 January the company was employing 'bully boys' who would ride in the rear of the TNT trucks armed with clubs. In a memo to me, Bob Finch, my executive assistant, added, 'When he says bully boys they are the toughest and biggest he has ever seen. They are paying them cash in hand £30 per night.' The informant also told Finch that most of the trucks in and out of Wapping were not being driven by regular TNT drivers, who had told management they disliked crossing picket lines but were being ignored.

Finch's memo said he believed the informant was genuine and it was worth checking out the worrying information. 'Should you advise the London district committee [responsible for the Wapping nightly picketing] to be very careful bearing in mind his indication of the bully boy tactics?' We did.

In the swirling developments around us in London and shuttling between London and Southend, it was important to keep focused that, crucial as it was, Wapping was not the whole story of the dispute with News International. My Union Jack Committee, drawn largely from the English provinces and from Scotland, Wales and Northern Ireland, were a useful reminder and so were calls, letters and some faxes from all over the country. But it was not likely to slip from my memory that my former branch members in Manchester, who delivered the *Daily Telegraph* from its new printing plant or the various titles that came out of Withy Grove, were very much involved.

On Merseyside the members producing the colour supplements were worried that by producing the supplements for the Murdoch titles they too were breaking the strike. And at Kinning Park in Glasgow, members had also been locked out and there were a considerable number involved.

Often with Tony Dubbins, I began a series of flying visits to the regions to rally the members involved and those on whose support we depended. And of course to continue to keep the media profile high.

Being a trade union official is a marvellous way to get to know one's own country and frequently it was a privilege for me to find myself somewhere – often in an out-of-the-way, remote spot – where our members made the paper or the ink with which the oldest manufacturing skill in the country is used to produce the printed word. From the Fort William paper mill in the Highlands of Scotland to the one in Ivybridge in Devon, from Frome in Somerset to the Weald of Kent, from Belfast to Bognor or to Bournemouth – I never knew from one month to another where the union's business would take me.

But my diary filled very rapidly in the early days of the News International dispute. On 15 and 16 February I was in Glasgow, on 6 March in Southampton, on 7 March with the Scottish Labour Party in Perth, on 8 March in Leeds and Bradford, on 13 March at the Wembley rally, on 14 March at the TUC women's conference in Leicester, on 17 March in Canterbury at Kent University, on 5 April in Newcastle, on 6 April on a march in London, on 9 April in Sawston, near Cambridge, on 11 April back to Glasgow and then Liverpool, on 16 May in Guernsey, on 21 May with Oxford University and on 24 & 25 May back once again in Glasgow.

Apart from the engagements at Wembley and in central London, these were some of the regional visits – but most days found me first at the King's Cross operations room, then often going down to Hadleigh, in meetings at the TUC, attending media sessions in London, meeting the executive or sub-committees and a score of other gatherings to do with the daily confrontation with Murdoch and his people.

My memories of the flying trips to the regions are a kaleidoscope of thoughts as one visit merges into another. But in Glasgow I remember most the feeling that came across to me from the crowded old conference hall – 'What help are we going to get?' I became quite impassioned and told the huge crowd that that truth was 'not much'. 'I would be misleading you if I told you anything else because the Thatcher employment laws have made it very difficult indeed for others to help us – much as they probably would wish. So we have got to stick together – all we have is each other.'

It was a theme I developed and the sensible people present in that Glasgow hall grasped I was telling them the truth as I saw it and not playing on their emotions and spouting rhetoric, which would have been all too easy.

It was from the second Glasgow rally on 10 and 11 April that our great Printers' March for Jobs began, led by a pipe band, with the banners of many trade unions in the city there in support. The idea had come from the original miners' march from Jarrow in 1936, which was a brilliantly conceived way to involve the whole nation in the pit struggle.

Although the weather was terrible twenty of the sacked Murdoch workers representing SOGAT, the NGA and the engineering union were given a send-off by the Scots and piped through the city to march to Preston, where, as it happened, the printing presses being used at Wapping had been built. The entire shop-floor workforce of Rockwell Graphics, who had made the Goss presses, clocked out despite a management threat to dock their pay. Two days later the marchers reached Manchester, where twenty-four newspaper delivery vans driven by my old branch members escorted the sacked printers to a reception in the town hall.

Meanwhile another contingent had set off from Newcastle via Yorkshire and linked up with the Glasgow contingent at Cannock in Staffordshire. A picket was staged outside the TNT depot from where the strike-breaking trucks had been coming. Eventually the marchers reached London, where a huge crowd of our London members greeted them on the Embankment and marched with them to the Wapping gates. In one sense it was the old traditional way of projecting a strike and not the modern media approach but in many towns and cities it struck a chord. Many other workers were beginning to reap the full impact of having rather impulsively voted the Tories back into power again and were perhaps beginning to rue their ballot box decision.

The unpopularity of the trade unions and how they were projected in the newspapers at the time had not helped – and nor had some of their decisions – but I was concerned that nothing if possible should come out of Wapping that ruined the chances again of getting a change of government. So how we handled the situation at the rally at Wembley, held a few weeks before the march on 13 March 1986, was crucial. Bravely Neil Kinnock said he would address the meeting and we knew that meant that television, radio and newspaper coverage was guaranteed. But so would any wrong, insensitive remark be picked up and sent round the country to be pounced upon by the right-wing Thatcherite tendency.

The rally was another effort at shoring up morale – vital as the High Court had just that week seized all our cars and assets and even prevented the union paying for a ballot on the pay award agreed with the general printing trade which had nothing at all to do with the Wapping dispute. So the tremendous support turning out from the TUC, many trade unions, Labour members of Parliament and also from all parts of the world as the international trade union movement rallied round us was very encouraging.

It is not until you come face to face with that kind of encouragement that you realise that the word 'solidarity' really does have depth and meaning. But was it as solid as it sounded, I wondered.

In my speech I called on Kinnock and Norman Willis, the TUC general secretary, for a pledge that the current anti-union laws would be repealed when Labour won back power. 'This will be seen as an historic dispute and a turning point in the general public's perception of trade union and employment law,' I told the crowded conference hall. 'SOGAT is a proud union with a very loyal membership and was founded 200 years ago – 185 years before Rupert Murdoch set foot in this country.' Indeed, as I pointed out, the traffic had been in the other direction with quite a number of our founders deported in chains to Australia.

'We will fight this dispute for as long as it takes for Rupert Murdoch and News International to get the message – and that is that we are not going to go away.' We could win, I said and 'win dignity, respect and the right to be a truly free people'. But I carefully added a phrase which did not close off the option of a negotiation – Joe Sheridan had taught me never to close the door for the other side.

Kinnock had to choose his words carefully too, and although it later became fashionable to deride his style, I defy anyone listening to him then in full flow not to be moved. He sneered his condemnation of News International management 'that connives in secret, deliberately provokes a dispute and then shuts itself in its castle surrounded only by its hand-picked hangers-on'. The word for that, said Kinnock, was feudalism. But the difference between the last age of the feudal barons and the new age of the press barons was that in the old days they offered protection in return for services rendered.

Stalag Wapping was about power and authority and not about technology. If the system had to be packaged in concrete, wrapped in razor wire, and delivered by a huge police presence then it really did not have much of a future as a system of industrial relations, said Kinnock. It was stirring stuff.

That weekend our rally at Fortress Wapping had a huge turnout both from our supporters and, ominously, from the Metropolitan Police who appeared to have engaged a higher gear – or had been told to by the shadowy influences giving them their orders, despite official denials to the contrary. So big was the demonstration that the Sunday paper distribution was held up for five hours, making them arrive too late for customers in many parts of the country.

Two SOGAT members listening to speeches by Labour MPs – not in any confrontation – were injured and taken to hospital as a TNT juggernaut simply drove into the crowd without slowing. One member had his leg injured but fortunately not broken as we feared, while the other member suffered a severely wrenched shoulder, a cracked rib and severe bruising. Worse was to come, was the hint from the helmeted police from behind their riot shields.

Among these tense gatherings were invitations to address not industrial workers or people on strike but university students who were extremely interested in what was going on. I went to talk to students at the University of Kent and twice I visited Oxford, once to meet the Oxford Labour Club and once, even more adrenalin-stirring, for a full-scale debate on parliamentary lines at the Oxford Union. It is generally considered that tomorrow's politicians – even the nation's next Prime Minister – are to be found within either the Oxford or the Cambridge Union so I felt it was time well spent.

The debate was hard hitting with Anthony Howard, then an assistant editor on the *Times*, Charles Wintour, a former *Evening Standard* editor, and Boris Johnson, then in the chair, all taking part. But I was glad to find that we won the debate that night overwhelmingly.

I was again with the students at Oxford on the night of 21 March and went into the events which had led up to the Wapping confrontation. But one thing

I did not tell the students – how could I have ever explained – was that the following day, Saturday 22 March 1986, I would be taking off from Heathrow with Bill Miles aboard Murdoch's private jet bound for Los Angeles to meet the newspaper tycoon face to face in secret.

I discussed in the Introduction how that meeting went and I will come back to the way it helped to move events forward in wringing from News International compensation for the 4,500 dismissed workers who, three months into the dispute, still had not received a penny – other than from our Welfare Fund – and whose families were really starting to feel the pinch. But I have little doubt that had details of the meeting leaked I would have been on a very sticky wicket. Tony Dubbins was not invited – only me. Sometimes trade union leaders have to take a chance to achieve what they want for their members. But they do not always understand it may be necessary to sup with a long spoon.

When I returned from LA plans were beginning to shape up for another major rally for Easter – in no less an exalted venue than Trafalgar Square, scene of many historic moments in working-class history. Some of our militants did not agree that we should seek permission – they would just have marched to the square and faced the inevitable confrontation. But quite apart from sacrificing the moral high ground it would have been a ham-fisted piece of public relations and the more sensible on the union executive responded to my view that we should seek official permission. The left doubted if we would get it, but they were wrong.

The go-ahead came in a letter from the Department of the Environment addressed, ironically, to the man in charge of day-to-day picketing, Bill Freeman at Caxton House in Borough Road. Freeman fancied himself as a tough-minded left winger who predicted my downfall.

A woman who signed herself Mrs H. E. Yokoyama told Freeman permission was granted for a public meeting in Trafalgar Square from 10 a.m. until sunset; he had to provide full details of what was being planned to the Commissioner of the Metropolitan Police. We were also given permission to have loudspeaker equipment using four speakers, the total output of which must not exceed 50 watts. Two could be positioned on the speakers' plinth and two others could be free standing.

It was all extremely well organised. 'Would you kindly ask the installers of the amplification equipment to refrain from draping the speaker leads across the mouth of the lions, if they possibly can,' requested Mrs Yokoyama. We felt it was the least we could do as she had been so helpful. She even told us how to get our electricity supply organised, gave us a list of firms which could supply the audio equipment, authorised banners in the square, permitted us to park six vehicles (which must not weigh more than 30cwt) so long as we supplied the registration numbers, and she asked us to bag up any rubbish so that it could be taken away for us. There was something incredibly helpful about Mrs Yokoyama and without seeking to patronise in any way, it all sounded very British. Or how the British had once behaved.

So for the second time I found myself speaking in Trafalgar Square. It was still pretty daunting and I defy anyone not to feel similarly. It was a tense moment but by now my microphone technique was under good control and I knew my subject – there really is no substitute for knowing what you are going to speak about. I know that sounds simplistic but it often surprises me to see people dying to get to their feet and speak – but without having really thought out what it is they want to say. Or how to say it.

Years later, in 2006, when I addressed the House of Lords on a debate to welcome International Women's Day, I recalled that we had seen amazing progress since I had spoken in Trafalgar Square in 1975 'when as a very nervous young union official I was terrified out of my wits but I had enough sense to realise that I was participating in something significant'. I am not sure that the second occasion was as significant as the first. But it was no less daunting.

Chapter 12

My main objective in meeting secretly in Los Angeles with Rupert Murdoch was somehow to edge him towards compensation for our members, most of whom were still not working. I also wanted to try to edge him towards giving our people some jobs there too eventually, although I was not optimistic.

I had little illusion about the possibility of getting many back into work within News International, although that was an obvious long-term objective. But attitudes had hardened inside and outside the Fortress Wapping gates and the chances of SOGAT- and NGA-trained printing operatives working alongside blackleg electricians seemed very remote but, I felt, worth a try. I could never go public on that thought and I did not concede it to Murdoch as he barbecued our lunch alongside his swimming pool in Beverly Hills but I did press hard on compensation.

To break the ice, though, I first chatted to him about his decision to change his nationality and become an American citizen. Wasn't it hard to cease being an Australian?

Murdoch waved it away. His only wish in life, he said, was to produce and publish newspapers. If he had to be a US citizen to publish newspapers there, so be it.

As a negotiating tactic I told Murdoch that the union conference in May might well take a decision to harden the tactics and I needed to have something to point to an alternative direction. (Privately I did not think the union conference would in fact want to strengthen the dispute.) He picked up one of the wrappers from the meat he was preparing and scribbled down notes on the points I put to him so I knew he had grasped them.

Back in London and straight into the thick of it I had little time to speculate on what might transpire but I anticipated that some kind of initiative would come from him. It certainly did. Suddenly it was announced that the Gray's Inn Road plant of Times Newspapers, including its composing room and printing presses, the editorial suite and the offices of the administration, were being offered to us in a straight deal to halt the Wapping dispute. In effect, the offer covered the old Kemsley building but not the more modern premises with an entrance actually on Gray's Inn Road. Nonetheless, it opened the prospect that the trade unions could launch and publish a new Labour-supporting newspaper, become 'employers' and take on printing work. But I said publicly that the plant would be useless to us without contracts for print work. Murdoch then offered to give us a contract for two years of print work and even to lend us advisers.

It was an audacious, eye-catching move, putting Murdoch into a more acceptable light and it certainly jerked new life into the news coverage of our dispute. But there was a deadline of 7 May by which we had to do a deal.

Barry Fitzpatrick, an official of our clerical branch, knew the site well and put his thoughts on paper, which were useful. Conveyancing and sorting out rights of way on site: who would pay? Relocation of plant – the computer systems located there, the switchboard and the essential offices services – likewise. Rates and general maintenance: how would they be covered until we got a profitable project going? What would happen to the skeleton staff left on site, such as the door security, firemen and electricians, at that time still being paid by Times Newspapers? There was a whole list of points like these raised by Fitzpatrick which did not encourage the thought of our union becoming a new Fleet Street newspaper baron.

I feared it was a snare. It sounded good but it was a project which could absorb an enormous amount of energy and might well stoke up inter-union rivalry among many of our people. The idea of trying to run a print works by committee was quite daunting. Gray's Inn Road did have a definite property value, though – if there was time the site could possibly provide a very steady income for our members involved.

The branches were not ready to make the move, however, nor to carry their members with them. Only Fitzpatrick's clerical and administrative branch were prepared to have a shot at it. Even so, I did not want to dismiss the proposal out of hand because it was the very first chink of light in the dispute and perhaps offered a way of finally getting the News International people round the negotiating table.

In the SOGAT journal my article was headed 'Trojan horse – or the way to go?' and began: 'It's not every day that a multi-millionaire offers you a printing press – and a contract for two years' work on it – as a "gift" to the Labour movement.' I rehearsed the attractions of a new serious newspaper supporting the left but explained we could only look at the proposal if there was real progress on the main dispute issue.

Suddenly I began to receive approaches from entrepreneurs and businessmen with proposals on how with their help SOGAT could become successful in printing, publishing and most certainly in property. When I drive past the old site now and see the splendid new building in Gray's Inn Road I do sometimes wish we had been able to hang on. But the chances were exceedingly remote.

I had some work done, though, on the minimum statutory redundancy pay to which our people might have been entitled in a normal industrial situation, so that if I were suddenly to be face to face with Murdoch and asked 'How much to settle?' I would be ready with a figure. It showed that any employee with two years' service declared redundant was entitled to a lump sum based on a week and a half's pay for each year of continuous employment between age forty-one and sixty-four for men and fifty-nine for women. There were lower figures for work between the ages of twenty-two and forty and a sliding scale for young people aged between eighteen and twenty-one. This was based on a maximum weekly wage of £155, which was not exactly a king's ransom but I knew it would be an acceptable bird in the hand to quite a few of my members, who were beginning to catch on to the fact, demonstrate as we might, it was going to be a very long haul indeed.

Back-of-an-envelope calculations gave me a round figure of about £30 million.

We decided to organise a mass application to the Department of Employment for unemployment benefit and for a claim for wrongful dismissal. It would mean a test case before an industrial tribunal – although we realised it could be interpreted by Murdoch as a sign that we were wearying of the battle and preparing to back down. It was a massive organisational task as every one of those on strike had to be given the appropriate paperwork and told how to make their claims individually. The branches set up a system to ensure that all this was completed in time because there was a legal deadline of three months after which it would be too late to make a claim.

But the development presented another opportunity which I set out in a report to the union executive on 6 May – a chance to end the union's sequestration and to get our hands back on the levers to run the union properly. In a five-page report to the executive, which was subsequently the basis of a letter to everyone on strike, I set out what had been done to rally support for our case around the country and the degree of success we had achieved. But it had to be accepted that other unions were handicapped in the amount of support they could give us because of the High Court stranglehold on us. They were, quite frankly, scared of the long arm of Margaret Thatcher's employment law.

Our branches could not pay the unemployment benefit which they would usually make to their members; 2,000 accident benefit claims could not be met; sick pay could not be paid – we could not even give sick members the fare to get to one of our convalescent homes; funeral benefit could not be paid; four branch offices had been closed down because of unpaid telephone bills and a number of officers' phones had been cut off; pensions could not be paid – even though members had contributed for years; over 50 per cent of the staff and officers of the union were not being paid – so the list went on. But the irony was that SOGAT was sequestrated and out of action not for Wapping but for calling on its wholesale distribution members not to handle Murdoch titles.

A meeting with branch secretaries agreed unanimously that they could do much more to help the News International dispute if they were free to operate. In my report I wrote: 'They felt that the union was sequestrated for an instruction that was not working. If it was, they would understand why we were to remain in the sequestration and all its consequences. In London the wholesale members have supported the National Executive instruction but this has not prevented News International from getting their titles to the 7,000 retail newsagents in the London area.'

I emphasised that going back to the High Court and eating humble pie did not mean the end of the dispute – far from it.

The executive heard me out, debated the issue thoroughly and then voted finally that we should seek release from the Order of Sequestration

Going to court and purging our contempt was a humiliating experience but it had to be done. The union had to pledge that it would lift all instructions to its branches to interfere in any way with newspaper production and distribution at News International plants. There was a hefty legal costs bill to pay for the company, the sequestrators and for our own legal costs, but we would then be in the same position as other unions in the dispute such as the NGA and the EETPU. It also meant that those in the News International dispute who were really suffering – about 1,700 out of the 4,500, we estimated – could start to receive £12 a week from the union if they were totally without work.

Finally I set out what then was the bottom line for SOGAT. There was a long way to go, I knew, but we still wanted recognition at Wapping and Glasgow, jobs and compensation for those for whom there were to be none; we wanted the printing of the northern edition of the *News of the World* put back to Manchester and distribution to go again through the wholesalers.

As to the prospect of acquiring the Gray's Inn Road plant, the executive agreed it might form part of a final package but in itself, that offer was not enough to settle the Battle for Wapping. Even so, it was a gear shift on the lonely road. But just how long was that road to be?

There was a deadline put on the offer by News International and it was quite impossible. They wanted an answer by 7 May, take it or leave it. We managed to get that put back to 30 May, as I explained in my circular to all the strikers, and there were the first tentative moves to get a meeting, which was what we had been seeking for months.

There was a preliminary meeting on 4 April but the first real confrontation took place at the Hyde Park Hotel on 16 April in 1986 and was quite a landmark event. Representing Murdoch were Bruce Matthews, Bill Gillespie and John Collier – Collier had once been the full-time NATSOPA official in Manchester. They were all managers we knew well. But we were under no illusion that there was any decision-making ability at the Hyde Park Hotel –

anything requiring a yes or no would be referred back to the boss. But there were signs he was still in the country rather than back in the USA, so that was slightly encouraging.

On our side I led as general secretary of the union with most members involved and Bill Miles was with me. Also in our eight-person team were Tony Dubbins and Alf Parish of the NGA, and the other unions were also represented. But most significantly for us was the attendance of John Monks, then head of the TUC organisation department but destined soon to be the TUC general secretary. Monks's involvement gave us more clout and his agreement to join us was welcome indeed. We were aware that he had a good relationship with Murdoch and we knew that contact might be useful in the days – months maybe – that lay ahead.

We had been working on a negotiating strategy although we knew we had few cards to play. What we had to try to project was that we were willing to negotiate and to be constructive. We had a meeting amongst ourselves beforehand to agree our line and then joined the employers.

In my opening statement I said we had revised our ideas for recognition at the Wapping plant. The unions were prepared to commit themselves to working for its profitability, efficiency, productivity, flexibility and job security. That was quite an offer from print unions in Fleet Street and one which before the opening of Fortress Wapping would have been snatched at by News International. But not now – the three managers sat listening politely but impassively as I outlined our ideas for a National Joint Council covering all the newspaper production plants and vesting trade union recognition in it rather than with individual unions. We also proposed an annual agreement, a conciliation and arbitration procedure which would be binding at the request of one party.

I went on to offer a commitment to avoiding breaks in production and single status – in other words all our members would be on the same footing and there would be genuine flexibility between skills. 'We consider these proposals to be radical and far reaching by any standards of British industrial relations,' I said, 'and truly believe they could lay the basis for a mutually constructive relationship between the company and the unions.'

I wouldn't say we held our breath for an immediate response but we were aware that we were offering a breakthrough to News International if they wanted one. But Matthews played for time and obviously needed to consult the boss. He said they would consider the union's document and suggested a further meeting.

Then he added that News International were very strongly of the view that any agreement would need to be legally binding because of the vulnerability of newspapers to industrial action. 'It is not enough to tell us that agreements would be honoured,' he told us. Only in the past few days the *Daily Express* had reached an agreement with SOGAT and other print unions involving a great deal of money. Yet within hours of signing it *Express* production had been halted by unofficial action. News International was determined not to be placed in such a position. He did not actually say 'never again' but we got his message.

After an adjournment Matthews came back to say that the company was disappointed it had not yet had a positive response to its offer of the Gray's Inn Road plant. They were therefore revising the offer so that unions in the wider labour movement could also explore if a labour-orientated newspaper could be produced.

It had not escaped our notice that such a publication could be a dagger blow to the *Daily Mirror*, which at that time – before Robert Maxwell's influence had had great impact – was still the best Labour-supporting newspaper in the country. It was quite a shrewd idea to get the labour and trade union movement engaged in undermining the main competitor to Murdoch's *Sun*, which had still a long way to climb.

The plant, Matthews said, was not 'clapped out' as had been claimed in some quarters (notably the *Morning Star*) and the offer was serious. It was not a red herring as had been suggested. News International would be willing to give professional advice on how to get a new paper off the ground and would extend its offer by twenty-one days.

Finally, Matthews added that the company was willing to offer £15 million, which would give an ex-gratia payment to those sacked individuals who were not employed by any other newspaper.

For our side I responded that the combined offer of the Gray's Inn Road plant and £15 million was not in itself sufficient for us to call off the dispute. We were still evaluating the offer of the plant and it could form part of a final settlement but the offer of compensation, which would barely cover statutory compensation, was totally inadequate.

So we left it there but – good news – we agreed to meet again on 22 April.

To trade union officials the prospect of further meetings like that gave us something to work on – something to encourage the members, to keep their hopes up and to stand firm. But it was important not to get carried away. Our people still stood outside the gates of Fortress Wapping and at Kinning Park in Glasgow seeing blacklegs going in to do their jobs and still saw the TNT trucks roaring out a few hours later laden with freshly printed newspapers. So long as that went on we were very much on the back foot.

While the Wapping conflict continued it needs to be understood that there was an undercurrent within the trade union ranks which was an added pressure. There was to some extent a left-versus-right pull for leadership of the issue – the left felt they could get better results by a more aggressive stance. There was also a tension between the London members and the rest of the union. But overriding was the view that a woman leading the dispute meant it would not be prosecuted with the single-minded determination and ruthlessness that a man would bring to it.

Bill Miles picked up that there was a feeling in London that they now had the dispute running well and they wanted to run it their way without me. The problem was to find a way to get rid of me. They hatched a plan that I should be forced to show I had not the stamina to continue leading the dispute and see it through. The best way of achieving this, the left believed, was to pile the pressure on me personally so that I would break down in tears and resign. The executive would of course have had a view if this had happened, but under SOGAT's constitution Danny Sergeant, as the No. 2 and my deputy, would have had to take over. The Londoners probably felt him to be much more pliable and less likely to oppose them. They would in effect have a figurehead who would do as he was told and not necessarily pursue the best for the whole union.

Miles told me about this a short time before I went into the morning press conference at the Britannia Street boardroom. It was not one of the bigger affairs when the world's press and television had been present – this was a smaller group of the industrial correspondents who were following the dispute each day. BBC television was nowhere to be seen. But the key people were there – the *Guardian*, the *Financial Times* and most of the faces I recognised as people who understood what the dispute was all about.

I sat in front of the trade union banner and after a brief statement took questions. The journalists came to an end and were starting to close their notebooks when I told them, 'Just before you go I have something to say.' I said I had picked up that there were some people around who were feeding the press a line that events were becoming too much for me and that I was not going to be able to see the dispute through – that, in fact, I was predicted to break down in tears. 'Now, do I look to you like that – do I look as if the whole world is somehow falling down around me? Whoever these people are, they are going to have to work very hard and they are not going to succeed.'

I paused and expected a flood of questions. But not one question was asked. One of the journalists said 'Thank you' and that was that. I believe some of the journalists had heard the rumours – certainly those more on the left and friendly with their colleagues on the *Morning Star* probably knew about the scheme.

I had not discussed my intentions with anyone when I decided to go public on the plan for a coup. It was gnawing away at me and one solution was of course to ignore it. But I felt I just had to get it out in the open. And I was feeling pretty good – I was not going to let it get on top of me. Miles told me afterwards, 'You probably did the right thing.'

Nothing more was heard of the coup except a lone paragraph in the *Morning Star* which declared, 'Picketing national co-ordinator Bill Freeman yesterday denounced as utter nonsense rumours that the London branches of the print workers' union SOGAT were seeking to split the union.'

Bill Freeman and Michael Hicks were the key figures in this kind of manoeuvring. Hicks himself was in Brixton prison and the *Morning Star* was running a campaign to get him freed from jail. From the beginning of the strike

Hicks seemed keen to get himself arrested. He was not actually directly affected by the News International action because his power base was the London wholesale distribution. Hicks saw an opportunity to become a martyr but it did him little good. Those around him believed he would emerge from jail on the shoulders of SOGAT members and be hailed as a hero. In fact his release hardly rated much coverage when he emerged from Brixton slimmer, fitter but not, I fear, much wiser.

Even so, the failure of the coup did not mean the left in London would abandon their efforts to seize control of the Wapping dispute. Another bid came when advertisements and flyers began appearing about a rally that had been called at the huge Methodist Central Hall in Westminster on 19 May at which I was billed to speak.

The event was being organised by the London District Council of the union and therefore involved all London branches. I was suspicious that my name was being used even though I had not received an invitation by letter or phone to speak. What was going on? In any case, as my assistant, Margaret Tothill, reminded me, I had already undertaken to go to Northampton to speak to warehouse drivers delivering paper to printers throughout the Midlands and Home Counties from the well-respected paper merchants of Robert Horne. I had already had to cancel a previous meeting and the members had been very patient and I did not want to let them down again.

It also weighed heavily with me that I had the whole union to run, but the London issue was sucking me in almost hourly so that the wider membership was receiving very little of my time or attention. Yet they had actually voted for me, unlike London.

I suspected that my name had been listed in the expectation that I might be unable to turn up. Then it would be said either that I was unwilling to give the time necessary to the dispute or, worse, that I did not have the guts to face the members.

The police contacted us to say they were concerned about my safety but I made it clear that I did not want them giving me protection. Not from my own members. I suppose it was proof that Special Branch were tapping telephones but it was also confirmation that mischief was planned, as we suspected.

I told my people to complain at the way the event was organised without any contact with headquarters but that somehow I would get to the meeting. However, I needed co-operation so that I could speak early and then get away to keep my date with the members in Northampton.

When I arrived at Central Hall it was absolutely packed. That hall holds several thousand people but only, occasionally, as many as on 19 May 1986.

People were leaning over the balconies and the noise was incredible. I was told it was the members in the News International dispute but my people were advising me there were people in the hall they did not recognise. The hall had just been packed. Anyone who wanted to have a go at me was welcome, it seemed.

I walked onto the stage and before I had said a word some started to boo and jeer me. Bill Miles was with me and so was Danny Sergeant, and we had some burly people, such as Peter Baker from Watford, one of my 'heavies'. They were not going to permit anyone to intimidate me. I had lots of friends in London too, and they were as appalled as us at the turn of events. They saw the extremists trying to intimidate me.

There were plain clothes police in the hall and there were also some very strange people who had very little to do with print or newspaper production. It was a very ugly scene.

I was determined to hold my ground and not be bullied off the stage but I had great difficulty in being heard. Still I made my point and then decided to leave as I was getting messages about missing my train to Northampton. I did miss my train and had to be driven there by Ken Tuppen, but we got a message ahead in time to the very decent people working at Horne's and, God bless them, they waited for me to arrive. When I walked in they applauded me – I went from anarchy to comradely order. It was quite wonderful and refreshing.

But it was clear the Central Hall event had been set up. I kept my counsel and made no complaint but the rest of the union was in uproar. There was clearly the possibility of headlines about the general secretary being defeated and snubbed by her members – just the kind that the organisers had intended. But it did not happen and they were frustrated again.

Even so others in the union demanded retribution and a very strong letter was sent to the officers of the London District Committee by the normally reticent and circumspect president, Danny Sergeant. But he was under pressure to react.

Sergeant protested very strongly at the snub to the general secretary and complained that although it was supposed to be a members' meeting in fact it had virtually been a public event. There had been no attempt to steward the event or check the credentials of people attending, he complained. 'I saw people for almost three hours jeering and slow hand clapping. Also the language of some people did no credit to this society.

'What was the purpose of requesting the general secretary to attend?' demanded the president. 'Was it to set members loose on her without giving her what we would expect when she was giving the National Executive Council report? As far as I can see there was no attempt to give her a fair hearing and it is the first time in my long association and experience to see such disrespect to the society's authority.

'There were people positively shouting for the whole of the meeting and were only interested in creating disorder and had no intention of hearing what was said other than to cause disruption.'

Sergeant concluded that he had received many phone calls from members outside London who were beginning to question the direction the dispute was taking. This was strong stuff from my deputy, who over the previous few months had, I felt, held back, even arguing to some colleagues that he saw it as his duty to remain aloof from the dispute. Well, that day had passed . . .

Almost inch by inch, it seemed, we managed to get some movement in the negotiations and slowly more money came onto the table. Then we were told Rupert Murdoch himself would meet us on 26 May at the Sheraton Skyline Hotel near Heathrow and Bill O'Neill, the Australian labour relations chief of News International, would be closely involved too. On our side we invited Norman Willis, the TUC general secretary, to join us, as it seemed as if events might be coming to some kind of head.

Murdoch made it clear when he opened the discussion that he was making his final offer to settle the dispute – which had turned very ugly and violent in recent days – and he would not be returning to the negotiating table. He added the front part of the Gray's Inn Road premises into the property offer, which did now make it quite a substantial proposition though still one which would be hard for the unions to handle.

His final offer for redundancy was £50 million – a considerable advance on the original £15 million – but there was no deal for recognition, no acceptance of our ideas on a joint working agreement. It would not work at Wapping, he said, and in any case it was not legally binding, which was what News International clearly wanted most. They had found that Thatcher's use of the law in labour relations worked and were not going back to the old days.

If there were vacancies at Wapping print workers could apply but there would be no priority over other applicants. 'Would those people already working at Wapping want to join the NGA?' asked Murdoch. 'I doubt it.'

We knew he had a point.

So we made preparations to hold ballots in each of the unions involved but were not over the moon at the likely outcome.

Meanwhile, the violence at Wapping and Kinning Park had been intensifying and there was no doubt that much more militant agitators had infiltrated our ranks. Attacks were also staged away from the production plants, which caught both the management and the police off guard. Wearing balaclavas to hide their faces, about 450 suddenly attacked a TNT distribution depot at Byfleet in Surrey. Lorries were badly damaged, a TNT manager was attacked and copies of the *Times* destroyed. At a John Menzies depot in Southend, another lightning attack terrified the staff and stopped the paper's distribution.

These kinds of incident were doing the union case no good at all – from holding the lead in the public relations battle we were suddenly being seen by the public as the thugs News International had claimed we were. Deep down I suspected they were not our members – though a few may have been – but by now every extremist activist group wanted to get in on the act, particularly the Trotskyist Socialist Workers Party, which saw Wapping as an extension of the miners' dispute.

The night of Saturday 3 May 1986 was when one of the major physical confrontations took place and events became very ugly indeed. Tony Benn was amongst the speakers billed to address the strikers and a big crowd was expected. But a much larger turnout ensued and there were two marches, one from the west and the other from the east, which combined into one major crowd streaming along the Highway. The police appeared to have been caught unawares and though they had blocked off the entrance to the Wapping plant at Virginia Street they could not hold the mob back. There was a charge at the gates and missiles flew everywhere as the police fell back. It looked as if the gates would give way when the mounted police suddenly charged into the crowd, striking out in all directions.

As I mentioned earlier, I saw some of it from the top floor of our bus headquarters and was horrified at the violence – but mostly what I saw was the police lashing out at ordinary people walking back along the Highway. What I had not seen was an attempt by a so-called snatch squad of crash-helmeted police to wade into the crowd and arrest those they had identified as trouble-makers, ringleaders or throwing missiles. But the police had miscalculated and were cut off by the crowds. In the heat of that moment the police involved were extremely vulnerable and the order was given without warning for a police charge to rescue the surrounded snatch squad, who risked being snatched themselves. Wynn Jones, the assistant commissioner I had met earlier, admitted that there had been no warning – 'there was no time', he argued later when he sought to justify why 150 people had been injured.

A BBC camera crew were thumped with truncheons, people were trampled underfoot by the horses and there were dozens of other individual incidents. I saw several people on the pavement walking away from the scene, who were beaten up by police wielding long batons who seemed to me to be out for vengeance. The police were in riot gear and appeared from nowhere and seemed bent on revenge and punishment. It was like a scene from behind the Iron Curtain.

It all happened so fast and was so ugly that it took my breath away and I felt my heart pounding. This was Thatcher's Britain.

The next morning the police were quick to get in their retaliation early! Jones held a press conference and showed a pile of missiles, lumps of concrete and iron palings, which he claimed had been taken from nearby railings by rioters. That hardly squared with what we were told by local residents, who believed they had seen police the previous day – before that night's clash – collecting items. Including some of their railings.

Few wanted to hear our side of the story but of course we did have the benefit of the BBC crew, who were independent witnesses to what had happened. And interestingly, when the details of those arrested were disclosed, it turned out that only twenty-five of the eighty-one arrested were print workers. But the police claimed to have suffered 175 injuries and some of their people were in hospital, including one woman police officer who was badly burned when a smoke bomb was thrown at her.

It was not a good night nor a very happy morning but our colleagues in the trade union movement were incensed, as their messages pouring in made clear. In the House of Commons Benn condemned 'the massive police attack on perfectly innocent people'. That did not quite add up either, but it was certainly true that the mass of those who turned out to march and demonstrated had not intended the violence to take place.

It was, even so, a strong signal that it was going to get even harder to keep the lid on the frustration as the printers felt their case slipping away.

I decided that it was time to involve the government and asked for a meeting at the Home Office. I was quickly offered a meeting with Giles Shaw, who, though a senior minister, was not the Home Secretary, but I accepted the offer to meet him. I made a short statement to the media before going into the Home Office, then newly located in Broadway, near Westminster. We were shown into a conference room, where I recognised several of the civil servants present – notably Michael Partridge, with whom I had worked at the Supplementary Benefits Commission. Hopefully he had briefed the minister that I was no firebrand and was a responsible person.

Shaw listened to my account of the events and then promised an investigation but they needed the numbers of the actual individual policemen involved to follow up.

That was the problem, I replied. I knew enough to look for numbers on collars or epaulettes but these men had no numbers. Either those on the other side of the table were good actors or they were truly shocked at my insistence that there were no numbers to be seen on the policemen involved.

We had no footage or news pictures to prove the point but subsequently, months later, following an inquiry by the Police Complaints Commission, it was established that some policemen had indeed been operating without means of identification.

But though it has never been proven I had always held the suspicion that while we had unidentified troublemakers, the police too had some strangers operating within their ranks. One suggestion is that they belonged to some secret unit – perhaps even the SAS – but certainly they were prepared to use a level of force on unarmed civilians which was not only unjustified but bordered on brutality.

I had promised the strikers that they had voted to come out on strike and they would vote on its outcome. I repeated this when we had a mass meeting again at the Academy in Brixton, where the fateful decision to vote on walking out had been decided the previous December. There was almost as big a turnout again. 'You come first,' I said. 'The National Executive had agreed that any final offer would be put to ballot. No one will take the decision to resolve this dispute without you, the members, deciding.'

This has always been my philosophy since I started negotiations back in the north-west and I had found it worked. I never liked the idea of deals in smoke-filled rooms between a few officials and management which were then somehow driven through. It meant the membership never really felt they 'owned' the issue which usually affected them most. Certainly holding the major ballot in December had meant the union could not be rubbished as Arthur Scargill had been for 'denying' his members a vote.

The final offer from Murdoch was in our hands after the 26 May meeting and each of the unions went about it in their own way. Tony Dubbins of the NGA recommended his members to vote against acceptance and did not even try to argue a case in favour. After all he had nothing to lose – his union was not sequestrated and he had far fewer members involved. He had probably sniffed the wind because out of some 800 of his members who attended a meeting to discuss the Murdoch offer, not one spoke in favour.

I looked at it rather differently, although I saw no purpose was to be gained in recommending the offer because that would have meant the militants piling on more pressure. There was also the danger that the vote would be lost and then I would be operating at a distinct disadvantage. But the ballot was a way to test out the strength of feeling so long as it was fairly run.

Chapter 13

With the sequestration lifted and control of our funds in our hands again, our union's biennial delegate conference could go ahead in Scarborough in June 1986 and there was just time for the ballot on Rupert Murdoch's final offer beforehand. I was determined that the event should not become a London show and that with the whole representation of the union present it would be time to take stock and get a fresh steer from the delegates. Whichever way the ballot went meant the conference would have to consider it.

At the last moment, as the ballot papers were going out to the members, some of the London activists tried to get an injunction against it. They argued that by distributing the voting papers in this way we were changing procedure since normally the papers would go to the chapels which would then distribute them. Some hopes. They failed to stop the ballot but its outcome was more to their liking since it showed 1,415 in favour and 2,081 against – quite a decisive turndown. Even so, the tactic of getting the result just ahead of the delegate conference meant the conference had to be given the chance to discuss it.

Just before the delegate conference we held a press conference in London to give the results of the ballot. I was photographed by the *Times* in quite a revealing moment. I was wearing a blue Jaeger business dress and the camera just caught me glancing upwards and possibly looking somewhat despondent – it was just one moment. But it appeared to show that what I was really thinking about was the ballot result. To my astonishment Danny Sergeant mentioned it at the conclusion of a conference arrangements meeting. 'Just one thing, Brenda,' he said. 'Before we go, could you please try not to look so despondent? Try not to look so down.'

This was after five months when my picture had been in print almost every day.

I do not know how I kept my temper at that moment. But I managed to restrain myself and answered, 'It's not about how we look – it's what we do. My mother always used to say you could tell from my looks how I was feeling and I suppose, Danny, the picture tells it all.'

There was a positive outcome from the *Times* picture, though. Jaeger had noted that I was wearing their designs fairly often – especially when on television – and quite unexpectedly a card arrived in the post from them giving me a 25 per cent discount on any new purchases. So that cheered me up somewhat.

Two big lads from our Belfast branch arrived and offered to walk down with me to the pavilion where the conference was being held. I suddenly realised they were concerned about my safety. To be honest I had not given it much thought. But as we neared the hall on this beautifully clear, sunny morning we could see there was a bigger demonstration than we had expected. On my way in there were shouts of 'you must support us' and 'this conference has got to give us backing'.

I was being urged to get into the hall quickly but I told the Belfast boys, 'No, I'm not doing that.' I stopped and stood my ground, and I looked at the mob. 'You know,' I told them, 'this union has backed you all the way through. Your people are here and they will get the chance to have their say. There is no need for this kind of thing.'

As I berated them on their manners, like a headmistress, I did not know there was a television camera taking it all in.

'What do you think your mothers and your families would think of you carrying on like this? You should be ashamed of yourselves.'

They quietened down but the scene was still being recorded and apparently went down very well with the viewers.

There was also a moment when one London delegate demanded to know how he was expected to meet the monthly payments on his £50,000 mortgage.

'If I go and tell the rest of the union you need help with that mortgage, you'll get nothing,' I replied. 'They're living in houses that are not worth half of that.'

153

It was a moment that summed up the gulf between the extremely well-paid London printers and the rest of the union membership. The London men by no means represented all those affected in Fleet Street but they got the media attention. And that labelled everyone else.

Inside the pavilion there was an expectant air and the majority of delegates clearly understood the importance of their decisions. But there were shouts of 'Judas' from some of the London members, which I ignored.

The conference arrangements committee had told me they planned to seat the London Central branch at the back of the hall but I turned down that plan. Seating was always rotated for each conference so sometimes delegates had a good view and then next time they might find themselves at the back. 'Put them wherever they would normally be placed' was my instruction. So there prominently in the central block were the London delegates, looking as if they had had a very bad night and were still suffering.

As general secretary I was to give the report on the previous two years' events, of which the Wapping dispute was clearly a peak. But so momentous and complex had been those events that there was no way I could deal with them in the ten minutes usually allowed the general secretary by the conference arrangements committee. This shouldn't have caused a problem – the president simply had to rule that the time cut-off would not stand and it would require two-thirds of the conference to overrule him. I told Sergeant there was a lot riding on this and it was a very important moment for the union.

To my amazement Sergeant would not hear of it and when my ten minutes was up he intervened, calling on me to wind up. 'But, President,' I said, 'this is a most important issue – we are all involved in this dispute and the conference is entitled to hear me account for my actions.' The conference reaction was obvious even to him. The delegates made it overwhelmingly clear that they wanted to hear me out.

I had spent a great deal of time on my speech – hours on it in fact. I wanted to be fair to everyone – even those who were against me. But I knew it was going to be crucial in swinging the conference behind the executive and preventing the Londoners breaking away. That could mean further sequestration, a major increase in violence – and losing the widespread public support we still enjoyed.

Looking back on my career, I am aware there have been several important speeches and some nerve-wracking ones, for example my first speech in Trafalgar Square and, later, my introduction speech to the House of Lords. But this was probably one of the most important of my career.

I went through the strengths and weaknesses of the dispute and the demands of some of the people involved. I warned that that union's assets were down from £5.6 million to £1.7 million, that our convalescent homes were at risk. But, I said, it did not help when one of our own branches took its own union to court – and the first we knew of it was when the newspapers rang us at home in the evening.

We needed to measure the degree of support that still remained. We knew some people had been taking redundancy and others had found work elsewhere. I looked straight at the London delegates and told them it did not help to be calling for increased action against News International when some of their leaders were secretly negotiating their own redundancy packets.

I singled out Ginger Wilson, the Father of the *Sunday Times* Chapel, who I revealed was secretly getting his own terms with the *Daily Express*, where he worked during the week. 'I know that because I am conducting the negotiations with the *Daily Express* and I know what is happening there. So it is good for him to take redundancy but it is not good for our members at News International to take their redundancy. Where's the honesty in that?' I demanded.

It was hard-hitting stuff and all his colleagues in the London delegation turned on a furious Wilson, who squirmed in his seat. They knew what was going on but they did not want to be publicly associated with such treachery. I could almost see them edging their chairs away from Wilson, who had been a thorn in my side for months, but if looks could kill, I knew he would have finished me off. So be it.

To those who were catcalling that I was selling the union down the river – a regular chant familiar to many trade union secretaries – I replied, 'That usually comes from those who do not realise there is no longer any river to sell them down.'

I knew I did not have the full executive behind me and not everyone in the pavilion agreed with me. Even so, I urged the conference to vote to keep the union together and rule that the Wapping dispute should continue to be the direct responsibility of the National Executive, answerable to the delegate conference.

I was playing the provincial card but it paid off. The vote not only went overwhelmingly my way but there was also a decision that the dispute should be pursued 'with all possible means consistent with ensuring the maintenance of SOGAT as an independent trade union'.

I did not spell it out but the vote meant the union could no longer run the risk of being sequestrated. I fully appreciated that the Scarborough decision meant the executive had an instruction not to allow the union to get back in court again if it meant risking its assets and the union's freedom to act on behalf of all its members. That was a major achievement from my point of view.

After my speech I was congratulated by many delegates but what I did not intend to forget was that when I walked on to the platform that morning the president, in front of several NEC members, told me, 'I have to remain aloof from all this – I must remain impartial.' When our union had its back to the wall, Sergeant wanted to sit on the sidelines.

It was a very long day by the time I had completed half a dozen television interviews and talked to the waiting reporters. But it was a very good one.

*

The outcome of the conference, while very satisfactory in many respects, actually solved nothing at the time. When we had packed our bags in Scarborough and set off home the dispute went on and the deadlock at Wapping continued. The violence very definitely increased and it was pretty clear that we could easily be in court again before long.

The journalists, who were defying the pickets every time they came into work and when they went home, were becoming increasingly concerned at the tactics of the people outside the gate. People were writing down the journalists' car registration numbers and taking photographs of them. On one occasion at about eight in the morning pickets arrived suddenly at the gates taking the few policemen on duty completely by surprise. The front entrance was quickly locked but that did not prevent the pickets from blocking it so that the journalists and white-collar staff trying to get into work were subjected to a frightening experience as they struggled for two hours to get into relative safety. It was nasty intimidatory stuff, although partly explained by the frustrations of those excluded from the Wapping development. It was not doing a lot for us in the public relations battle, however.

Though the behaviour at Wapping was frightening it was nothing like the mob violence that was breaking out at various TNT depots and other plants involved with Murdoch's papers. Just before the Scarborough conference opened the News International wharf at Deptford, where rolls of newsprint were stored, was firebombed. It resulted in one of the biggest fires in the history of London. There were other well-organised incidents all over the country and it was clear to me that some people had a quite different agenda. And I doubted if many of those involved were actually print workers. However, in this situation I felt more assured now that the conference had ruled that the NEC and not the Londoners were in charge of the dispute.

Even so, on 31 July we were not surprised to find ourselves in the High Court again. Murdoch successfully sought injunctions to limit the number of pickets to six and to ensure that any demonstration could only pass the Wapping gates and not obstruct them. In that respect it was very much like the way picket numbers in America are limited and forced to keep moving if they demonstrate outside a building. TNT also took out injunctions against the print unions.

The judge reminded us tartly: 'Freedom of speech has never extended to intimidation, abuse and threats directed against those going about their lawful business.' And he warned that any unions which did not restrict their pickets to six would be liable to heavy fines or sequestration.

Yet within hours of this very serious shot across our bows a mob of about 200 attacked a TNT depot at Thetford in Norfolk, smashing vans and trying to set the place alight. There was nothing for it but to issue a very strong warning to all our branches in London to co-operate with the new order from the High Court. I knew they would not like it but I also knew that the union conference decision fully endorsed our instruction.

While this kind of development was the daily diet there were plenty of other issues to keep us all on our toes. Firstly we were pressing the TUC very hard to expel the electricians' union, the EETPU, from its ranks. The TUC never likes to see a union outside the fold and not surprisingly wriggled but we were determined to have the issue on the agenda at the annual conference in September. And Eric Hammond was his usual intransigent self – he too had no intention of backing down nor of halting the supply of workers so that Wapping production could continue.

I recalled that the remarks of his predecessor, the late Frank Chapple, were right. He once told me, 'You think I am awkward? Wait till you come up against Hammond.' I quite liked Hammond personally, though. Once I surprised him by turning up to his union's reception at the TUC conference. Plainly I was not expected to make it but I went along to the electricians' hotel and breezed in. For a moment Hammond looked as if he had seen a ghost but then he gave a broad grin and came over to greet me. He was at his charming best and was the perfect gentleman. That night anyway.

With the months slipping by there were several sessions at Congress House as the print unions mounted their case but the other trade union leaders sitting round the room were none too keen. In their hearts they knew they might one day be in the dock because the so-called 'poaching' of members was a constant problem.

One particular piece of evidence played into our hands which we felt proved the EETPU's deliberate deception. We had heard that Tom Rice, a national officer of the electricians' union and responsible for print members, had, before the start of Wapping, travelled to America with Christopher Pole-Carew – a dark figure in our world because he was renowned for ruthlessly beating a journalists' strike in Nottingham and locking them out for a year.

The pair together had toured American newspaper plants such as *USA Today* and the *Washington Post* – much as we did with the union fact-finding team I had led. And we found out that the pair had initially met in the home of Woodrow Wyatt, once a Labour MP but now extremely right wing and outrageously anti-trade union in his views. Suddenly confirmation of our suspicion of complicity came in *The End of the Street* (Fleet Street of course), a quickly written book by Linda Melvern, a journalist, which delved into the dispute. So an impartial observer had pinpointed the deception we knew existed but could not prove.

The TUC continued to squirm and in the meantime Hammond produced an extremely well crafted defence brief which skilfully sailed round the lies, seeking to paint the EETPU as more transgressed against than transgressor of the fraternal guidelines observed in the trade union movement for 150 years. Hammond claimed that, far from seeking to divide the movement, his union had sought to act as broker and bring the two sides together. Yes, his union had met Pole-Carew but so had the print unions. And Rice's visit to the USA was no different to ours.

It was skilful manoeuvring around hazardous rocks. Hammond even quoted from the *Guardian* of 20 November, which reported a leaked memo from News International. 'KRM [Murdoch] telephoned to say that he had spoken to EH [Hammond] and all was satisfactory. EH was thoroughly prepared to go ahead and also accepted that should there be an emergency need to start without the *London Post*, this would be acceptable to him even though he would prefer not to do it, given the chance.'

Well, that should have sunk Hammond. Not a bit of it. His brief commented that this dynamite was being interpreted as a go-ahead to Murdoch. Such an approval had never been given by Hammond or any other officer of the EETPU.

Hammond summed up: 'We have not retaliated to this record of provocation. Technical change has always been a familiar part of our members' lives . . . our concern has been to see that they are successfully harnessed, not fearfully rejected.' And Hammond reminded his members that his union was not alone in facing charges of duplicity. 'What about the "SOGAT conspiracy" involving the then Sogat general secretary [Bill Keys] to push the EETPU out of Fleet Street with secret meetings at country hotels . . .?'

Which was where I came in.

It was a good attempt to pass the blame but it did not deter us from pressing Norman Willis, the TUC general secretary, to face up to the problem. If the electricians could get away with it then any union could take a shine to another's members and the upshot would be chaos. Tony Dubbins on behalf of the NGA was particularly vitriolic in his pursuit of the electricians. But in our hearts we knew we were not getting anywhere. Yes, there was sympathy – and indeed disgust at the actions of the electricians' union – but the powers that be at Congress House were not really going to do anything about it. Hammond had won – at least for the time being. It was another sign that gradually the dispute was slipping away from us.

The biggest question on my mind, however, was the financial position of the whole union. From being a relatively wealthy organisation it was hovering near bankruptcy and whatever donations were sent by well-wishers went into a separate general fund to alleviate hardship. None of it came to bolster the union's own resources.

It was becoming clearer every day by August that we were heading for a financial crisis. Everything we did in connection with Wapping was an unbudgeted cost – increased travel, heavier postal charges, more and more phone calls. Our costs for lawyers were going through the roof, not only for our advice but covering Murdoch whenever he went to law and won his costs. We even had to pay the charges of the sequestration firm which he had chosen to freeze all our assets. Losing our cars and then having to pay the sequestrators to get the use of them again was galling.

I asked Mike Molloy, head of research, and Denis Bartlett, our financial secretary, to pull all the figures together and to do some projections for the months ahead. Their memo made sombre reading and included the following figures:

- Legal advice, SOGAT's representation in court, representation in regard to pickets and unfair dismissal: £250,000
- Likely fine if we came to sequestration again: £25,000
- Sequestrators' costs: £504,000
- Sequestrators' solicitors' costs: £30,000
- News International's costs: £30,000

An astonishing figure was £40,000 for an impending bill from our London clerical branch, which had sued us and won, so that SOGAT nationally was liable to a £40,000 bill to cover the branch's lawyers and judgment against us. Plus our own legal costs. In the midst of Wapping it was pure madness. But sadly not untypical. The real killer, however, was a projection for what we were liable to face under injunctions already granted, which Molloy and Bartlett estimated would be £2,750,000.

All that totalled over £3.6 million.

In addition they put the cost of further campaigning at £200,000; paying unemployment benefit for twenty-six weeks to mid-August they thought would come to £460,000; the amount for meetings, rallies, faxes and copying and the usual overheads to fight a union battle was estimated to be a further £250,000.

In the middle of all this came a request from my personal assistant to tell him if he should continue with the cost of leasing a fax machine for a further three months at a cost of £672.75 including VAT! Definitely, I told him by memo.

The total overall was £4,559,000. Big money even for a trade union with more than 200,000 members.

The banks put in some heavy bills for stopping our funds from flowing. In many cases the costs were higher than our team estimated but they were not to blame because, as Bartlett explained in a memo to me, 'I have checked the arithmetic of the various costs of the banks but, frankly, we have no yardstick by which to say whether the various costing methods are acceptable or not.' They would all come out of our money held by the sequestrators.

Looking at the bills the banks put in was quite revealing. The one from National Westminster, as it was known then, was horrendous at £33,352 and Barclays was not far behind at £26,935. But others were much more reasonable, which may have had something to do with the political attitudes of their staff and customers. The Yorkshire Bank put in a bill for a mere £500 and the Bank of Scotland settled for £2,355.

I was extremely annoyed at the National Westminster bill, which almost seemed to include the cost of new wallpaper at 3,000 branches. To broadcast the actual sequestration to each branch cost an amazing £3,000 and we were asked to pay for 157 hours' work of a sub-manager, 88 hours for clerks at £9.34 an hour and several other hard-to-swallow charges. Through an intermediary at the bank, David Seven, who was the bank's likeable political adviser, I let it be known I was so angry I was considering publishing the bill, which I did not think would go down well with all its customers.

The union subsequently received a compensatory cheque from NatWest and I dropped it. The money was worth more than the publicity at that time.

In the midst of this I had a cash crisis of my own. By now all my anonymity had evaporated and since I was so frequently on television it meant everyone felt they knew me, judging from the way they talked to me when I was in Marks and Spencer. Quite a lot of them knew where I lived too, at 42 Gibson Square, Islington.

It is a nice square that survived almost intact from World War II bombing and I liked living there particularly for its convenience. One advantage was that every registered London cabbie knew it because they told me Gibson Square is on the first route they learn on what they call 'the Knowledge' – their much-admired memory of London's road geography. When some writer wanted to knock me, my home came out sounding like an exclusive Georgian mansion but actually it was a three-storey terraced house typical of all Islington and many other London boroughs before the war.

Knowledge of my home was not confined to the cabbies and occasionally some nasty items would come through the letter box, usually anonymously. So others had also noted my address.

Foolishly I often left my car keys and my handbag on the hall table without giving it much thought even though I was still carrying a large amount of union funds in cash. Suddenly one day I realised my handbag was missing. Every possible place it might be was searched but it soon became obvious that it had been stolen. As I was in the house, talking to my partner or perhaps to my driver, someone had silently inserted something like a credit card and pushed back the front door lock. My handbag was all too obvious to the intruder.

Although I could see the publicity implications there was no alternative but to call the police. Two constables arrived and took details and I did see an eyebrow rise when I said there was up to £3,000 in notes in the missing handbag. One asked if I often carried that sort of sum, to which I replied truthfully, 'Yes, quite frequently.' But I did not say why and the police made no mention of my role even though, surely, they knew who I was.

I expected news of the robbery to be picked up by the media but somehow it did not leak out even though my loss was solemnly recorded in the local station files. In the office I confessed to David Washington, the union's finance officer, who was not too worried either. He had known me, fortunately, for many years in the north-west and even said he thought the loss might be covered by insurance. Still I was very relieved a few days later to be told my handbag had been found in a car park off nearby Upper Street. All my credit cards – which I had hastily cancelled – were there and so were my keys. But of the cash, unsurprisingly, there was no sign.

Back at Gibson Square and, too late, we put in a new lock and a safety chain. I no longer left my handbag in the hall. I did not want a repeat of a rather nasty personal dilemma.

My cash problem was of course small beer compared to the crisis facing the union. We were quite plainly going to run out of money. Either we cut back on our campaign or we had to raise some more funds to carry on. I put a full report before the executive and they voted strongly to put out an appeal for a levy to the membership.

We needed to pull out all the stops in the appeal and to get across to the members just how serious was the situation facing the union. We decided on a special effort in the union journal, now extensively redesigned and much more attractive to read thanks to the efforts of David Evans – now Lord Evans of Watford – and his colleagues then at Centurion Press, which specialised on supplying print and design work to unions. This message would then be used as the basis of a special fund-raising leaflet. It was Evans's team, incidentally, who had redesigned the union badge and masthead for SOGAT which had helped to take it out of the 'Co-op style' and yank us up to date. Important, I felt, for a print union which should be a style leader.

I decided the time had now come for some new, top class photographs and got a message to Jane Bown, renowned for her work in black and white. She had taken pictures of me some years earlier in my career and I had always been impressed with her work, which appeared for many years in the *Observer*. Bown went to work on photographing me for an hour or so one day at a corner in a TUC corridor and the results were outstanding.

My picture on the front cover of the November issue of the union journal looked the reader straight in the eye with the appeal 'I have to spell out to you without emotion or exaggeration just how serious a situation SOGAT is now in . . . the brutal truth is that the union is financially crippled.' I urged the members to support a ballot for a levy of 58 pence a week for six months in addition to the member's usual contribution. 'This is not crying wolf,' I wrote. 'It is deadly – very deadly – serious.'

The levy would be time limited and in effect was less than the price of a packet of cigarettes, a basket of vegetables or a pint of beer a week.

I spelt out in detail the bill for legal costs that the union faced and also the amount that the London branches themselves had paid out: London Central had spent more than £500,000, the Rirma branch had spent £750,000 and the clerical branch £400,000.

'Colleagues, it depresses me deeply to have to make this appeal,' I declared, 'but the Wapping dispute is the most bitter in the history of the union. It is physically and emotionally draining; it has diverted my energies away from the introduction of improved services to you and the need to modernise and see the union better managed. I think you know me well enough to accept that I would never – not for a moment – make such an appeal unless the union faced a very serious situation. It really does, believe me.'

The ballot paper, headed 'Special Levy Ballot', needed to be returned to the branch secretaries by Thursday 18 December – a week before Christmas.

The appeal made quite an impact within and outside the union and amongst the leadership we congratulated ourselves for giving it our best shot. Most of the big branches rallied round and the journal carried endorsements from Dennis Hill of Yorkshire, Roy Gunning of Belfast, George Lamont, the Scottish district secretary, Tony Walsh of South Wales and others.

When Norman Willis, the TUC general secretary, saw the appeal, as usual he had a joke. 'Blimey, Brenda, we're trying to wrap this dispute up – this will keep it going for years.' I was not so sure. Again the appeal presented an opportunity to the members in the provinces to show that their patience with the London dispute was running out. They could see the Wapping dispute was draining the union – why drag out that process longer than necessary?

But while we waited for the result of the ballot, outwardly the union appeared to continue its very determined campaign and we made a special effort to enlist some big names to our cause. Colin Welland, who wrote the screenplay for *Chariots of Fire*, sent a strong call: 'Rupert Murdoch is not just the unacceptable face of capitalism – it is the evil face of capitalism. He must be resisted at all costs.' The message from the comedian Kenny Lynch was also brief and to the point: 'The whole business was planned months in advance. It was disgusting and should be opposed as rigorously as humanly possible.' John Williams, that wonderful exponent of the classical guitar, told us: 'Yes, I support your campaign for the boycott against Murdoch's actions.'

Tom Watts, who was playing Lofty in *EastEnders*, appeared at a fund-raising event in south London wearing a 'No Sell-Out' T-shirt and told the audience, 'You know where I stand. The fact that I am here I hope says that.' Not surprisingly Mike Harding, the musician and folk singer, was also standing firm. 'I support your campaign against Murdoch and send best wishes for a successful campaign.' Glenda Jackson was there too – long before we realised she had aspirations to become a Labour MP. She said, 'I have cancelled my delivery of the *Times* and the *Sunday Times* and I have never read the *Sun*,' she told us. Good for Glenda.

Ben Elton wrote, 'I offer my best wishes in the struggle against a man whose evil pursuit of wealth and power has led him to act like a common thief.' Robbie Coltrane commented, 'The blatant, opportunist use of the present anti-union laws by Murdoch represents not only the mistreatment of the workers concerned, it represents a precedent for any unscrupulous employer bent on weakening the rights of all working people. He must be opposed.' Pete Townshend, the musician, declared, 'What we are facing is not the Labour movement's resistance to change, but the press barons' resistance to pass on the benefits of change to the greater mass of their long-standing employees.' Mick Groves of the Spinners folk group added, 'The Thatcher government would appear to settle for a return to Victorian times, but Rupert Murdoch won't stop until we return to feudal times. We might remind him this is Britain, not Australia or America.'

Sadly, despite this level of support, the membership itself was not so sure; in the fourth ballot since the strike began they rejected the imposition of a six-month levy. It reaffirmed where the bulk of the membership stood on the dispute, now in its eleventh month.

Chapter 14

Although we were staring into the abyss so far as money was concerned I had no alternative but to press on and outwardly present a picture of determination and firm belief that our case was just and strong. As indeed I felt it was.

Now that the threat of sequestration was lifted – even if just temporarily – it did mean that other unions could help us financially and several offered loans to help us get over our cash flow problems. The trouble with this was that eventually the loans would have to be repaid and after nearly a year the fraternal feelings were not so sympathetic as they had been at the start of the strike. The NGA of course was willing to help, but I could not help wondering if there was an ulterior motive – the weaker SOGAT became the easier it would be for the NGA to absorb our union once the dispute was over.

Bill O'Neill had now taken charge of the negotiations for Rupert Murdoch. He was tough and determined, but I also felt that he could be trusted and had a much more direct line to Murdoch than some of his other colleagues possessed. Christopher Pole-Carew seemed to have faded out of the picture – and I cannot say we missed him.

We met O'Neill at the Grosvenor Hotel on 22 August and a week later at the Copthorne Hotel, near Gatwick airport. The hotel was chosen not so much because of it being near Gatwick but more because it was half way to Brighton, where we were all gathering for the annual Trades Union Congress, at which the future of the EETPU was high on the agenda.

We appeared to gain a little ground in that Murdoch's 'final' offer was not so final. The total of the overall offer went up to £55 million and it included an improvement to four weeks' pay for each completed year of service to those who worked full time for News International. There was a raised ceiling of £205 on weekly earnings and there would be a minimum payment of £2,000. There were also payments for the part-timers.

In addition the concept we had put forward of a National Joint Council was accepted but it was a rather hollow victory because the management insisted we could only deal with conciliation and communication problems. They added, 'None of the four print production unions will at this stage be individually or jointly recognised for the purposes of collective bargaining.'

There was also a condition that the improved offer would only be confirmed if we, as general secretaries, agreed to recommend it. Although I had largely achieved my personal objective of wringing some real compensation for my members out of this squalid situation I judged it would be counter-productive to recommend the new offer. But I won my argument that all those who voted to strike were still entitled to vote on the offer – even if they had now found other jobs.

On 8 October we announced the ballot result and it still was deadlock: SOGAT members voted 2,372 against and 960 in favour, the NGA voted 556 to 116 and the engineers 107 to 47.

There was also a new growing problem in that News International were quietly contacting individual strikers and offering to do a personal deal with them. For people who had been without steady income for nearly a year this was rather attractive, even though most hated taking what they felt was 'blood money' from Murdoch. But he had taken the view that he was unlikely to get a deal with all the unions and there might be some movement begun by picking off our members one by one.

What started as a trickle of about 200 willing to settle became a strong flow after the ballot rejection and soon the figure was over a thousand. The trouble with this was that there was still little incentive for people to settle the dispute and they might as well continue to vote against in the hope of getting a better offer. Certainly they had seen Murdoch raise his sights several times since first he had declared he was not intending to pay out a penny to people who had gone out on strike and therefore dismissed themselves. The argument went, 'He must be hurting and that's why he wants this over. Let's keep the pressure on. We're in no hurry.'

Against that, of course, printing at Wapping was much more efficient. Big savings were now being achieved – there had not been a halt in production by industrial dispute from the day News International departed Gray's Inn Road and Bouverie Street. So money was flowing in nicely from Murdoch's cash cows such as the *Sun* and the *News of the World*, from which he could finance his wider world activities and his early soundings in Hollywood with the movie industry.

Meanwhile the nightly demonstrations at Wapping and Kinning Park still continued with the larger Saturday night rallies. And the violence at depots and distribution centres around the country went on even though security was stepped up.

News International decided to add to the pressure with a return to the courts and on 20 January they sought to recover the cost of their additional security measures. I knew it would not be long before we were back in court, but the last thing SOGAT needed was another heavy legal bill. Four days later there was suddenly ample proof for the public – and the judges – to see, when the biggest-ever clash took place between the police and the demonstrators.

Tensions had been high because of the death two weeks previously of Michael Delaney, just nineteen years old, who had no printing connections but obviously felt indignant at the TNT lorries roaring through Wapping, where he lived. He banged on the side of a big truck and shouted 'scab' but the driver did not hear or see Michael and the wheels went over him. There were a number of incidents like this during the dispute but this one affected me deeply and I wrote a letter of condolence to Michael's family. By contrast, neither the *Times* nor the *Sun* reported the incident, which did not go down well with those outside Wapping that Saturday night.

The other death that still disturbed me was of a young child, aged about three, who fell through the open tread stairs at Congress House, the TUC headquarters in Great Russell Street, where her parents took her while attending a meeting in the very early days of the dispute. It had never happened before but somehow the child slipped, fell through the staircase and was killed when her head hit the hard floor. Another innocent casualty from this vicious dispute.

The demonstration on 24 January was planned to be a major event because it was the twelve-month anniversary of the start of the strike. Our stewards, under George Holmes's guidance, knew they had to try to keep control but did not think it would be easy.

That seemed even more unlikely when the marchers assembled near Bouverie Street and Holmes was tipped off by an officer in the City Police, 'You're going to get a thumping tonight – watch out.' There was seldom any trouble with the City Police but they only controlled a small part of the march route, the rest being in the hands of the Metropolitan Police.

The estimate of the numbers gathered in Wapping was around 12,000 and there were certainly many more than those involved in the strike. But the anniversary represented an important landmark in the Labour movement's challenge to the Thatcher employment laws, and many trade unionists, some MPs and lots of hangers-on were determined to be at Wapping that night. The result was a powder keg to which, in my view, the Metropolitan Police were quite willing to put a match.

I sent Holmes to make contact with the police officer with whom he was supposed to liaise and to pass the message that I wanted to see plenty of uniformed police around the entrance and policing the whole event impartially. 'Tell them we want no games tonight of mounted police hiding round corners and then charging out on people.'

There were certainly plenty of police about but there was also a hard core in the crowd who planned more than an anniversary event. According to the police attempts were made electronically to jam their communications and a wire was unfurled across the Highway to try to bring down police horses. A lorry was overturned and the scene was becoming very ugly as other police in full riot gear moved in.

Over the mike I called for calm and told the police to stop being so aggressive but it was like pushing water uphill. A pitched battle ensued with paving stones, iron railings and ball bearings employed against helmeted, visored police thumping out with their long truncheons. It was all quite appalling and frightening, and it was doing nothing to retain the support and sympathy of the public which we had managed to retain for most of the year.

The kind of violence which had so damaged Arthur Scargill's reputation at Orgreave was very evident that night at Wapping. But just as in the mining incident there was plenty of evidence that the police were looking for trouble and working to a plan that night in east London.

Interestingly, next morning when the tally was counted there had been sixty-seven arrests, of which only thirteen had anything to do with printing. The police claimed they had thirty-nine policemen injured – it always was fascinating to see how policemen in full riot gear could get so knocked about at times like this – eleven horses hurt and nine police vehicles damaged. There were also widespread injuries amongst the crowd, some quite serious, but many not recorded. A lot of people had bruises, cuts and broken bones next morning.

Thankfully, though, no one had been killed. I did not feel we would be so lucky as I watched the violent scenes, quite appalled that this was happening in the capital city of a democratic nation and at what damaging film footage we were helping to send round the world.

Fortunately we had plenty of witnesses – people such as the left-wing MP Dennis Skinner and Peter Shore, the local MP, who were able to tell colleagues what had happened. And a lady called Barbara Cohen, who was leading a team of observers, declared that the police had been to blame by raising the tension after a peaceful march. So for once Wynn Jones, the police commander in charge, was not able to have it all his own way next morning when the nation started to demand answers.

On Sunday morning my phone hardly stopped ringing, not only with calls from union members outside London wanting to know what had happened and if I was alright. There were also calls from the TUC, from fellow union leaders and from Neil Kinnock, the leader of the Labour Party. He had no option but to speak out against the 'hideous' violence which he knew was doing Labour's election chances no favours, and the TUC general secretary, Norman Willis, urged me that the demonstrations had to end.

Easier said than done, I told him. I could give an instruction but there was nothing in my power to prevent people from converging at Wapping night after night unless we could find a way to end the dispute.

The union executive was due to meet on Thursday 5 February and suddenly this looked like the moment to seize to bring Wapping to an end. But I had to have something in hand which would force the issue. Shock at the reaction to the violent scenes might present me with a fresh negotiating opportunity and I tried to contact Bill O'Neill. We had also picked up rumours that News International were preparing to return to the High Court to seek an injunction against the union. But O'Neill was not in Britain and could not come immediately.

Could I go to New York? If I left the country I would almost certainly be seen and the media – and the more militant – would suspect I was on my way to see Murdoch. Somehow I needed to slip away and get back without my absence being noted. Concorde seemed to be the answer but my partner wisely pointed out that there was no way one could board Concorde at Heathrow without being spotted by the assiduous news agency which monitors all comings and goings at Britain's airports.

No one watched who was flying on the French Concorde, though, he told me. Or at least only Frenchmen, it seemed.

The Concorde trip via Paris was so secret that John Harris, the partner at Thompsons who looked after us, took money for the tickets from his personal account at Abbey National and reclaimed it later from his office. Meanwhile I kept a diary date at Newcastle on Monday 26 January so that no one in the SOGAT offices would see my travel plans changing.

Bill Miles was not usually thrown off balance but he did find it surprising when I told him to make sure he had his passport. Then I told him to be ready when I returned to London for a secret trip to New York.

We caught up with O'Neill at the Hilton at John F. Kennedy airport on Tuesday 27 January. We stayed the Monday night at a hotel near Charles de Gaulle airport and took the morning Concorde, joining O'Neill in the Hilton coffee lounge. I outlined my thinking. I now had the bulk of the union behind me with a conference vote retaining all power in the executive, where I thought I had a majority. I also had instructions to keep the union out of the courts.

Were News International thinking of returning to the courts seeking an order for contempt following Saturday night's clash? O'Neill said that was possible but he had no knowledge of it. However, he went off to make a long distance phone call to Geoffrey Richards of Farrer & Co., Murdoch's lawyers, to check it out. Richards confirmed he was getting the issue back into the High Court, where the judge would quite likely throw the book at us for 'disobeying' the strictures against violent demonstrations. There was very good video footage of the violence, photographs and depositions.

While O'Neill was on the phone, to his amazement he heard a woman caller in the next phone booth asking for 'copy', which was the way journalists used to dictate their written material to typists – in Fleet Street many copy takers were my members. Then O'Neill heard the journalist tell her office that she had 'been in the hotel for an hour and it seemed as if they have come up with a plan to bring the strike to an end'.

'How on earth did they get wind of this meeting?' O'Neill asked when he came back to the coffee table.

The funny thing was none of us had seen a journalist we recognised and no one had attempted to talk to us. Strange.

In the hotel lobby the place was full with television cameras, lights, recording gear and plenty of journalists, but no one seemed interested in the two Bills or me as we walked through. Quite by coincidence, we found out, we were meeting in the hotel where a New York strike was being settled, but we never did discover what it was about.

I did feel there was a glimmer of light beginning to show at the end of a very long tunnel, though, as Bill Miles and I caught the Air France Concorde back to Paris just three hours later that fateful day. I began to appreciate the praise Sir David Frost held for the supersonic plane – there and back in a day and no one had missed us. Miles, who had a heart condition, had a night's sleep in Paris, but I carried on to London.

I felt slightly uncomfortable about it but the ends really did justify the means. We had given the dispute our best shot, had won some compensation for the strikers, many of whom had now found other work – though never as good pay as the halcyon days of Fleet Street provided. Above all I had kept the union together – we had not split like the miners.

I had been taught by my old boss Joe Sheridan in Manchester that it was a trade union leader's job to keep his union together even if it meant taking the blame. 'Sometimes', he told me, 'they have to blame someone to purge their own guilt and that is usually you – even if it hurts.'

I was about to find out. Something about being 'sold down the river' was the phrase that came to mind . . .

John Harris of Thompsons told me the next day that Farrer & Co. had sent them a draft of the application they were considering making within a few days to the High Court seeking an order for sequestration of SOGAT. 'It is patently clear that the demonstration last Saturday was organised by your clients, that it was anything but peaceful, disciplined and orderly and that no effective steps were taken to control it,' said Farrers. 'This represents a calculated and flagrant breach . . . which in our view will justify the sequestration of all the Union's assets and the imposition of a very substantial fine. We will arrange for the service of the proceedings shortly.'

Well, that was pretty clear.

To make their intentions even clearer to any in London in doubt, the draft order to the court, apart from naming me as general secretary, also listed Bill Freeman, Michael Hicks and Michael Britton, three of the most active in the day-to-day Wapping street scenes; Ted Chard of the London Central branch; Charlie Cherrill of our London machine branch; and Chris Robbins, secretary of the London clerical branch. So no hiding behind my skirts this time!

Eldred Tabachnik did not need to study the order for long when we went to see him. 'If that gets into court you're finished,' he advised. 'I don't want to know about it.' His very strong advice was that we had no chance of winning.

It was Murdoch's mailed fist without much hint of a velvet glove. So it was on the dark evening of 2 February I slipped out of London, riding not in my union car but Harris's Rover saloon as he drove Miles and me secretly to his home in Barnet. I was very worried that we might be being followed and twice I asked Harris to stop to make a check but it seemed all clear.

We were shown into Harris's front room and a few minutes later Bill O'Neill arrived with Geoffrey Richards of Farrers – I was finally face to face with the actual writer of the memorandum which told Murdoch how to get around paying compensation by cynically forcing a strike. Actually I got on rather well with him as we all levelled on how to end the strike. In a way we were all laying our cards on the table, I suppose.

Harris's daughter, Gail, had prepared dinner and we all sat round the family table to work out the way to end the dispute. I made it clear that I regarded the strike as lost some time ago and going nowhere. We needed a way out of the impasse. My colleagues and I could see that going back to court would either mean total humiliation and a virtual end to the union – or, if we won, would be an enormous shot in the arm for those who wished to carry it on. But, I added, all our legal advice was that we had no chance.

Yet the truth of the situation also was that the strike was at the fag end – only a small number were still supporting it – and by now a very large number, quite understandably, had settled privately and taken their compensation. More than half of those who voted for the strike had in fact settled with News International and taken their money. So should we be carrying on with minority support, probably smashing SOGAT to pieces?

O'Neill and Richards explained that the dispute was now having little effect on production or distribution but there was a mounting tally of ugly incidents and people were going to be hurt badly or even killed if these went on. They would also like to be rid of the daily demonstration outside the Wapping plant, which they could live with but which the staff hated. And they confirmed that News International was well advanced with its legal case to take us to the High Court but they realised it probably would mean the end of SOGAT. Once the process started, though, there was little that could be done to halt it.

It was a very practical session as we worked out the procedure, but at the back of my mind was the fact that we had won from Murdoch £55 million in decent compensation and I really did not want to risk losing that at the eleventh hour.

There was also the question of the News International pension fund, in which many of those on strike had invested big sums. It was agreed that fund would be preserved and News International remained true to their word – unlike Robert Maxwell.

Maybe I did not fully appreciate it at the time but News International was still quite sensitive about its reputation in the country and wanted to do the decent thing and move on – although not if it meant taking back any of the strikers. But they were willing to give an assurance to me that eventually some of the less militant might eventually find their way back into Murdoch's plants. They would be able to apply for vacancies, which would come through my office. That was quite a breakthrough.

Most of our people wanted to move on too. For twelve months everything affecting the union's general membership had had to take second place to the News International dispute. I was determined to give my time to the most important negotiation in the industry, between the British Printing Industries Federation and ourselves, but I knew that out of every day, Wapping gobbled up at least three hours of my time and it was a serious detraction to running the union.

The members in the provinces had been very tolerant and understanding but there were signs that here too patience was wearing thin. No one had refused to pay their contributions but I was very conscious that we were on a knife edge.

We had to have a formal end to the dispute. It could not just fizzle out, because at any time there could be a flare-up – maybe an ad hoc Saturday night punch-up – and we would be held responsible and back in court. But in the absence of a ballot the full union executive could vote to conclude the year-long strike.

The session at John Harris's dinner table was very businesslike as we looked at what we had to do and what News International had to do to tie up all the loose ends so that I could present a comprehensive report to the SOGAT executive, which was due to meet on Thursday 5 February.

It was decided Farrers would send the union a formal letter warning of News International's intentions if the strike was not resolved and also setting out again its compensation terms. That was the catalyst I needed to get the issue formally before the executive as an emergency item.

To circulate in advance an executive paper would have given the likely opposition time to prepare and mount a campaign – even possibly a demonstration at Hadleigh, as we saw at the beginning of the strike. Most of us knew in our hearts that something had to happen – the speculation in the newspapers alerted them if nothing else.

So there was a tense but rather resigned air in the wood-panelled executive boardroom at Hadleigh as we gathered on 5 February, just over twelve months from the beginning of the final major industrial confrontation in British industrial history. We had lost. Even so, we all knew we had given it our best shot.

We also agreed that Harris would be at the executive meeting and would keep in touch with Richards by phone.

Before the meeting started I talked to some of my London supporters, loyal people such as George Holmes, and told them that I did not expect them to vote on my side. I knew they would have been lynched. Even so, to hear the determined opposition from seven of the London contingent – none of whom wanted to be seen less militant than the next – was remarkable. Yet it was also self-indulgent. So long as someone else took the decision to call off the lost strike they could not be blamed.

I was pretty sure I would have that honour thrust upon me.

I reported on the developments, the advice of our counsel, Eldred Tabachnik, that we stood no chance but that if we moved smartly we might be able to salvage the compensation and the pension fund. The executive agreed that Harris should go and telephone Richards from my office. He came back and said, 'It's a deal.'

When the president called for votes the result was twenty-three to nine to call off the dispute. I am not sure I heard a collective sigh of relief around the boardroom but the expressions on several members' faces convinced me we did have the right decision that fateful day.

I had prepared a press notice before the meeting and immediately the executive meeting ended it was issued to the news agencies and copies run off for the press, who had arrived in force at Hadleigh. For many of the journalists too this was the culmination to a story they had followed for more than twelve months and was one much nearer their own profession than was the usual run of labour relation matters.

After explaining the reasons I said, 'This has been a very difficult decision for the executive to take. But what they were faced with was the sequestration once again of our total union and a fine.

'This has been a bitter dispute. It is a disgrace to our so-called democracy that working people can be sacked and treated in the way that our members were at News International. The laws which this government have enacted have done nothing for the average family in Britain but everything for employers, who choose to be ruthless and treat their workforce like a set of old clothes to be thrown away without any regard.'

It was obvious, I said, the law had to be changed – a clear hint to those planning the Labour argument at the next general election. 'We will never forget this dispute and the ravages of it will be evident for a long time to come,' I summed up.

Until now the full story of how we engineered the ending has never been told. And both Bill O'Neill and I have kept our mouths closed for a very long time.

Looking back I have no qualms about my decision to call it a day. I had to judge the right moment and the right mood of the majority of the executive as representative of the wider union. There has been plenty of strong criticism, notably from the extreme left, but I have never had second thoughts.

I received many letters from ordinary SOGAT members, and one in particular sums up how they felt. Eddie Kirkpatrick was from Liverpool but a loyal member of my old north-west area. On 5 February, the very day we called off the strike, he wrote to me from his home in Pitville Avenue, Mossley Hill:

'I want you to know that I appreciate some of the extremely difficult situations you have had to deal with since being elected general secretary. I can also imagine the mental torment you must have endured in reaching the decision to end the dispute.

'In the present climate of anti-trade union legislation there was no other conclusion to this dispute. It would have been madness to have allowed Murdoch, not only to destroy our members' employment, but to destroy SOGAT as well.

'Brenda, I know it's not much, but my thoughts are with you and I assure you of my support and confidence. If there is any way that I can be of assistance – just shout.

'Sincere best wishes, Eddie.'

Never a day without cameras: outside SOGAT's 'battle headquarters' in
Britannia Street, near King's Cross, during the Wapping dispute.

One of the leaflets produced jointly with other unions during the Wapping strike.

SOGAT • AUEW • NUJ • NGA

My Dad wants to work but Mr Murdoch sacked him.

DON'T BUY

The Sun
NEWS OF THE WORLD
THE TIMES
THE SUNDAY TIMES

5,000 families like Emma's have now lost their breadwinners **THEY NEED YOUR SUPPORT**

At the huge Wapping Rally we held at Wembley, Neil Kinnock, then leader of the opposition, led a standing ovation for me. He made a brilliant speech himself.

In Nelson's shadow, leading the anti-Murdoch protest rally in Trafalgar Square. The crowd looked impressively big from the platform.

In 1975 I organised a big event in Manchester to mark International Women's Year. Among the highlights was seeing a policewoman leading the parade on horseback.

Seeing young people get their foot on the housing ladder was a very satisfying occasion when I was chairman of the Housing Corporation.

Above at a dinner on board HMS *Victory* to mark the end of my chairmanship of time with the Armed Forces Pay Review Body; *left* as chairman, reviewing airmen at the passing-out parade at RAF Halton in February 2005. (Crown copyright)

With newly graduated students at Croydon College, October 1994. I loved handing them their hard-won qualifications and congratulating them. (*Croydon Advertiser*)

My first honorary degree – appropriately from the University of Salford,
the city where I was born.

In my robes on becoming a member of the House of Lords, with Lord Murray of Epping (*right*) and Lord Dean of Beswick. (UPPA)

Relaxing in Lanzarote after Wapping, with Bill Miles and Eve Horwood.
They came to spend Christmas with us shortly before Bill died.

In the garden at Gibson Square.

It was good of him to put his thoughts down like that and I much appreciated it at the time.

The following day, after languishing on the inside pages for some weeks, we were back on the front pages. Not surprisingly the *Times* led with the heading 'Sogat pulls out of Wapping dispute' and a sub-head 'News International ends legal action and reopens cash offer'. So it was good to read the deal confirmed in print. Alongside a photograph of me in a cream blouse, black cravat and long necklace, they had picked up my quote: 'As regards a sell-out, there is nothing left to sell out. We have not been able to stop the papers.'

Murdoch was quoted saying, 'This has been a sad and unnecessary tragedy. The tragedy has been drawn out for thirteen months despite two serious attempts by the company to bring it to an end, including an offer of a printing plant, equipment and cash. It is in everyone's interest that it ends now.'

Tim Jones, who had covered the dispute fairly and honourably for the *Times* throughout, noted that since the dispute started about twenty union members had died, and their widows would be offered double the termination terms.

Interestingly there was not much crowing in the leader column of the newspaper. Its headline was 'Hard lessons of Wapping' but it appeared to try to be reasonably even handed in its comments. They respected my views, it said, about the anti-union laws which I had condemned. 'Our ideal is daily to take part in open democratic debate with those whose ambitions for British society are different from our own but whose commitment to our democratic processes is as strong.'

The leader concluded, 'Hard lessons have been learnt at Wapping. If they are heeded the fight may not have been totally in vain.' Interesting.

The *Financial Times*'s coverage, under the guidance of John Lloyd – later editor of the *New Statesman* and the *FT* magazine – had been outstanding. Helen Hague, his deputy, a young woman with whom I got on well, covered the press conference and she also wrote the front page lead. She speculated that the London hard core would try to prolong the dispute because they were angry that there had not been the ballot I had promised. They had a point but it ignored the impact of the return to the High Court, which would probably have made it impossible for the union to operate, let alone conduct a ballot.

Inside the 'Pink 'Un' Hague did a Woman in the News profile – usually each week it was about a man in the news – headed 'A time to attack, and a time to retreat'. I had made no secret, said Hague, of my underlying belief in realistic manning levels and new technology. 'That said, when the sackings were announced, Miss Dean put her formidable public relations skills to work on behalf of the workers. Night after night on television she pointed to what she called the cold and calculated sacking of 5,000 workers, making sure that clerical workers, cleaners, telephonists and messengers were mentioned in an attempt to correct the image of the "Fleet Street fat cats".' To which quietly I pleaded guilty.

At the mass rally in Central Hall, Westminster when I was shouted down, Hague reported she heard one jibe 'she's a film star'. She also wrote that the consensus among newspaper executives was that I could have averted Wapping if elected to national office sooner. Well, maybe, but the Fleet Street 'keep out' attitude was well embedded in London. In a letter to me, my predecessor, Bill Keys, said he regarded his failure years earlier to get acceptance of 'A Programme for Action' in Fleet Street as his major defeat.

Hague summed up predicting I would be wooed by the Labour Party and said one newspaper executive had told her, 'If Kinnock's got any sense he'll give her a Cabinet position if he gets power. She's the acceptable face of both feminism and trade unionism.'

The *Guardian* pulled out quite the worst picture of me they could find in the photo library, which had me wondering about the politics of those on the picture desk. However, Patrick Wintour, son of Charles, with whom I was on good terms, reported to his customary high standard. Throughout the thirteen months Wintour had followed events closely and, in particular, explained the complexities of the employment law well. He was extremely well informed but always checked to get the other side of the story.

He was wrong, though, to describe our executive meeting as stormy, which I do not recall. I had attended far worse. There was an air of resignation, people were worn down and many of them had to endure almost daily criticism and abuse so, generally, people were rather restrained.

One fact that did emerge was that out of the 4,500 members who went on strike only 680 remained out by the time we took the executive vote.

The *Independent*, the new, refreshing competition for the *Times*, also made our decision the lead, and it was under the byline of David Felton, one of those who refused to cross the picket line to go into Wapping. He quit the *Times* for the new paper. Inside, another 'refusenik', Felton's labour staff colleague Barrie Clement, did a background piece in which he commented, 'Despite the polished manner of Ms Dean, the public never took the printers to their hearts as they did, to a degree, the miners.'

The *Independent* leader was headed 'Hard times beyond Dockland' and explored the dispute well, arguing that, just like everyone else in Britain, trade unionists were going to have to change. Membership of the unions was in sharp decline and the unions had to adapt. 'Although Brenda Dean is very much the acceptable face of trade unionism, the scenes outside News International have been as disgraceful as anything which happened in the miners' strike.'

After the press conference there were dozens of radio and television interviews with people such as Ian Ross, Michael Green, Mark Mardell and many others, quite a few from abroad.

Eventually I was able to get away from Hadleigh after some commiserations all round with the staff, who had backed us up so solidly throughout the thirteen-month trial of strength. Ken drove me home and I was lost in thought until I dozed off.

From Gibson Square I rang Bill O'Neill and told him the deed was done. He recalls me saying, 'I have had a dreadful day.' Maybe, but what I do remember was that I told him how financially crippled the union was now and wondering aloud if there was anything that could be done to help us.

We agreed I would put it on paper and O'Neill would give it to Murdoch.

Chapter 15

Next morning at Gibson Square I sat once again at the trusty little Apple Mac, which had well and truly covered its costs in the past thirteen months pouring out speech notes, drafts of press releases, articles, papers for the executive and notes for lawyers. I don't think I could have coped without that tiny box of a computer, which is today a collector's item but was state of the art just twenty years ago.

I sent Bill O'Neill copies of the correspondence carrying through our decision to end the strike and said that from what I had heard of the London meeting it was really all over. 'The members present were very depressed and some were in tears. They were more or less unanimous that the dispute was over and there was not much point in going down to Wapping again, although some may turn up tonight as one last journey to end the dispute.'

In a personal letter to O'Neill I listed all our legal costs, how our £1.4 million share portfolio had gone and now we faced a legal bill from our own lawyers of around £1 million. We also could be liable to a claim for unemployment benefit from our members of £294,000. We would probably have to take mortgages on our two convalescent homes. Add to that a bill for £450,000 sequestration costs, the bank costs and others, and the union was in dire financial straits. Fortunately News International had agreed to pay its own legal costs. It was these amounts which I asked if they could be raised on a private and confidential basis with Mr Murdoch, I explained.

O'Neill had undertaken to discuss these costs with Rupert Murdoch when he was next in the country in March and I offered to meet him then.

I added a handwritten postscript: 'I hope you agree that in handling the press side of the decision I did not "run you out of town"! The same cannot be said of the *Sun*'s attitude to us.' Under Kelvin McKenzie, the *Sun* had been its spiteful self, unlike the measured attitude of the *Times*.

Twenty years later McKenzie told how he used to drive through the picket lines in his Jaguar with three SAS bodyguards, give a quick beep on the horn and the V-sign and then, not surprisingly, as the crowd surged forward, shot off down the Highway at 100 miles an hour. (What were the police doing about that?) 'I enjoyed that,' he said. 'I hated those people. I hated the fact that they earned so much money and did so little work. I hated their rather thick, ill-educated attitude to life.' I am not actually sure McKenzie, then or now, puts forward a greatly superior, educated, attitude to life. Certainly not one worth emulating.

I was not very hopeful that my letter to O'Neill would produce results and I hated putting out the begging bowl but it was worth a try. But on 11 February a rather curt letter came back from him, in which he told me he had had a conversation with his boss. Yes, they would meet their 'quite high' legal costs but he added, 'We believe it inappropriate to consider your request for the £450,000.' So we were on our own.

Looking back on the year, a lot of the events merge into each other but I gave some thought to how I felt and the lessons I learned. The imbalance in industrial relations legislation introduced under Thatcher had left us very embittered and in some respects our laws were worse than in some dictatorial regimes. I am pleased that under Tony Blair the law is again more even handed, both for the unions and for the employers. Industrial relations in Britain have not suffered as a result. People again now have the basic right to join a trade union, which I regard as one of the hallmarks of a democratic society. I am proud still to be a trade union member.

But what about so-called secondary action? This is today still a divisive issue and I am not adamant that the clock should go completely back to the pre-Thatcher period. On the other hand I believe there is a case for a more even-handed legal situation and it needs reviewing. SOGAT was sequestrated for secondary action when it tried to stop newspapers being distributed by the wholesalers. But it is forgotten that we were operating a fully legal strike, had held a ballot and were meticulous in following the strict letter of the law.

Meanwhile News International was able to dismiss its employees, transfer the point of production and, by setting up a series of new companies and transferring production and distribution to them, make it impossible for us to pursue a legal dispute. The law of the land was 100 per cent behind the company.

That has nothing to do with so-called secondary action – that is using legislation loaded against working people to frustrate their basic democratic rights. In my view that is unfair and the imbalance needs correcting.

When one is in the midst of such a situation there is little opportunity to consider oneself. The campaign went on seven days a week, week in, week out. It was totally draining. Yes, I became a national figure but the price for that was loss of personal privacy and it is not until you have lost it that you understand just how valuable it is.

I did feel pretty lonely at times. It was my decision as general secretary to persuade the executive to have the ballot which led to the strike but I did keep wondering if I had done the right thing.

I sometimes thought about the effect it was having on my father and mother living in Cleveleys – not a hotbed of socialism at the best of times. Were they getting sniping remarks when shopping or in the working men's club to which my dad would go? And what about my younger brother, Bobby, who was a manager in the printing industry? Did he feel a backlash from the lithographers and printers he managed, I wondered. What about my nieces at school, when their aunt was so often on nightly television? I worried that I might be making life difficult for them. Children really just want to melt into the background and not stand out in any way. Were they quietly cursing their famous aunt, perhaps?

Was there more I could do about the strike? Had I missed a trick anywhere? I knew I could not work any harder and every working hour went into the dispute. But that did not prevent me from worrying.

I clung to my personal values and integrity carefully. In my heart I knew that once I compromised on those I risked losing the respect of those around me and the many who were watching. Never did I tell the executive or the members anything in which I did not believe. There are so many union leaders in the past who have told the membership what they wanted to hear and for a while been a hero. But they usually came unstuck and I was determined not to go down that road. I was not going to lie in any situation. And I was not playing any games with people's lives.

That is not to say I was not a wheeler-dealer – I do believe in that and consider wheeling and dealing an essential part of being a negotiator but it does not mean one has to lie. Or cheat.

My Christian faith was truly a comfort to me. I quite often said my prayers and asked for guidance. (Years later I was proud to become the president of the Christian Socialist Movement Appeal.) Sometimes I would slip into a back pew in Christ Church, Blackfriars Road, over the bridge from Fleet Street and where nowadays the *Daily Express* is located. It is interesting how that came about.

Twelve of our branches held their meetings in the John Marshall Hall at the church and, located in the midst of the offices and homes of so many 'in the print', it held a special place in people's hearts. Some of the crucial votes of the London branches on the Wapping issue were taken in the hall. The vicar at the time was the Rev. Peter Challen, who took a great personal interest in what was happening – he saw the impact on families. Often women and children accompanied their breadwinner to Christ Church and Challen believed there was a genuine attempt to resolve the dispute.

He discussed with the trade unionists if the church could make some kind of gesture. In a chat with him the idea came up of some kind of commemoration and I agreed that the union would make a good contribution to its cost. Challen brought together a group to discuss a theme and the Arts in Labour group was contacted. From that initiative, the sculptor Ian Walters responded to the church and said he was interested.

Challen actually wrote a poem about the crisis. When I read it I was touched. All these years later it still reads well. His poem was titled 'Remember Wapping – a Group's Suggestion for the Theme of the Sculpture'.

> Remember Wapping!
> Not in scale, as that kind of lying;
> but in significance, as that kind of dying
> to old technologies without resurrection

in our methodology.
When will we learn,
when will hearts turn, and
our inhumanity to others
give way to new ability
to share?
In the unforgettable 80s
skills were aborted,
view-points distorted,
inevitability exhorted,
and dignity contorted, when
our real humanity to others
was placed only after
earnings per shift or share!

Remember Wapping!
In this house, and hall, of God,
we must recall capital duly subordinate
to the labour that begets it;
properties subordinate to shared use
by those who generate,
in living participation, the working health, and
all the wealth
of people.

Nowadays Walters's name is well known, particularly for the bust of Nelson Mandela at the Royal Festival Hall by the Thames. He also made a magnificent bust of Harold Wilson, busts of Oliver Tambo, Archbishop Trevor Huddleston and Tony Benn, and a monument to the International Brigade. In 2001 Walters went to South Africa, where Mandela sat for him for nine hours – the longest he has ever posed for an artist – and it is this work which may well soon go up in Trafalgar Square. I certainly hope so.

Walters's bronze memorial to Wapping was splendid and Challen brought together another group which discussed the work and its implications. Interestingly, along with the workers was a policeman, taking part quite on his own initiative. He was involved at Wapping and felt uncomfortable at what was taking place.

The group agreed they wanted the bronze to be placed in the John Marshall Hall and the poem Challen had written, together with a second he wrote about the sculpture after the discussion, mounted alongside.

I felt quite moved when I was asked to unveil the sculpture at its dedication in 1989 and there is a framed photograph of me in the wall with Challen and Walters.

Challen's second poem summed up how the group was feeling at the conclusion to the Wapping dispute:

'All Wapping's Unacceptable Faces – the Group's
Response to the Finished Piece'

Did it really happen in the 80s?
Was it us?
Are we managers or workers, women or men,
categories driven by survival,

or persons uniquely resolute
to face and effect resounding change?
Could the tale repeat itself, have we learnt anything?
Why feed so avariciously on
daily diets of prejudice and spite?
Called news, it still breeds enmities.
Can faith discern good news in all this shame?

All lost in change and so protested painfully,
only for powers to field policemen seeming ready to talk,
yet so swift to strike;
strikers who retaliated,
bitterness engendering, or did the strikers strike first,

for policemen to react?
No matter – no one cared to yield.
Unacceptable faces everywhere, thus
this sculptured relief.

Look again; it's constantly revealing,
horse's head and pounding hooves,
mediaeval jousting, visors of vengeance,
razor wire and barriers of shields, new prejudices surfacing,
with sticks and stones.
There seems a hand in offering,
only to show the same is snatching back.
It grasps a sheath of five million notes,
the labour of five thousand other hands,
the price of settlement, yet no peace.

Print on old matrix, then the new screens,
rolling sheets of prejudice, feeding the hand that offers,
and takes back;
portraying the unacceptable faces
of all our greed.
Occasional impartial news, more often
sensations that ignore all feelings.
What is Good News in all this dis-array?

Let Wapping never come again.
Let faces turn, acceptability be found
in each and every gift and talent;
whether of pen, print or type, modern or cathode ray;
new technologies, with sensitivity, displacing old.
Let living communities arise to replace the drive for gain,
the survival race, that none can win;
salvation has a human face . . . for everyone.

Sadly, as I concluded this book came news that Ian Walters had succumbed to cancer. But he fought to the end and managed to complete the bust of Mandela and *The Bronze Women*, a 7-foot statue to be erected shortly in Lambeth.

The other big issue to examine after the strike ended was the role of the police. Their actions during the miners' dispute, when they used plenty of strong-arm tactics, had given a warning. But the argument had been that the miners themselves had indulged in violence, they had not held a ballot on their strike and the government had a duty to ensure the continuation of electricity supplies.

That kind of thinking hardly applied in our strike. For a start newspapers are not vital to life and limb and we had a clear-cut ballot result in support of an official strike. Our members had been flung out of work without warning and a variety of legal tactics had been used against them.

From the beginning I went on record saying publicly that we condemned violence and we were not looking for a fight with the police. I declined to criticise them. It was our decision to set up a liaison with the police to explain what we were doing and for several months there was no real clash. But it was the police who provoked the clash on 3 May, repeatedly charging the crowd with horses, helmeted men hitting out wildly with batons, hardly appearing impartial and seeking to keep the peace.

When I was interviewed afterwards I said we had not been given any warning over the loudspeaker that the police were going to charge – as the police chief, Wynn Jones, subsequently admitted. 'You talk of police in riot gear – this was the police in riot,' I said. 'Our people are calling them "Murdoch's Cavalry" and it's dreadful what has happened here tonight.'

That was not just our view – the BBC's house journal *Ariel* printed in some detail on 7 May what had happened to their television teams. Christopher Morris, an experienced journalist who was at the scene was quoted: 'The first BBC crew to be attacked were cameraman Phil Warren, recordist Baz Solanki and lighting technician Tony Fallshawe. They tried unsuccessfully to break the camera but did knock out the lights with a well-aimed blow with a truncheon. Tony Fallshawe's second set of lights were shattered too, a short time afterwards during another charge by baton-wielding police.

'Across the road the second crew, cameraman Ian Fairclough, Steve Taylor and lighting man George Vint, experienced an identical attack. Another set of lights was smashed to try and stop us filming.'

I was sent *Ariel* privately with an attached comment – 'interesting that the BBC did not see fit to run this story or use the footage at the time'. Yes, very interesting. Yet surely that was news – an impartial account by their own staff of what was happening in the Highway. Edited out by whose decision? Had someone high in the BBC been given a nudge from within Whitehall to keep off the grass?

The police appeared to me to be working to orders and made little attempt to fulfil their publicly accepted role in a democracy as independent keepers of the peace.

The issue came up at a SOGAT executive meeting when the strike ended because quite a number of members were urging that the union should take the matter to the Police Complaints Authority. After a long debate the executive voted against making a formal complaint – partly because they wanted to close the chapter on Wapping. But also because they saw no point in co-operating with the Establishment. The executive did, however, agree not to stand in the way of any individual member who wished to complain.

The Haldane Society, a society of lawyers which has a reputation for integrity and enjoys good relations with government, produced some strong evidence of police over-reaction early in 1987. The society said that a Mr Andrew King, a Wapping resident, had a nasty moment when taking four children home from school, one in a pushchair. While he was crossing the road in heavy traffic the pushchair became stuck and toppled over. With two policemen nearby Mr King shouted for help.

At once he found himself surrounded by police, dragged away from the children and put in a van. Moments later, the children in tears, were bundled into the van too. The Haldane Society said Mr King was held in a police cell for two hours.

At his trial for obstructing the highway a PC Chitty (no. G195) claimed Mr King had gone into the road and taunted the police, shouting, 'I'm here now, you wankers, and there's nothing you can do about it.' Not surprisingly the magistrates threw out the case and awarded costs against the police.

The same policeman supported a colleague in a case in which one of the few black print workers, Denys Rama, was alleged to have struck a policeman twice in the face. In court Rama denied the charges and claimed he had been set upon by the police. Their prosecution admitted that at the police station, when Rama saw a police doctor, he was told he probably had a broken jaw. The policeman said he had been forced to do a rugby tackle on Rama, which did not explain why he had several injuries to his face. The case was thrown out at Southwark Crown Court.

There had been so many detailed accounts of ugly incidents like this that when I was contacted by the Police Complaints Authority I decided that, yes, I would agree to be interviewed and tell what I had seen. The problem for the PCA, they told me, was that although they had plenty of camera footage and news pictures, no formal complaint had been made to them. I decided to give them one. Quite a few individual policemen were in deep trouble, I was told, and if a complaint was made some would probably go to jail.

I was amazed to discover that the Haldane Society, despite its report and the cases it had uncovered, was refusing point blank to co-operate with the authority. I can only imagine the lawyers involved felt their views would be labelled as too left wing and would be brushed off. Similarly no politician, trade union leader or individual union branch would co-operate with the inquiry. Later a number of policemen declined to make statements which might have incriminated them.

I was at the PCA's offices for several hours as I detailed my experiences to an authority member, Noel Taylor, telling what I had seen and done both on the night of 3 May and at the final violent confrontation of 24 January 1987. I found Taylor a most thorough man who carefully checked everything. He had conducted inquiries into the Brixton and Toxteth riots so was not overawed by adverse police reaction. He was known as Captain Taylor because he had held a top post with Shell Tankers and was a qualified marine officer.

I have learned subsequently just how difficult the Metropolitan Police made it for Taylor and his police investigator, Chief Superintendent D. J. Wyrko of

Northamptonshire Police, who had a team of eleven of his own policemen working with him. If the Met could have achieved its ambition either to get Wyrko off the case or to compromise him in some way I am sure that would have been done.

Apparently, Peter Imbert, head of Thames Valley Police Force put Wynn Jones in charge of the Greenham Common anti-nuclear protest. So when Imbert moved up from deputy to be head of the Metropolitan Police in 1987, the most coveted position in British policing, Jones was on the team.

The PCA did have a number of successes – one in particular was getting a trial halted at Southwark County Court. It was able to prove that a police sergeant giving damning evidence against a man had never been in the same area as him. Yet the sergeant was quite prepared to give evidence on oath as he had done in several other Wapping cases.

One other discovery of which I was unaware at the time was that on the night of 24 January 1987 members of the City of London Police came in as reinforcements to the Met. The police injuries list contained 153 Met people but also 41 from the City. That perhaps explains why the City of London police officer had warned George Holmes that night that our members were going to get a thrashing – did he know it was going to happen?

It was three years before the authority published its final – and very fair – report into events at Wapping on 24 January 1987. But before then charges were brought against twenty-four serving Metropolitan policemen and two who had retired. Earlier 146 Met men and 93 from the City came under investigation. In all fairness these figures have to be set against the fact that 1,200 policemen were on duty that fateful night.

Those charged ultimately appeared before the magistrate at Bow Street. They were suspended and the cases were then adjourned and silence ensued. Months elapsed and eventually the men came back to court, whereupon the magistrate dismissed the case on the grounds that the men concerned had suffered enough in the long wait. I suspect this was exactly what those in charge of the Metropolitan police had in mind.

Without being hypersensitive I believe this was part of a master plan in Whitehall agreed somewhere in the bowels of the Home Office.

The police are politically aware nowadays but they were not babes in arms in that respect twenty years ago. They knew what they had done during the miners' strike yet survived all criticisms. I believe they either knew, or felt, they had a blank cheque from the government in 1986.

Murdoch himself was not averse to political lobbying and had an open door to No. 10, as did people such as the late Woodrow Wyatt, an EETPU supporter and owner of a printing plant himself. He was an adroit political lobbyist and had the ear of ministers and the Prime Minister. There were a number of similar shadowy figures around who had been involved in the Grunwick union recognition dispute and urged within the right-wing Conservative ranks that to crush the printers meant defeating the last stand of organised labour.

I am reasonably certain, without wishing to sound paranoid, that my home telephone number was tapped during the dispute. There were several suspicious incidents. On one occasion when the phone handset was replaced, immediately the phone rang. When it was picked up there were some very odd sounds at the other end. On another occasion there was a leak in the newspapers of a matter I discussed on the phone but I told no one in the union. Odd!

Anyway I worked on the basis that my phone was being tapped. It was amusing really because years earlier I was sounded out in Manchester if I would be willing to assist MI5 with activities in the trade union movement locally. I had a chat but was glad I had turned them down.

Maybe my attempt to avoid violence and to keep firm discipline was doomed, not helped by the intervention of Trotskyists and miscellaneous troublemakers. I took it up in a letter to the *Police Federation Journal* in April 1987 in which I protested strongly at a photograph published the previous month showing an array of items that police claimed had been used against them at Wapping. The caption was 'Look what Brenda Dean's peaceful supporters left behind'.

I recounted what I had seen on the night of 24 January, when the demonstration had been completely reasonable until their baton charges and asked the journal's readers if that was what they wanted. 'All this does raise the question as to whether the police are any longer a neutral force, acting impartially to enforce the law on all sides, or whether they are themselves becoming protagonists in individual disputes, acting on behalf of employers (and the government) in helping to defeat and undermine free trade unions. This is a serious matter for your members as well as mine.'

I suggested the police should ask themselves if they wanted to create another Northern Ireland on the mainland or a police state. 'Surely that isn't really what you want, is it? In that case perhaps a cool reappraisal of recent events would be valuable. But an inquiry at Wapping must be part of the process. If your members have behaved correctly, what are you afraid of?' I summed up.

There was no reply in the next edition of the *Police Federation Journal.*

Albert Meltzer, who was an independent observer during the Wapping demonstrations, published his findings on the World Wide Web. They make interesting reading. He said the police acted like an occupation force and he never accepted the argument that a few 'bad apples' had over-reacted. 'The attack on demonstrators to defend Rupert Murdoch's scab operation was violent but it was not uncontrolled. It had one guiding purpose – to get his papers out on time.'

Mr Meltzer was standing in front of the SOGAT platform taking notes and someone next to him was using a camera when a woman, unknown to him, stood up to speak. 'I heard a voice from the police ranks clearly shout, "That's Brenda Dean," and a chorus went up from the ranks, "Let's get the bitch."' On hearing the cry 'Get the bitch' the police charged forward, claimed Mr Meltzer, but a shower of stones and marbles stopped their attack on the platform. 'The question remains – why would police officers want to "get the bitch"? What could they have against Brenda Dean? The only reason I can think of is that they were following the instructions. There was no other motive. The police did not appear undisciplined to me. Even in retreat they maintained their ranks,' summed up Mr Meltzer.

Chapter 16

Back in 1976 at the TUC conference in Blackpool I was up to my eyes in a dispute between the union nationally and Express Newspapers, then headed by Jocelyn Stevens. I had not met him at the time but we did meet subsequently and we got on well together. Stevens was an unpredictable buccaneer alright, but newspapers were deeply ingrained in his blood. When some months later he launched the *Daily Star* from Manchester I was honoured to be invited to the big night.

This dispute, however, was as usual a problem between the *Express* and the London branches and they wanted our Manchester delivery drivers to stop distribution.

My members were a great bunch of men – or lads, as I insisted on calling them – and I felt confident that if I asked them to stop then they would. But why should they? Here was yet another London row and I saw no real reason to bring out my members in support, losing pay and running the risk of employer exasperation. It was a dispute which, frankly, should not have been taking place.

On the other hand I knew the London people would see it as a test of my resolution and determination. 'Can she deliver?' I could hear them asking. The union nationally had its doubts and Bill Keys, then the general secretary, sent Bill Miles to Manchester with the intent, I suspected, of 'stiffening' me up. I needn't have worried about my Manchester members because they backed me to the hilt but not before asking Miles to leave the meeting so that they could talk to me alone as their union negotiator. Quite a coup.

So all this was on my mind as I arrived rather late for the *Daily Mirror*'s annual reception at the Imperial Hotel.

As I have often said, in my work I have met lots of males but very few real men. But I did bump into one right then, at – of all places – the TUC conference. As I came into the room for the *Mirror* reception someone I later learned was named Keith McDowall quite cheekily asked who I was looking for.

I spun round and said, 'What makes you think I am looking for anyone?' It was quite a put-down and immediately I was rather sorry because he was obviously deflated. I little realised that I had just met my life partner and that in the struggle ahead he would be my real confidant.

It had been a little rude and really Keith was at the receiving end of my inner resentment and reaction to the male culture all around me. So I went back to talk to him as a way of saying sorry. That decision was to change my life.

He told me his name, and that at the time he was director of information at the Department of Employment, working with Michael Foot and Albert Booth, so we had something in common. But I soon learned that for thirteen years he had been on the broadsheet *Daily Mail,* where he became industrial editor specialising in labour relations, trade union affairs, economics and Labour politics. So we had even more in common than I at first thought. Subsequently Keith was in charge of press and public relations at British Shipbuilders and then moved to – of all places – the CBI, where he worked closely with Sir Terence Beckett, former chief of Ford of Britain, whom Keith said he had always admired.

Without Keith I doubt my life would have been enriched by the enormous range of people I met through him nor would it have had the wider perspective which enabled my career to develop in the way it did.

Keith was always there for me, which was an enormous support because of his vast experience and ability to see 'the big picture', and with his journalistic experience he saw the angles I missed. It helped me to avoid so many potential blunders, particularly as he not only knew the newspaper scene but also so many characters in it. Many's the time I came back home feeling rather heavily laden with what seemed an intractable problem to sit down over supper and a glass of wine, talk it through with Keith and suddenly see a way through. While our different jobs obviously could cause a problem we were careful not to compromise each other and since I was then still in Manchester as branch secretary there was not a direct clash.

We set up home together and had a splendid fourth-floor flat in Mountjoy House in the Barbican, overlooking St Giles' Cripplegate, where Milton worshipped and Maria Callas recorded some marvellous operatic arias. We had some good parties, to which came quite a few politicians such as John Smith and journalist friends including Ian Ross, then with the BBC as industrial correspondent, and the late Roy Nash, *Daily Mail* education writer. (Roy married Joyce Nash, a former headmistress, who went on to become senior commoner on the City of London Corporation and on the way demolished quite a few anti-women citadels herself.) So among the journalistic fraternity our secret was known but no one saw it as a gossip item at the time.

When I was about to become general secretary of the union, however, there clearly was the potential for an embarrassing situation. I would now have a national profile and few reporters would be able to resist the temptation to mention my involvement with a top official of 'the bosses' union'.

Before I took the decision to go for the top job in the union I discussed it with Keith. I was well aware of the possibility that, should I win the election, then my success could have a dire effect on his career. Quite a conundrum to face and not one I relished. But when I raised the issue with Keith his reaction was immediate and positive – 'You must go for it' was his response. And in saying that he did not just mean go for the job – with it came his wholehearted support and personal involvement.

So, when I won, Keith resolved he had to tell Beckett and went to him to offer his resignation.

'Oh, that'll be the print lady,' said the CBI director general, who clearly knew all about us although he had never said a word. One can only assume that MI5 had again been at work. Beckett declined Keith's resignation offer and subsequently I met him and the then president, Sir David Nickson of Scottish and Newcastle. I later faced them at the National Economic Development Council when I became the first woman to be in the TUC team and they both came to our wedding party years later at The Reform Club. (It was the first – and last – time they had jazz at the club!)

I also got on well with the British Shipbuilders team, which included John Parker, now Sir John, who heads National Grid, and the late, charming, Admiral Sir Anthony Griffin, BS chairman. He turned out to be a very good ballroom dancer when he took me onto the floor at a BS dance in Newcastle. The admiral told me that cadets like him, when at Dartmouth, were all taught to dance since they might, he explained, one day have to partner someone like the wife of the British ambassador at an embassy event. They think of everything, it seems, in the Royal Navy.

Quite a few of my members, certainly in my old branch, also knew about Keith and what he did, but he got on well with them and here again people seemed to take our decision in their stride.

As Wapping loomed Keith and I were in Lanzarote in what *Private Eye* called our 'love nest' where I did a lot of thinking – and talking with him – about the imminent crunch situation. Actually it was quite a comfortable two-bedroom apartment at Costa Teguise, where one of our friends and neighbours was Lord Marsh, ex-MP and former chairman of British Rail.

I needed someone to talk to and assess situations and Keith's journalistic and government relations experience was invaluable. Over the months ahead Keith's skill and writing too were vital – I could see why he seemed to be held in high regard by so many employers. His personal input with articles for our union magazine, and his advice on the approach and line to take with the media, and sometimes with Whitehall and government, helped enormously in the Battle of Wapping. Gosh, did I (and my union) benefit from his input behind the scenes!

I realised the Wapping dispute could have spelt disaster for us and our relationship, such were the stresses of thirteen months in the media eye. After all, who really wants their home invaded at any time of the day and night with calls and intrusions? That was why Keith decided we needed an answering machine so that at least we could have dinner without the infernal phone demanding to be answered.

Still the fear at the back of my mind that it could all wreck our relationship proved to be groundless. We grew closer together and came through that traumatic period not just intact, but stronger.

Our boat deserves a mention too. It was called *La Bamba* and it was moored on the river Medway at Upnor. Some weekends we could be anchored down near the Isle of Grain, in one of the creeks such as Stangate, and it was the perfect place to switch off. So near London – and Hadleigh because we could look across the Thames to the lights of Southend – and yet a million miles away with only the kingfishers calling us. The dear old river Medway, muddy as it may be, and *La Bamba* did a lot to give my mind a rest during the trials of the Wapping era.

Chapter 17

Months before the Wapping crunch there had been discussions between the National Graphical Association and our union about the possibilities of merging. This all had to be put on ice for the thirteen months of Wapping, and afterwards time flashed by as we started to lick our wounds and try to rebuild, most notably the finances of SOGAT. In fact we did rebuild more quickly than any of us thought possible, mainly through good financial management.

Even so, the speed of technical change affected a far wider area than just Wapping. It seemed clear to me that the whole world of communication was going to be turned upside down. Merging with the NGA would simply provide a breathing space. What we needed was a much wider consultation in the communication field with the aim of establishing media as an independent trade union sphere of influence.

I shared these views one day with Alan Tuffin, then general secretary of the Union of Postal Workers, when we were chatting before the TUC General Council at Congress House. Tuffin agreed that a wider 'communications union' would be a route worth exploring. Otherwise one by one unions in this field, busily competing with each other for membership, would wither away in the process.

Tuffin felt the telecommunications union might well join with his union but could also be attracted to the idea of a major media union. Telecoms after all, at that time, were the key to everything. Then if SOGAT and the NGA came together, followed by a merger with the two communications unions, we would have a combined membership of just under 500,000.

Tuffin and I were quite excited with the concept and each of us obtained the support of our executives. We commissioned some preliminary exploratory work by Peter Hain, then the research officer in the postmen's union. This was well before he became an MP and went on to be Leader of the House of Commons and Secretary of State for Northern Ireland.

Hain reported back that the concept was feasible. But before we could make further progress the NGA reacted strongly. They got wind of the project and threatened to pull out of amalgamation talks with SOGAT if we continued talking to other communication unions. As our amalgamation was one of the first stages in the plan, SOGAT was forced to suspend the talks. The postmen and the Post Office Engineering Union achieved their merger, however.

So the chance to build a whole new union in a field that has mushroomed in the last twenty years and, as we all know, changed the face of the world, let alone Britain, slipped through our fingers. It was a tragic case of a missed opportunity. It rather aptly summed up the approach and thinking at the top of the NGA.

Inevitably, the question of SOGAT merging with the NGA began to be discussed within the industry and became quite a topic. Neither leadership really wanted to go down that route. The culture of the rival unions was so very different but both recognised there was really no alternative and it would herald very big changes. Manning conditions throughout the printing industry were getting tighter and tougher. The branches, where power really lay, could see how vulnerable they were by divided ranks. And I could see the trade union movement was never going to be as powerful as it had been in the past.

Whenever they could, the NGA chapels tried to elbow our members out of jobs, arguing their members were skilled whereas our people were semi-skilled – and therefore inferior. If you look back at the 200-year-old roots of the print unions which had gradually combined to create SOGAT, you can see this was patent nonsense; you could hardly have a higher skill, for example, than bookbinding, papermaking or box-making.

Our people handled tasks such as inking and many mechanised processes but it was true that they never handled the compositors' 'stick', which gave the NGA their so-called skill status, even though all type, even headlines in newspapers and advertisements, was set by machine. It was just that the typographers then charged out the work as if they had set it by hand! Come to think of it, that was perhaps where the skill came in . . .

But I felt that to protect the future of our members we had at least to explore the road to amalgamation. That was certainly what many employers wanted – the prospect of negotiating just with one union rather than a number, often in membership competition with each other, was quite attractive. On the other hand, having to negotiate with the 'No Go Area', as many employers regarded the NGA, was not going to be easy.

In an article in the SOGAT journal some months after the Wapping dust had settled I set out the case for exploring a merger and stated bluntly that, if it came about, it would be for the benefit of the members, not the officers. I also argued the case strongly in favour at the union's 1988 conference. There had been too many amalgamations suddenly conceived because the general secretaries were about to retire or one of them could see a way to bump up his pension by an agreement to take early retirement. This merger, I said, would be different. It certainly was.

Tony Dubbins and I were virtually the same age with me being slightly older. He would, however, be elected president of the TUC just ahead of me as he had seniority. As it turned out I had departed by the time my turn came around – much to Keith's disappointment because he always fancied having on the mantelpiece the TUC president's magnificent silver gilt handbell. But Dubbins's and my ages meant that if an eventual merger came about there would have to be an election and one of us would then become general secretary of the new combined union. And the loser would become deputy general secretary.

The negotiations to work out the structure, the rules, the finances, the location of the new headquarters and eventually the name of the new union took about two years. Both unions had negotiating teams. It was hard work and very time consuming. Quite apart from working out how it would all take place, the laws for unions had all been modernised and were quite complex. The days of the old Registrar of Friendly Societies, which had presided over the trade union movement for a century and a half, had passed into history.

And it was not only the head offices that had to be merged. All over the country there were rival branches of the NGA and SOGAT which would have to sink their differences and sort out their finances, their offices and of course their procedures.

In terms of office systems SOGAT was considerably ahead of the NGA. I was proud that our union was one of the most advanced in computers and had a system linking every branch to head office. So each day headquarters knew how it was faring financially. Our office at Hadleigh was nearer London than that of the NGA, located at Bedford.

Eventually, though, agreement was reached. I addressed the NGA conference and Dubbins came to speak to our delegates. In SOGAT we produced some really good literature including a question-and-answer list and even some joke material. It was one of the biggest campaigns we had conducted but it was well received. When the vote came 74,883 members voted in favour and 13,078 against. The NGA produced 51,859 in favour of merging but a surprising 19,212 against.

Then of course came arrangements to decide who would hold the top jobs in the combined union, which was to be called the Graphical, Paper and Media Union. I was delighted that we had won our point to have the word 'paper' in the new union's name and inserting 'media' meant it could cast its eyes around the evolving new world of electronic communication too. I was under no illusions that it was going to be a tough fight with Dubbins. While I had made friends in the Wapping campaign I had also made enemies amongst those who felt my line had not been sufficiently aggressive and that I had not been sufficiently extreme.

This was particularly the case with the branches in Liverpool, Glasgow and, naturally, most of London. The Liverpudlians had always been a thorn in my side dating back to Manchester days. Although I had many good friends and supporters on Merseyside the branch leadership itself, often in turmoil internally, had always been jealous of the success of the Manchester branch. The Glasgow branch was led by Allan Watson, who I never trusted. He always flirted with the left wing and I suspected Dubbins had offered him a free hand in Scotland if the NGA triumphed in the ballot battle. The price was probably that Watson delivered the Glasgow vote.

Despite denials, I was under little illusion that everything that was being said within the SOGAT executive was being fed back to the NGA. At local level NGA branch skilled members were also telling our semi-skilled people to vote to join them and their wages would rise. Tempting.

The NGA line was that in Dubbins they had a real trade unionist at the helm while SOGAT offered 'a film star' who preferred to be on television rather than thumping the table. It was possibly a way of justifying the uncomfortable fact that their man had been less than effective with the media during the Wapping campaign. It was also being said that I was very dictatorial, which I was not. Really the NGA whispers were describing their own candidate, not me. In the years ahead, even months, they were going to find out that truth.

My own attitude was that I would fight the good fight but play it straight. After all that had happened I was not about to get down in the gutter now. Those were my values and I stuck by them. My supporters wanted me to make promises on pay but I was not prepared to lie about something I doubted if I could deliver. I knew the craftsmen would never let it happen. I was also aware that although the NGA was smaller than our union, its members voted well and produced a higher return in ballots than we did. Maybe, though, once again, the women membership of SOGAT would ride to my rescue?

Arthur Bonner, who was an NGA branch secretary in London, told me privately after the merger had been completed that he and other local NGA officers had been told to spend as much as they needed to get the vote in – and to get it right for Dubbins.

The original date for vesting the new union was 1 July 1991 and if this target date had been met SOGAT, which had polled extremely well in the campaign to merge, might have carried the day. But a fly in the ointment came when a retired SOGAT member went to court to challenge why Danny Sergeant and two other officers had not offered themselves for re-election after five years as I had done. I had not actually been required to stand for re-election but had taken the view that this would prevent the union being dragged into time-consuming expense in the courts. I was not challenged and easily won re-election. Here again, Sergeant's hesitation and tendency to sit on the fence had landed the union in difficulty.

But it was a godsend to the NGA. The ensuing complications were seized on to force a three-month delay – a golden opportunity to whip up further their strong campaign for their candidate for general secretary.

I remember the day of the ballot result very well. On 29 May 1991 I was in the Thompsons flat at Congress House when Ted Chard, one of our national officers now, formerly the London branch secretary, phoned me. He was a scrutineer for us at the count, held by the Electoral Reform Society. 'I don't know the figures, Brenda, but from the size of the piles of voting papers it is not looking good,' he reported. I knew he was conditioning me to be prepared for defeat.

A little later I received a call confirming the official results and there was no room for argument. Dubbins had beaten me by 78,654 votes to my total of 72,657. The NGA had achieved a 70 per cent turnout, while we had done well but achieved only 65 per cent. But a quarter of my members had voted for Dubbins and only 15 per cent of his members had voted for me.

I have always argued that if you believe in the ballot box you have to accept the outcome even if the results are not to your personal taste.

I went home to Islington. Keith came out and met me at the door. We went in and I didn't cry but it was upsetting. But I knew I had to do the decent thing and I picked up the phone and rang Dubbins. I congratulated him on the result and said I was prepared to work with him as deputy general secretary. Easier said than done, I was to find.

When I went to Bedford, where it had been decided the new union would be based, I ran into a wall of non-co-operation. There is no other way to describe it. I could feel the atmosphere – it was quite awful. My key staff, for example Margaret Tothill and my driver, Ken Tuppen, felt it too. Some of our own people such as Mike Molloy, our research officer, had sold out earlier on the promise of an NGA job and there was little help to be found there. Everyone it seemed had been poisoned against us, and we felt isolated. It was anything but brotherly or fraternal. There was also a very macho atmosphere and if you did not join in the Friday afternoon drinking session – a very heavy affair with the pace set by Dubbins in his office – then you were out.

Dubbins gave me the task of sorting out the branch network, which was always going to be something of a nightmare and full of pitfalls. It was a very poisoned chalice, really, but I decided to get stuck into it. There was a joint working group of people from both unions and it was going to be a long job. I expected the first meeting to be tense but that atmosphere continued. Everything I did I found challenged. The NGA people had obviously been conditioned against me and at first it was very tough going.

I worked extremely hard at it, though, and gradually I started to make some progress although there were two of Dubbins's close confidants on the committee – placed there, I felt, to keep an eye on me. But having completed that task, and with the report on the future of the branch network well received, I felt it was never going to work out for me personally. I had given it my best shot but I knew in my heart my days in the trade union movement were coming to a close.

I sat down and typed out my thoughts on what was going wrong and whether I should stay. I still have that list. The first item says 'Systematically frozen out'. After all these years I still believe that was the case.

What is remarkable is that nowadays I meet so many from the union who tell me how much they regret my leaving. Well, so be it, they had their chance, but no regrets. So I resolved it was time to go although I had no idea, after thirty-two years, eight months in the trade union movement, where I was going.

I drove to Bedford with two draft press notices in my briefcase – one if Dubbins agreed I should leave in good order and one, which he would not like at all, if he decided to make life difficult for me. Keith had helped me draft them.

I had asked to see Dubbins in his office at about half-past seven in the morning and over the weekend the tom-toms must have been beating. Two of his closest allies were waiting for me at Bedford. One of them asked, 'You're not getting fed up, are you? You're not thinking of leaving?'

'Well, what's that got to do with you?' I parried. 'You'll probably be glad to see me go.'

'Oh no,' he said. 'We now realise we have been given a real bum steer about you. We've enjoyed working with you. You're dead straight. You've done a good job on this branch amalgamation. And furthermore if you want to challenge Tony you'll find the executive will back you against him.'

I said, 'Do you really think I have gone through all this to see the union tear itself apart? People will be forced to take sides. He was elected by the members, straight, bad or indifferent. That was the members' decision and you've got to put up with it. But I don't.'

I don't think they meant me challenging Dubbins for the general secretary's job but they wanted me to take him on in the executive. He was running riot and people were beginning to feel very insecure. They were seeing a real bully at work.

I saw him shortly after this encounter in his large, comfortable office. Sat behind his desk, he appeared rather tense. It was not a meeting of two colleagues, but a business meeting. I said I had tried but it was not working out. I had thought about it and I thought the best thing was for me to go.

This clearly was not unexpected and he took it in his stride. 'Well – when do you want to go?'

I told him I would be happy to go immediately but I wanted to tie up the branch amalgamations and I wanted to depart properly and in the best interests of the union. 'You will not find me', I said, 'nasty or bitter.'

I gave him the paper I had worked out listing my redundancy details. I stressed I was not asking for any special terms – just the deal that all others displaced by the merger had received. And I asked him to tell the executive at its meeting, later that morning, that I was going.

It was all very low key and Dubbins made no attempt to dissuade me from leaving. But he did ask, 'Why do you want to go?'

I laughed. 'You're joking, Tony. If you don't know now you'll never know. It will never work out between you and me because you don't want me around. Everything you have done has told me that.

'If you had been as you have been with me this morning we might have had a chance. But you have never talked to me, nor consulted me about anything. The place is run like a boys' club: if you are in and agree, OK; if not, you are out.'

I gave him the draft press release which I said I wanted released if I parted on amicable terms. I kept the nastier version in my handbag.

Very soon the press calls started to come in. Bad news, as we know, travels fast.

I also received a personal call from Charles Clarke, then running Neil Kinnock's office. 'Why didn't you tell us you were going? Your name would have been on the list of new peers that went in last week.' Ah well.

Bill Jordan, the engineers' leader, and John Edmonds of the GMB union rang to sympathise.

The journalists mostly took the line that they were not surprised but wanted me to let my hair down. It was a temptation I resisted. I was not going to put the boot into my union after all I had been through – and after all that the trade union movement had given me.

A personal statement went out under my signature, dated 13 May 1992. I said it had been a year since the ballot for a new general secretary and though I had tried I conceded I had found difficulty in my new role. 'It is therefore with a very heavy heart that after nearly thirty-three years of employment in the union I informed the general secretary this week that I had decided to take redundancy and would leave at the end of June.'

I denied rumours that I had a new job to go to. 'I do not. I have no alternative employment to go to and have not sought any.

'My decision to leave has been like sustaining a bereavement. But I leave with no bitterness or recriminations.'

A GPMU press statement stated the executive had accepted my decision with regret.

Ken Tuppen took me home for the last time – though I little knew then that later, he would join my husband's team in the flourishing public affairs business he built up.

I wrote a farewell article for the union magazine which I said I had found very hard to write. I had spent the weekend wondering how I would write my last article for the union after thirty-three years. The trade union movement had given me my start and trained me. 'From that beginning I have been able to rise to the top, been given the chance to do something for my fellow men and women, been allowed to see some of my ideas come to fruition – above all to help to establish ONE UNION for print, paper and packing.

'But now the time has come to go and I suppose I feel like that French singer, Edith Piaf, whose theme was 'no regrets' because, to tell the truth, I have very few indeed. A few, yes, but this is not the time nor the place to list them. And in any case they will get smaller, and more into perspective, as time passes.'

Proud memories I listed were raising £25,000 for the street children of India and Peru, supporting the miners and their families in their strike, giving the children of striking cross-Channel ferry workers a Christmas party, hosting children from the earthquakes in Armenia, and inviting to Britain the tragic youngsters from Chernobyl – many of whom would be dead within twelve months. That was, I recalled, 'the caring face of trade unions we rarely get the chance to read about in the press'.

'Yes, I would pursue Wapping again – although I would have preferred a stronger hand and might have wished that those who felt they knew it all and could run their own shows – till they hit the buffers – would have been willing earlier to respond to leadership, to plan ahead and use their brains rather than rely on brawn.

'Definitely, no regrets,' I concluded. 'Bye for now . . . Brenda.'

Perhaps there was one big regret, brought back to me recently when the GPMU, formed from the amalgamation of our two unions, folded its tent and was absorbed by Amicus, basically the engineering union. That communications plan, killed by NGA intransigence and a desire to dominate, got them nowhere in the end. Still, Tony Dubbins got a job . . .

Chapter 18

The day after my resignation from the union my life changed noticeably. I wouldn't say that the telephone stopped ringing, because there were many calls at home from well-wishers both in the union and wider afield. But it rang much less, the faxes slowed and the post was a much lighter burden for our delivery man.

The letters continued to come in, though, some critical but mostly from the members and others in all walks of life who had felt for me in the struggle and wanted now to express their sympathy and understanding. Some were very touching indeed. I could quote from hundreds because they still lie in the SOGAT box files on the dispute.

Most people asked the same question: 'What are you going to do?' For the first time in my life I had no idea. I was being quite truthful when I told SOGAT members that I had no secret job up my sleeve and I was right in saying it felt like a bereavement. There was that numbness and feeling of helplessness one associates with a death close in the family.

Keith had set up his own business from home and had taken over the office from which I had often worked during the Wapping dispute. The Apple Mac had gone and been replaced with a much faster box of tricks. But he set me up an office in an upstairs bedroom and bought me one of the first laptops made by Apple, which was a design icon at the time. There was not a lot for it to do, though. I had a couple of part-time posts, which were useful but not too demanding in terms of time.

However, I had been invited to become a member of the newly created Independent Committee for Supervision of Telephone Information Services or ICSTIS, which was independent but funded by the industry. It was not a government initiative but an attempt by the industry itself to combat some of the unscrupulous operators who were moving in.

All kinds of nasty scams were being discovered and fortunes being quickly amassed by people, for example, offering very explicit sexual titillation over the phone. And the longer people were kept on the line the more it cost at premium rates. It was bringing the money in, too, for the operators, such as British Telecom and Vodafone – but not doing a lot for their reputations. I spent hours with other committee members at the ICSTIS office listening in to this filth and making a judgement on whether the so-called service should be shut down. The trouble was that as fast as we shut one down, another sprang up in its place or there was simply a name change.

At first BT, Vodafone and the other companies had been rather tentative but later we had the full support of the network operators. By then they accepted that being seen to do the right thing, rather than just rake in profits, enhanced their reputation with the public. And in any case the premium rate business was booming so they could afford to clean it up.

Louis Blom-Cooper QC was the committee's genial chairman and its members were drawn from quite a wide cross-section of public life. As I had time on my hands I was able to put in quite a lot of it into ICSTIS and found the young team, most of them intelligent young women, fun to work with. And remarkably cool and unspoilt by the cesspit around them. One was a young, attractive barrister who went on to take silk and become a QC – Patricia Scotland, later to become a member of the House of Lords and an extremely competent government minister.

I had no idea then but two years later I was to become the chairman of ICSTIS when Blom-Cooper stood down. I shook the industry one day by imposing a fine of £90,000 on one operator.

ICSTIS became an excellent example of an industry willing to self-regulate without the Man from Whitehall's input. Nearly twenty-five years later it is still doing an incredibly good job.

One of my indelible memories of the period was the role British Telecom played in helping support ChildLine, the organisation devoted to helping children who have been or are being abused. I shall never forgot going to listen one Christmas with Esther Rantzen, ChildLine's founder, to the desperate calls coming in and how relieved the youngsters were to find, at last, somewhere, they could obtain help and advice. And a shoulder to cry on, so to speak.

The director of ChildLine was Valerie Howarth, who worked extremely hard to build it up. She was also on the board of ICSTIS and I was later delighted when her name was among the first twelve chosen to be selected by the Appointments Commission to come into the Lords as non-party peers.

Meanwhile my old friends in the paper industry came up trumps as I looked around, and I was invited to become a non-executive director of the paper manufacturer Inveresk plc by its chairman, Stefan Kay. Although I took membership of committees in my stride this was to be my first experience of what it meant to be a company director – the trade union movement often sneered, but I discovered there is considerably more to being on a board than is generally realised.

Over the years the legal responsibilities – and risks – have become extremely onerous. At Inveresk I also became a trustee of the pension fund, renewing my interest in what to many is an arcane subject. In the trade union world I had learned just how important it is to have people who really understand pensions as trustees and I have kept up that specialist interest. If everyone had been sharper, Robert Maxwell might not have been able to damage so many people's lives by stealing their life savings.

Another good employer contact, Bob Gavron, who had built up St Ives plc, which printed the *Economist* each week and other publications, also came to my aid. He arranged for me to have a part-time consultancy role, which apart from filling in some time for me also provided some income.

I was not broke because I had received quite a handsome cheque from the union once the final settlement was worked out but I felt I was too young at forty-eight to think about retirement and eking out my savings. And too young yet to draw the old age pension. But who was going to want to employ a former trade union leader? I knew I carried 'baggage' and there would not be many as brave as Inveresk or St Ives which would consider finding me a role.

A career in politics was perhaps the way for me to go? When I was branch secretary in Manchester I did once decline an invitation in 1983 to succeed

Frank Allaun as MP for Salford East. I decided at the time to stay with the trade union movement which had always held more attraction to me. But I was now much better known and might be able to find a seat, but I was still not sure I wanted to start to work my way through a new undergrowth like Labour Party politics at that time. Nor did I relish the domestic upheaval it was bound to involve – nursing a new constituency, late nights and wearying travel do not do much for a happy home life. Mind you, had it been New Labour I might have thought differently because the brand of change that Tony Blair brought – started by Neil Kinnock – was very much more to my pragmatic taste.

Nonetheless, I did work hard in support of Neil Kinnock in the general election of April 1992 because the party's opinion polling had told them that, flatteringly, I was 'the acceptable face of trade unionism'. Kinnock and Charles Clarke, his chief of staff, took a decision generally to keep trade unionists off the platforms and out of the media – even though they drew on the movement for fighting funds. But they asked me to share platforms in various parts of the country, mostly marginal constituencies, and in this way I made contact with a number of newcomers, subsequently to become ministers when Tony Blair swept the board in 1997.

The outcome to the general election was very disappointing, though. Keith and I had been at a BBC election night party and found it rather subdued so we went to the Labour Party headquarters in Millbank when the results started to come through. The early result at Basildon, which the Tories easily held, predicted the likely outcome and we went home.

Kinnock, in my view, has never had the full credit for clawing back more than a hundred seats then, which made the 1997 result much more attainable, and it was sad to see him stand down so quickly and humiliatingly. From my point of view a change of government would possibly have opened up some opportunities.

Keith continued to be very reassuring. He had taken the plunge and quit the CBI, where he had become a deputy director general. There was a change at the top and it was obvious to him that he would no longer fit in. So at fifty-nine he had thrown it all up and resolved to set up his own business. He explained it felt at first like diving into a cold swimming pool but have confidence, he told me, and events would fall into place.

He thought I would be able to be self-employed and develop what has now become known as 'a portfolio' of jobs and tasks rather than work for just one organisation again; he forecast that new opportunities would open up and I just had to be patient and have self-confidence.

Not for the first time he turned out to be dead right but I was not sure of it at the time. Yet the pace did certainly begin to quicken. One interesting assignment was with Mentorn Films, for which I worked on a training film in labour relations. I was much more comfortable after Wapping in front of the television camera so I enjoyed sessions on negotiating, recruitment, chairing meetings, handling a dismissal and the other myriad tasks that cross the desk of the human relations manager. The series is still in use and occasionally I receive a royalty cheque.

Another interesting one was to be asked to serve on the Stamp Advisory Committee of Royal Mail, an assorted group of lay people who give their views on the themes and designs chosen for new postage stamps. It was a very interesting assignment indeed to anyone like me with a printing industry background, for postage stamps, I believe, are miniature works of art.

The revolution in stamp design in Britain is genuinely one of Tony Benn's real achievements brought off when he was Postmaster General in Harold Wilson's government. On the face of it there was not a lot to do at the Post Office, which was probably the reason Wilson sent Benn to the job. But Benn saw a chance to break out of the tradition that the nation's stamps only showed the monarch's head and did not even mention Britain. After all, the view went, everyone knows Britain invented the postage stamp so we do not need to name the country. Such arrogance takes the breath away.

Since the breakthrough, for which Benn personally had an audience with the Queen to convince her he was not a twentieth-century Roundhead, intent on sweeping monarchy away, Britain has had some really wonderful stamp series. They have become collector's items. I have a huge collection of first day covers. But there is enormous pressure on Royal Mail to get a series devoted to a single issue and making the small selection for the year uncovers a minefield of special interests. The lay committee ensures that an outside view is sought and advice taken. But Royal Mail has to be commercial and some of the biggest sales are remarkably ordinary. Cats, dogs and horses have achieved some of the biggest sales.

When I was serving there was great pressure to have a good series for the fiftieth anniversary of D-Day but what to include and what to omit was a nightmare. There are only five or six stamps in a series.

A fellow advisory committee member was Professor Alan Livingstone, principal of the renowned Falmouth College of Art and Design, who became a good friend. Some years later he recruited me for his campaign to win funding and locate the Cornwall Combined University at Penryn, bringing together his art and design students with the Camborne School of Mines and other student centres. Thus Cornwall for the first time ever had its own university and could offer young people in the county the chance of a place locally rather than move away and possibly never return.

During this period Sir Ron Mason, former scientific adviser to the Ministry of Defence, was chairman of the then shadow board of University College London Hospital and he approached me in 1994 to join him. Later I became deputy chairman. It had to be approved of course by Brian Mawhinney, minister of state at the Department of Health, but it was my first step, gingerly, into health, medicine, hospitals, doctors and back into the world of government quangos.

At that time there was a desperation to break the logjam which had been holding back many new building projects in the NHS. London urgently needed new hospitals but the only way the Treasury would give the go-ahead was if there was a private finance initiative, or PFI as it soon became known, in place. That was not easy in hospital construction. We also had the problem that the hospital services were in great demand and had to continue in the midst of any new development.

Our group consisted of several buildings, in addition to the worn-out Middlesex and University College hospitals. There was the Hospital for Tropical Diseases; the Eastman Dental Hospital; the National Hospital for

Neurology and Neurosurgery, one of the world's foremost specialist centres on brain disorder, in Queen Square; the Elizabeth Garratt Anderson Hospital, specialising in women's ailments – about ten in all. Each separate facility was worn out and the staff were working under great difficulties.

Yet we were sitting on a property bonanza. The values of some of the sites were soaring – in particular one still-empty area known as the Odeon site, at the corner of Tottenham Court Road and Grafton Way, where a cinema had been destroyed in World War II. UCLH had never had the money to develop it.

When Labour came to power in 1997 our opportunity came to get the project on the move. There was considerable political lobbying needed and Whitehall corridors to tread before we began to see the way forward. The magnificent old building of the Middlesex Hospital would have to close, including the fabulous chapel on the ground floor, and that was likely to meet resistance. And many medical staff would have to decamp.

Piece by piece, though, we were able to complete deals which enabled us to acquire the site on the corner of Euston Road and Tottenham Court Road, which is where the magnificent new UCLH hospital was opened by Her Majesty the Queen on 20 October 2005. By that time I had moved on but I am immensely proud to have played a small role in what was at the time the biggest building project in the National Health Service.

One other spin-off was bringing a dynamic young woman to Mason's attention. I thought Valerie Amos would make a useful addition to the board. I little thought that later I would be her sponsor when she came into the House of Lords in 1997. And that she would become the first black woman to be the Leader of the House of Lords.

By now the late and dear John Smith had emerged as the new leader of the Labour Party. One day I went to see him in the office of the leader of the opposition in the House of Commons. He asked me how I was coping and I gave him a frank assessment without being too downbeat. Then he told me he 'would keep my name in mind' for a short list of new working peers he was being asked to submit to 10 Downing Street. Under Margaret Thatcher the number of Labour lords had been very limited and the Labour Party was desperate for an infusion of new and younger blood. It was a wonderful offer by Smith to consider me and would at last allow me to be able to answer the question 'But what are you doing now?'

I had no idea where this new road would lead but I was keen to take an early step on it. I thanked Smith warmly and found my way out into the sunlight from the quiet corridors at Westminster. There was probably a large smile on my face. My life might be going to change again.

In fact it happened relatively quickly. Just before he went off on holiday in July 1993, Smith telephoned and told me, 'I wanted six peers but only got three, Brenda, and you are to be one of them.'

Wow. I really had not taken it for granted as it was indeed a nomination coveted by so many. Smith's other successful submissions were Joyce Gould, who had worked hard and long at Labour Party headquarters, especially battling against the Trotskyists during Neil Kinnock's era, and Simon Haskel, a businessman who had advised Smith over a number of years.

A few days later No. 10 were in touch to confirm I would accept a nomination by the Prime Minister, now John Major. It was due to be announced in the *London Gazette* on a Saturday morning. We were in Falmouth, where, with his business doing well, Keith had bought a house on the waterfront and moved his boat to a nearby mooring.

My brother and sister-in-law were coming down to join us and Keith persuaded my father to come too. Dad said he did not want to cramp our style and tried to cry off but Keith managed to get him to travel to Cornwall. None of my family knew of the impending announcement. John Smith had rung through and said the announcement would come at the weekend, on Saturday morning. 'Tell Keith and go off and enjoy yourselves,' he advised.

But when we were out sailing the boat on Friday afternoon in Falmouth's beautiful harbour the mobile phone rang to warn that the list was leaking and No. 10 had decided to bring forward the announcement to that afternoon. Soon afterwards the phone calls were coming in fast and I was below in the forward cabin taking them and giving interviews on radio and speaking to newspapers. As the boat sailed on, most of its crew were blissfully unaware of what I was doing but curious that I was spending so much time on the phone. But I suppose it was not all that new to my family.

We came ashore and managed to prevent them hearing any news programmes. Keith had booked a table for dinner at a favourite country hotel, Trengilly Wartha, near Constantine in Cornwall. Still my father and brother had no idea of anything special. Not, that is, until Keith ordered champagne, raised his glass and told my father, 'Congratulations, Hugh, your daughter is now a peeress and a member of the House of Lords.'

'You what?' said my father. And to me, 'Is he kidding?'

The news was repeated and he needed to sit down. You do not think when a baby is born in an air raid, rides on the back of your bike and checks your wages slip, that one day she is going to end up in the House of Lords.

Like me, I think he felt how sad it was that my mother was no longer alive to join in the celebration.

Most members of the Upper House, unless they are hereditary, will tell enquirers just how hard it is to hit upon an appropriate title. If, for example, there had been no other Dean in the Lords, I could just have used my own surname. But there were two others already in the House, so to avoid confusion the rule is that the name of a place is added to the personal name and that becomes one's title.

But not just any place. The Garter King of Arms, who works out of the College of Arms, a splendid office on Queen Victoria Street, near Blackfriars, has to approve before the title can be 'gazetted' – that is, placed in the *London Gazette*, which is the oldest continuously published newspaper in Britain and probably the world.

I went to discuss it at the Garter King's office. The holder of this illustrious office was ill so I saw his deputy.

He asked if I had thought about a title. As a joke, I proposed Dean of Wapping.

Garter No. 2 squashed that instantly. His job, he explained, was to ensure that the Queen was not embarrassed in any way. Involving the sovereign's name in anything to do with a squalid labour relations confrontation just would not do, he implied.

Well, how about Dean of Manchester?

'Oh no, my dear, a big city like that is reserved for a countess.'

'Give me time,' I said and suggested something to do with Thornton-le-Fylde, an area with which I had strong connection. That was acceptable but I had to prove the place existed, because there was no reference to it in the College of Arms' very large book of place names in the United Kingdom.

The Fylde country, in God's County of Lancashire, has a great history. Once the Fylde teemed with trading activity as shallow-draught merchant vessels sailed into the ports among the marshes. It was where I had bought my own first house. My father and brother both lived there and when Keith and I married in 1988, after he had left the CBI and would not therefore cause them any embarrassment, we got married in a little church at Thornton-Cleveleys. As Keith was divorced John Chennel, the vicar, defied his bishop to marry us and he and his wife became long-standing family friends. It was also where my dear mother's and father's ashes were placed.

I phoned Garter's office and told him I still proposed Thornton-le-Fylde. But despite all the historic records in his office, no trace could be found of any such location. If I could prove that such a place did once exist I could go ahead. If not I would have to start again, it seemed.

There is a Poulton-le-Fylde, indeed there is a railway station there, but nothing it seemed existed to show Thornton-le-Fylde. I rang the town clerk of Wyre Borough Council, who was most unhelpful. 'Never heard of it,' he said, clearly not keen to have my name on any map near him.

But the local librarian was much more helpful. Yes, it did exist and a call to Directory Enquiries confirmed it. But better still, the librarian suggested, if I went to the crossroads at Cleveleys, there were still premises there where once operated the now defunct William Deacon's Bank. Engraved on the stonework it declared 'Thornton-le-Fylde branch'.

Bingo.

I rang Garter and reported on my research. My two independent sources were confirmed and I had my title. I was offered a coat of arms, if I wanted to pay for one, but I thought for a working girl from Salford that might be over-doing things. As would the purchase of robes.

Initiation into the House of Lords is today much better organised by the political parties and the more experienced people help newcomers. Nowadays new peers have a mentor to steer them on their way. When I entered the Upper House Ted Graham, then opposition Chief Whip, was very helpful, but one had to find out the rules, the practices and the etiquette mostly for oneself. Nothing was written down and though peers would answer questions it still left one to find out as best one could.

My sponsors for the induction ceremony were Lord Murray of Epping Forest, the highly respected former general secretary of the TUC, and Lord Dean of Beswick – Joe Dean, a prominent member of the engineering union and a former leader of Manchester City Council, who turned out to be a great pal. Sadly, neither Joe nor Lionel – always 'Len' to the newspapers but Lionel to his family and friends – are still with us.

The robes I wore were loaned to me – the House authorities have a small stock in store – but the hem had to be pinned up. It is for most women peers. The hardest part of the ceremony was when all three of us turned together and doffed our hats. Being trade unionists we practised and were delighted to be told by others we were much better co-ordinated on that day than the Conservative peers who were introducing one of their nominees.

Once installed in the Lords, most importantly I had to find a desk. There were not enough to go round in those days in opposition, but even when in government, there is a scramble to find somewhere to work.

The other big worry for a newcomer is the maiden speech. Until you have made one, you are not permitted to take part in any debate nor ask a question, although you can vote. There are some people who have never got round to making this first speech, and the longer they leave it the harder it is to launch forth. Public speaking, though I am still likely to be nervous, did not worry me unduly but this was a very major speech in my career.

I let the whips know that I would like to put my name to speak on the debate on the Queen's Speech, which is really an expression of the government programme for the session ahead. The debate ranges far and wide and it is not too difficult to find somewhere to slot in. So it was that at 4.33 p.m. on 25 November 1993, I stood, heart pounding a little, to put to use all that I had learned about speech-making since the first time Joe Sheridan, back in Manchester, took my career in hand.

The convention is that the maiden speech should not be politically controversial and the object is to paint a picture of your background and experience so that the House learns more about their new member – the distinguished sociologist Lord Dahrendorf was also taking his plunge later that afternoon.

I said it was true that I was perhaps well known for my role in the News International dispute but that the bulk of the 240,000 people I had represented in SOGAT were from paper and printing and had an excellent labour relations record. Printing was the fifth largest manufacturing industry in Britain and had a net trade surplus with the rest of the world. So I was about more than just Fleet Street.

I put down a marker on my attitude to the Conservative government's record on employment law and noted that unemployment had risen by 34 per cent since 1988. I also pointed out that accidents at work were running annually at 1.6 million and, as a result, the nation was losing thirty million working days. So I sailed near but was not considered to be too controversial.

It all came to an end pretty quickly and suddenly I was on the last lap. 'It is my intention to listen to those with opposing points of view with tolerance and good manners. I hope too that, in the spirit of consensus and compromise, agreement and understanding will on occasion prevail – qualities which I like to think that the British people will insist are brought back into the way we work at all levels in public life in this great country of ours.'

Exactly ten minutes. The ordeal was over and I was now a fully fledged member of one of the friendliest, most experienced, most tolerant – and wisest – debating chambers in the world. I felt very honoured.

My other big achievement by then was that I had found a desk. Once you had a desk you could have a direct telephone and somewhere to which your mail can be delivered. And there was already a daily mountain of mail, not always wanted, but occasionally containing perhaps a letter which may open up a new window on the world.

Among the welcoming people on our benches I came to know fairly soon was Lord Ennals, formerly the Secretary for Health and Social Security. While I had followed the pensions debate I had never had much to do with health but

Ennals seemed to want to talk. Once he had been the international secretary at Labour Party headquarters, before winning the Norwich North seat in the Commons, so he had a wide circle of contacts. In World War II he was a captain in the army. Among his many roles, he told me one evening, he was president of the Institute of Occupational Therapists and enquired if I would be interested in going along with him to a meeting at their headquarters in Southwark.

My mother had suffered from rheumatoid arthritis and I was aware how important the therapists had been in her life but I knew little more than that about the profession. Imagine my surprise when Ennals introduced me to the board of the institute and suggested I would make an ideal person to succeed him as president! I was not actually bounced but it felt rather like it . . .

They were such nice and enthusiastic people, however, that I soon came round to the idea of being president, which I was assured would not be onerous. A little alarm bell rang because over the years I have discovered that tasks predicted not to be onerous generally are, and that a job that can be fitted in 'within a few hours' rarely works out to be the case.

The Princess Royal was the patron and as usual she was no passenger. She took a great interest and wanted to be kept well informed. I went to see her at Buckingham Palace on one occasion with officers of the institute to discuss an event it was planning and found the princess also to be an excellent handler of a meeting. Maybe she had been trained by a trade union... Over the years our paths have crossed on a number of occasions and I have found her warm and friendly. She is always on top of the topic in which she is involved. I am not surprised that she completes more engagements than anyone else in the Royal Family.

I have also been privileged to work closely with Prince Charles and served on his Business Trust for five years. There was a very enjoyable overnight stay at Sandringham I particularly remember. Here again I speak as I find and for me the prince is an excellent operator. To meet some of the young people running their own businesses after financial launch-aid from the Prince's Trust is very impressive; the prince has been a real pioneer in this field. Among my treasured possessions are a silver letter opener with the Duchy of Cornwall emblem and a signed, mounted photograph of the prince, thanking me for the support I gave to the trust. This was particularly the case on the issue of rural housing, to which the prince is very committed.

Keith and I were privileged to attend Charles's fiftieth birthday party at Hampton Court Palace, though I was extremely lucky to avoid being carried out on a stretcher when a huge stand showing some of the prince's paintings fell over and just missed me.

But back to the therapists – an early task I was asked to preside over was selecting a new chief executive as, within a few months of my taking over from Ennals, the current one announced he was planning to move on. So here I was into headhunting a professional in a field which was completely new to me. But it worked out well and we made a good choice in recruiting Sheelagh Richards.

Just as Ennals did, after ten years I located my successor and introduced her to the institute. Baroness Wilkins is doing a splendid job and, being wheelchair bound, probably has a more direct knowledge of the work of occupational therapists.

Ennals subsequently did me a great turn when he put my name forward again to succeed him but this time as a non-executive director on the board of Takare plc, which operated a chain of well-run private nursing homes. We were due to meet the chairman when Ennals was suddenly taken ill and within a few weeks was dead. Looking back I think he knew and was carefully sorting out his affairs but he never said a word about such matters.

Strangely, I was on my way to the memorial service for Lord Ennals when I was due to meet the Takare chairman, Keith Bradshaw. He suggested we went together and collected me in his car at the Palace of Westminster. Before we reached the church, Bradshaw invited me to take Ennals's place and join his board. 'But you know nothing about me, Mr Bradshaw.' I said.

'If David was recommending you, that's fine with me,' came the reply.

Once again Ennals seemed to have tied up everything nicely.

This was to be my third post on a plc. The second was with a firm that ran a group of companies in Britain and France manufacturing shoes – the Chinese and Vietnamese had not at that time taken over the worldwide industry. But the company was not well run and it collapsed. Though I lost no money personally I was conscious of the importance of my reputation and it was a salutary lesson.

Takare looked different, though. It had invested £300 million in about 100 newly built nursing homes containing around 12,000 beds, employed 13,500 professional staff and seemed to have a good future. But there was a snag. Although local authorities wanted to get out of elderly care and use such well-run private nursing homes, the Treasury would not actually provide the funds to do it.

So Takare was under pressure from the City. They used the same ratings as they would for a commercial organisation selling a product. They also wanted a traditional management structure and did not like the idea of having Bradshaw as executive chairman. So in came a man named Chaim Patel. His company was called Court Cavendish and had about 1,500 beds.

The plan was to merge two companies under the name Care First, and Patel, an entrepreneurial figure, was to become the new chief executive. He was certainly a man in a hurry. He told colleagues he intended to be a millionaire and to have a seat in the House of Lords. Quite quickly, it appeared.

It was not long before there were clear signs of strain in the boardroom. Though I was new to business I was not all that surprised.

I got on extremely well with Bradshaw and we have become firm friends, often travelling together with our other halves to follow the fortunes of the English cricket team. With him and Pam we have been to South Africa and the Caribbean. But there was more than cricket on our minds as the boardroom struggle turned quite nasty. Eventually, however, a deal was done. I supported Bradshaw and the company was sold to the private hospital group BUPA. I think the public were the loser because the Takare homes I visited were well run, the staff quality was high and the buildings very modern. But sadly there is still a long way to go before sufficient funding is available to enable local authorities to buy a high standard of care for the elderly.

Chapter 19

In 1991 I was sounded out on whether I would be willing to serve on the Armed Forces Pay Review Body, an independent body at arm's length from government, which tried fairly to assess service pay and conditions and recommend them to the Prime Minister and Secretary of State for Defence. The diligent Mike Horsman came to see me from the Office of Manpower Economics and explained the role of the body.

I said I had never had any experience of military service and knew very little about the lives of soldiers, sailors and air personnel. In any case I had my doubts as to whether a Conservative government would want a trade unionist getting too close to the services.

No, a trade unionist with an independent frame of mind was wanted, I was assured. Traditionally there had always been a trade unionist member but I would be the first woman.

I was wrong. In my post came a letter signed by John Major, the Prime Minister, inviting me to serve for a two-year term. Little did I realise that in the years ahead I was going to learn and know a great deal about the splendid people, men and women, who make up our three armed services and are a credit to this nation.

After my term I came off the review body in 1993 because it is extremely difficult to put a reasoned case for a pay increase or a rise in an allowance when the Chancellor of the Exchequer of the day lets it be known he will not agree an increase above the level he has decided. Not much point in having an independent body. Kenneth Clarke, then Chancellor, seemed intent on blocking the award, which I felt I could not accept. I could resign but then I would become the story rather than the fact that the government was not paying the services what we felt they were worth. It would have been a one-day sensation but only have a temporary impact. I did not threaten because a resignation threat can only really work once, but before the final decision was made I went to see Gordon Hourston, the board chairman, to explain my decision and quietly bowed out.

Now that I was free from the joint responsibility of membership, I could, if necessary, come out and say why the Armed Forces Pay Review Body felt so strongly about the award. As it happened it was not necessary to speak out. I had reckoned without the wily Malcolm Rifkind, the Defence Secretary, who sought an early morning meeting with the Prime Minister, just before Cabinet met, and won Major's support for the pay award. The service people were paid in full.

Eventually, though, pay awards were staged, which was very demoralising for both the service personnel and indeed the review body. Clarke backed off. Perhaps he decided it was not worth the candle.

Two years later, in 1995, I was approached and asked if I would consider coming back to the review body as chairman, the first time a woman had ever held the post. At first I doubted if I was the right person. How would the services take to a woman? 'Oh,' said Horsman, 'that has already been checked out. The armed forces want you.'

I was pressed very hard and eventually found it very rewarding – though not financially. In my period the work was totally unpaid, which I personally preferred. It gave the members an independence which impressed the service people. Occasionally if one came across someone with a grudge or a cocky barrack room lawyer, one could say, 'I don't have to do this – I am not paid. I am trying to understand your problems and maybe do something about them. It's up to you.' It usually worked. Most servicepeople, though, were very interested in us and I had some fascinating experiences seeing them at work. And where they worked.

So it was that over the years I went down in an Upholder class submarine, out on patrol in sensitive areas of Northern Ireland, into Afghanistan and Basra and Al Amara in Iraq, on a high-speed patrol boat in Hong Kong harbour, and out with the Royal Marines to Belize. I was taken up in helicopters, one of which in Iraq fired off its anti-missile flares, much to the concern of all aboard. I flew at speed aboard the Queen's Flight executive jet, and went on the lumbering Hercules, usually slow but safe, although one was recently shot down in Iraq.

In complete contrast I found myself aboard the aircraft carrier *Illustrious* for the D-Day anniversary when it fired the official salute. A magnificent occasion and a memory to treasure.

On other occasions I found myself dining with officers of all the units stationed at Bulford Camp and Tidworth on Salisbury Plain, and staying the night there in the splendid house of the Adjutant General; dining several times aboard HMS *Victory* – including an all-services farewell dinner when I concluded the pay review chairmanship; attended a candle-lit dining-in night at Fighter Command headquarters, RAF Stanmore, seeing the Battle of Britain control room and inside Lord Dowding's office; and visiting RNAS Culdrose in Cornwall, the Fleet Air Arm station, that actually employs over 2,000 civilians and is the largest employer in Cornwall. I stayed that night with the commanding officer, Captain Peter Fish, and his wife Marion, who became firm friends when later they retired to Falmouth.

I suppose one of the most amusing incidents was when with a couple of review body colleagues I went out to see our soldiers engaged in very lifelike war games and firing real ammunition in the wilds of the Canadian prairie. Literally miles and miles from the nearest civilisation, in a training and exercise area where there are no 'facilities' as the saying goes in service circles. But there comes a point when a girl just has to spend a penny and we were miles from the base camp. The only thing to do was to get the soldiers to form a circle and face outwards while I got on with it as quick as I could. I must say they were all gentlemen, but it must have made them chortle afterwards.

Playing with tanks and guns is all very well but it did not interest me very much although I realised I had to show some in what were the men's big toys. What seized me was talking to the servicemen and women and finding out about their conditions – always without officers present. Often they would have their case prepared and one could tell if an officer had been helping behind the scenes but generally I found the servicepeople could express their point of view with the same directness and simplicity which I was used to finding on the factory floor.

I always made it a point, too, if there were married quarters, of asking to meet the wives of serving men. I found it went down extremely well because the women had wanted to say things and felt fobbed off by someone like the sergeant major or warrant officer. Yet the wives could give an insight to service conditions which we wanted to know even if their husbands felt they should not reveal it or were too proud to speak up.

Each year, when we had gathered all the facts and figures that we could, the time would come to sit down and work out what the pay award, allowances and charges should be. Could the Treasury be persuaded to foot the bill? And would something here have a knock-on effect on servicepeople somewhere else? It was a delicate balancing act and usefully in this area we had the splendid back-up and research of the Office of Manpower Economics, headed by Horsman and Christine Haworth as our team leader. Horsman's civil service background was the former Department of Employment and Haworth came from Defence, so they were accomplished in producing briefs and arguments to support a pay award.

Fortunately I also became a member of the Senior Salaries Review Board and so was able to keep a close eye on what the generals, air marshals and judges were getting.

It usually needed very careful judgement and timing to put forward a good case and my experience now of how Whitehall and Westminster worked was invaluable. I got on well with George Robertson and Geoff Hoon, successive Secretaries of State for Defence, but I also made sure that the senior civil servants knew our approach.

I did not threaten but, as I have said before, I am never against wheeler-dealing. If the Treasury set a limit which the evidence told us was not just on, we managed to find a way around it to arrive at the point we wanted to be. Perhaps by increasing allowances instead of pay, for example. I regarded it as all part of the negotiation process really – headlines can be a five-minute wonder but what the service people received was our priority.

Always leave the door open for the other side to be able to exit without embarrassment.

I am sometimes asked, in view of my background, if the three services should be allowed to join trade unions. I do not believe the question should be allowed to arise. So long as the government treats the services fairly on allowances and conditions, not just pay, that will be the case. It is really in the government's own hands to avoid the short-term thinking on pay which could provoke the issue.

What is known as 'overstretch' – in effect giving the services more tasks for which they do not have further manpower – is living dangerously. Service personnel must get adequate time at home to see their families and sort out domestic problems and the only answer would seem to be more recruits. Not for the first time the British have evolved a system like the Armed Forces Pay Review Body, which neatly meets the need and I have been told is the envy of some servicemen in other nations such as the United States and Australia. The Americans may draw more when on active service but are poorly recompensed when back home.

We have to ensure that Cabinet ministers and senior civil servants understand and pledge that our system has to be fair and honest and not open to financial cheese paring or manipulation. The services cannot expect to run rings round the pay system but they have a right to know that their pay and conditions will be reviewed fairly and impartially. And regularly. In that way I believe we will maintain the best regular army in the world, a splendid navy and a top class, well-equipped air force. Britain cannot really demand much more but it should be willing to pay for it.

There was a warm letter of thanks from the Prime Minister when I signed off. 'Under her chairmanship the AFPRB has successfully continued to deliver, year on year, recommendations both fair to service personnel and acceptable to the government. I am in no doubt that this has been accomplished because of her leadership, independence and determination to understand the issues that are important to service personnel, and her insight and appreciation of the workings of government.

'To have successfully discharged this responsibility to the full while juggling many other commitments, not least as a member of the House of Lords, is no mean achievement. She will be a difficult act to follow.'

My defence connections have certainly broadened as a result of my interest in service pay and allowances. One, which came as a surprise, was an approach by a Conservative peer asking me in confidence if I would consider becoming the chairman of the Lords Defence Committee. Defence is more a Tory field of interest than it is usually for members of my party. The Defence Committee members include at least four previous Chiefs of the Defence Staff – the most senior post in the services – former defence ministers and a number of people who have held senior rank, some of them in wartime service.

'I am honoured, but why me? I asked. 'I have never been in the services.'

The reply was that news of my activities as chairman of the Armed Forces Pay Review Body had filtered through and it was felt on all sides of the House that I could contribute to the work of the group. I could hardly decline. So I became the chairman of the committee and I continue to find the experience stimulating and extremely interesting.

The most unusual outcome from the work with the services resulted from a telephone call to our car as we were on the road to Heathrow in late October 2000. We were off to an annual jazz cruise we have been attending for sixteen years.

Geoff Hoon at the Ministry of Defence was asking for help to solve a dilemma for the Labour government though it was not a problem of their making. It was at the receiving end of a nasty campaign, mainly in the *Daily Mirror*, involving the civil servants' unions and the public services group of the Transport & General Workers' Union. There was, too, a whiff of competitive membership recruitment in the air.

People who worked overseas for the Commonwealth War Graves Commission were on the verge of striking, it was claimed, because their overseas allowances were being cut. Emotions were being whipped up before the impending Remembrance Day early in November and there was even the threat of a demonstration by the Cenotaph in Whitehall. The Royal British Legion with its branches up and down the country had become involved as had the Women's Institute – a formidable alliance. *SAGA* magazine, which has thousands of senior citizens as its readers, many of whom served in the Second World War, also weighed in with a major article condemning the callous acts of the commission.

As a result letters of protest poured into the commission's headquarters and to ministers and local MPs. There were letters in the *Times*, and even Michael Palin, the much-travelled actor then in the midst of a major series on BBC One, pitched in with criticism.

Among the scare stories being circulated was a suggestion that the cut in allowances could mean some of the thousands of war cemeteries around the world might have to be closed. Another shocker was the suggestion that only British gardeners could tend the cemeteries adequately – somehow it seemed the French and the Belgians were not up to the job. Whoever was master-minding the press campaign of the civil service unions was certainly earning his corn. The fact that the war graves are not the total responsibility of the British government was being totally ignored. It rather ruined the story, I suppose.

In fact the Commonwealth War Graves Commission has an illustrious record going back to the worst battles of World War I when just collecting the dead from the battlefield was a major problem. While its headquarters is in this country at Maidenhead, Berkshire, its committee of management includes representatives of Australia, New Zealand, Canada, South Africa and India as well as the United Kingdom.

Hoon wanted to announce as soon as possible that I would conduct an inquiry and wanted me to agree over the phone. He seemed to think this move might quieten things down and at least cool off the threat of demonstration in Whitehall. He was probably right that, whatever the government said, there were some people not at all squeamish about the facts and willing to lay the blame solely on the Labour government.

I agreed to take on the job although I had little experience or knowledge of the work of the War Graves Commission. I did, however, make three conditions: the work had to be completely independent of the Ministry of Defence; my report would be published in full, warts and all; and if necessary I would have full access to the minister. All these conditions were met immediately and I had an excellent session with Sir Roger Jackling, the second permanent secretary, to clinch them.

Fortunately a system I have always used came to mind. In a hurried task like this good quality back-up staff is essential and it was accepted that I could draw on the support and know-how of the Office of Manpower Economics. As soon as we reached Heathrow I got a call through to Mike Horsman and told him he had a new job on top of all his other duties. Horsman leapt at it – and he admitted that his hobby was studying interesting historic battlefields and the story they tell. Job comparison and pay allowances were also meat and drink to him. I knew I could rely on him and his team.

Temperatures were rising in Parliament on the issue and my appointment was announced in the House of Commons and also to my colleagues in the House of Lords to try to cool matters. I had a number of well-wishers.

As usual when one lifts the lid, there was more to this situation than appeared at first sight. The commission had been in the throes of appointing a new director general. Some internal candidates had put their hats in the ring and not been successful. A new man was about to take up the reins. So this was not the time for a grass roots staff upheaval.

Richard Kellaway, a senior career civil servant, had been selected, but he hardly had time to get his feet under the table before the issue exploded on to the front pages. The unions had timed it well. Kellaway and I met quickly and he issued a news release on behalf of the commission welcoming my appointment. I was 'to conduct an independent review of proposed changes to the pay and allowances of its team of gardeners and other UK-based overseas staff'. The unions also gave my arrival on the scene a tentative welcome.

I met the whole commission in mid-December and told them how I planned to proceed. I felt I needed to know more about what the War Graves Commission actually did and with Horsman and some others had already paid a flying visit to a number of World War I burial grounds in France and Belgium. It was bitterly cold in early November walking through the magnificently tended graveyards and devastating to note the ages of the young men for whom these were the final resting places. These graves were maintained by British gardeners, although many had settled locally, married and brought up their families.

I also went to see some World War II sites, notably Cassino in Italy, where the horrendous battle took place in 1943–4 in which so many nations fought – British, yes, but also French, Polish, Canadian, New Zealand, Indian, Polish and American soldiers all fell there. As did so many Germans and Italians. We also went to nearby Anzio and some of the other cemeteries in the area, all involved in trying to take the mountain on which Monte Cassino monastery had stood, commanding the approaches to so crucial a crossroads.

It all made a deep impression on me and I fought the tears. I defy anyone not to be moved in those pristine, quiet, magnificently tended commemorations to youth cut down in its prime.

In Italy I also met non-British gardeners, recruited from around the cemeteries, whose families often had many personal memories of the actual battles. A job for them with the commission is sought after and handed from father to son. Any idea that they were not quite up to the job was not only untrue but deeply insulting. As to pay, of course they would have liked more, but there was nothing like the level of complaints that were coming from the British staff.

What had happened was that our government had decided that local allowances in the Foreign and Commonwealth Office would no longer be assessed centrally, all departments affected then falling into line. From 1995 each department had to fix its own rates. The War Graves Commission found itself on the spot because it needed to come to a new agreement with its own staff and so froze the allowances temporarily. Unfortunately, at the time, sterling was going through the roof and pay in local currency was falling.

Moreover, it had been years since there had been a proper review of what the gardeners were paid – and whether, for example, it was right still to be paying for overseas staff to send their children to the UK, all expenses paid, for education. That had been Foreign Office practice and others had been only too happy to tag along. Now it seemed to be over.

With the support of Horsman and his team we got on with the task because I felt it essential not to lose the initiative. By 14 March 2001 I was able to attend a meeting of the War Graves Commission held at Canada House in London and present my findings.

It had been much more complex than I expected but the announcement of the independent review had taken much of the heat out of the issue. Even so I had personally received about 200 letters of protest, over half of them prompted by the *SAGA* magazine piece. I made a series of recommendations bringing in a new pay scheme which faced up to current conditions while gently phasing out the older set-up which was so deeply entrenched. The cost was broadly neutral in the first year. I said it was not my job to run the organisation and the commission's own people now had to negotiate it through with the unions.

The commission accepted my findings and so did the unions. I made sure they were in the picture – wheeler-dealing again, I suppose.

At the conclusion of the inquiry I wrote to Sir Roger Jackling, who had been very helpful. I told him that I had personally written back to everyone who had complained to me although I was still receiving protest letters as the *SAGA* magazine was passed on. Or being read in the doctor's waiting room.

I contacted Paul Bach, then editing the magazine, and asked if I could now write a response to the critical article which had led to much of the anger amongst people who had not perhaps had all the facts. He was very open and offered me space for 1,400 words, all of which he printed with a photograph of me standing by the war memorial in St James's Park, opposite the parade ground.

A lot of us, hopefully, had learned from the events of the past six months.

That rounded things off and the issue went quietly away. But I keep in touch because today I am proud to be a vice president of the War Widows' Association.

Chapter 20

The year 1997 looked like being general election year. Early in the year I had a telephone call from David Blunkett, then shadow Education Secretary. I had had very little to do with him as education then was not really my field. He told me the Conservative Education Secretary, Gillian Shephard, wanted to announce an inquiry into the funding of higher education which would involve the thorny issue of financing the nation's universities.

In the run-up to an election the normal situation is to avoid anything controversial or, if the problem is so urgent, an attempt is made to get bipartisan support. This is what was happening. Blunkett said my name had been put forward to serve on an inquiry committee and he thought it a good suggestion. When one considers the breadth of the knowledge and experience in the world of education I wondered why no teaching union name had been considered. But everyone knew that some of the unions in education were hardly on speaking terms so I did not press it.

It would be a fairly new field for me. I had not been involved in vocational training, although I had been involved in some training in the printing industry. Still, I could sniff the challenge of change in the air – and that was the attraction. I told Blunkett that if the Labour Party wanted me to do the job, I would have a go.

The key man leading the project was Sir Ron Dearing, a distinguished former senior civil servant from the Department of Trade and Industry, who had a reputation for sorting out hot government potatoes. This one was certainly piping hot. Dearing had been involved in the nationalisation of aerospace and shipbuilding, had been chairman of the Post Office and carried out, successfully, a number of delicate tasks in Whitehall. He was equally accepted by Conservative and Labour.

Dearing was to take charge of what was officially to be known as the National Inquiry into the Future of Higher Education. It quickly became known as 'the Dearing committee'. For me, this was going to be an opportunity to see a master at work.

When I saw the names of my colleagues it was a little daunting. There were seventeen of us in all and I was the only one without a degree – not one I had studied for, anyway. I was rather proud to have had an honorary degree presented to me at Salford University, by Professor John Ashworth, the vice chancellor. And others had followed, notably from Central Lancashire, Nottingham, Manchester, City, London Metropolitan and Exeter. But they hardly compared to the string of letters after the names of people such as Sir Richard Sykes, chairman and chief executive of GlaxoWellcome, Dr David Potter, who created Psion, or Sir Ronald Oxburgh, rector of Imperial College and former chief scientific adviser to the government.

There were three other women on the team. One was Judith Evans, head of personnel at J. Sainsbury plc, who also had a background in higher education. Then there was Pamela Morris, former head teacher at the Blue School in Wells, on the court of the University of Bath and much into career development and routes into higher education. And also Professor Diana Laurillard, pro-vice chancellor of the Open University.

So most of my colleagues seemed to arrive with a background in science and technology or higher education. Had they found the right lay person in me, I wondered?

But apparently Dearing himself had asked for 'that trade union lass' and it seemed to be my entry pass to an almost completely new world. Although thinking back, I had been a member of the Literacy Trust and from 1995 to 1998 I served on the Council of the Open University. I had a feel for university funding, too, because for five years I was a member of the Council of City University and at this time I was serving on the governing body of the London School of Economics. So the world of academia was not completely a closed book to me.

Still, there is one thing trade union experience had taught me – never be daunted by apparent brain power on the other side of the table. Sometimes it cannot tell the wood for the trees . . .

That was certainly not the case with Dearing. He set off at a cracking pace and clearly had no intention of slowing down. He knew he had to deliver before or soon after the general election. He was also very clear that this was a once-and-for-all chance to try to get university funding finally sorted out – because of the bipartisan agreement – so this was not to be missed.

He worked himself extremely hard, despite not being in the best of health, and had no compunction about doing the same with us. Quite apart from serving on the main steering committee we were divided into working groups into which were brought others steeped in various aspects of higher education. I found myself put to chairing the team looking at Staff and Use of Resources. This accounted for the major part of the budget spend of the universities. Among our team was Sir Geoffrey Holland, former permanent secretary of the Department of Education and then vice chancellor of Exeter University, Professor David Chiddick of De Montfort University, the highly respected Sara Morrison from GEC and several others of influence. But Dearing also slotted me in to the team looking at Funding and Student Support.

That did not mean he let us slip away, however – the chairman had us all on parade for the main working party as the individual team reports came back. It was hard but fascinating work to watch a master at handling committees and bureaucracy refuse to be bogged down and remain determined to steer us to good conclusions. It was a privilege.

When I joined the committee I felt in my own mind that I was against the concept of tuition fees being paid by students themselves. I had grown up with the concept of free education at the point of delivery, had seen many from the working class reach university as a result, and saw no reason why it should not continue. But by the time we came to our conclusions and signed off in July 1997 I had changed my mind completely. Having heard the arguments and become extremely concerned at the way in which we were seeing some of our famous universities in decline I came round completely on the issue.

I was also concerned that only about half of the students came through traditional routes. The remainder were mature and part-time students paying their own tuition fees so the system was not even handed for all students. So, reluctantly, I accepted that students – and their parents – had to make a contribution.

As Dearing put it in his foreword: 'We are particularly concerned about planned further reductions in the unit of funding for higher education . . . if these are carried out, it will have been halved in 25 years. We therefore recommend that students enter into an obligation to make contributions to the cost of their higher education once they are in work.'

The last inquiry of this nature into higher education had been by the Robbins committee in the early 1960s, which had taken two and a half years to complete. The Dearing committee hit the target with a highly detailed report of 460 pages in just fourteen months. We made ninety-three recommendations for change.

On the day the report was publicly revealed at the Commonwealth Institute the main hall was crammed. Everyone wanted to hear Dearing give his report. When he spoke he revealed that the whole report had that morning gone on the Web, which was quite revolutionary thinking in those days. He said that as he spoke some thousands of hits on the website had already been made. The shape of things to come.

I am rather proud of my bound copy of the report, signed personally by all my colleagues. I made some good new friends on the committee with whom I am still in touch. I little realised then that some years later the issue of tuition fees would nearly tear the Labour Party apart and that the Prime Minister, Tony Blair, would have to sail very close to the wind to get it approved by both Houses of Parliament. I still feel very strongly that the Dearing committee's decision to recommend a student, or family, contribution was the right one.

As we toiled on the report the general election was suddenly declared to take place on 1 May 1997 and this time Labour – or New Labour as it had become – swept the board, winning 413 seats, while the Conservatives managed 165 and the Liberal Democrats 46. We were in Falmouth working for the Labour candidate, Candy Atherton, who was to become one of the newly elected women MPs. Despite our weariness, we still went to London for the result. We were fortunate enough to have invitations to the Festival Hall and were standing, just, when at dawn Tony Blair came outside and told his supporters, 'It's a wonderful morning.' It certainly was. And to top it off as we drove wearily to Islington, on the car radio came confirmation that Atherton had won Falmouth & Camborne.

That weekend, which was a bank holiday, we were back at Falmouth and Keith was on the boat when the phone rang. It was Tony Blair calling personally from 10 Downing Street. I remember the enormous pleasure it gave me, after waiting for a Labour victory for eighteen years, to respond, 'Good day, Prime Minister.'

To my amazement, I found myself being offered the post of Minister of State in the Northern Ireland Office, in effect No. 2 in the ministerial team.

Keith had pulled my leg and said I would get a call but he forecast it would be to send me to Trade and Industry, where the late Jean Denham had made a success. And without telling me he left a message on the London telephone giving our number in Cornwall. But Northern Ireland? I explained I was engaged in the important work of the Dearing committee. Could I telephone Mo Mowlam, who was to be the Secretary of State for Northern Ireland? No problem there. But when I added, 'And could I have time to think it over?' it clearly was not the form. Usually MPs and peers, phoned on the morning after a general election, are falling over themselves to report to their departments and ready to go.

I was not, No. 10 noted.

I got Keith back off the boat and discussed with him the proposal that I should join Mowlam in Northern Ireland. Mo and I were good friends and apparently she had asked for me. But, as Keith pointed out, I had no experience of Northern Ireland other than occasional visits to our branch in Belfast and was not steeped in the confrontational style of politics and personalities in the province.

Keith had accompanied James Callaghan there when Home Secretary and served with William Whitelaw, the first Secretary of State for Northern Ireland, as his press secretary for two years. 'They'll mock it as "petticoat government",' he predicted. Even so he felt I should take the post as an experience because the chance might never come again.

I was not so sure. Why, I wondered, when I had my life all nicely worked out, had I to throw up everything for a helter-skelter life, shuttling back and forth to Belfast? And as the peer in the team, most likely I would have to take over the duty minister role at weekends. (Keith said he would come over, but not every weekend – he felt he had paid his price to the province.)

One other consideration was that I had had some experience of what being a minister involved, as in opposition I had been a Labour whip, responsible for marshalling a group of peers into the voting lobby, and a junior opposition spokesman on the National Heritage brief, and I also spoke for the front bench on employment matters. I felt it tied me down and I much enjoyed roaming further afield, working on a wider brief than just party politics.

I picked up the phone and rang Jonathan Powell, the Prime Minister's chief adviser, and said I did not wish to go to Northern Ireland. Sorry.

Was I quite sure? If I did not want to travel to and from Northern Ireland, how about being a Labour whip?

Yes, I had made up my mind and in any case I had an undertaking to complete the Dearing report into higher education. Clearly this was not considered too much of a problem by those closest to the Prime Minister. It could easily be fitted in . . . or someone else could take over.

I was not so sure. I really did think the problems of further education mattered. But in any case I had made up my mind.

Once again, a decision was to change my life considerably, because very soon a completely new door was to open. Change was on the way again . . .

*

I would not say I was close to Tony Blair but I knew him and Cherie, his wife, quite well, partly because their Islington home was not more than 200 yards from ours. When they came to our place they told us they wanted to move from Hackney to Islington. We did not realise it would virtually be over the garden fence. But from our upper bedrooms we overlooked their back garden (where we found out later some of the negotiation with Gordon Brown had taken place). And as both our properties adjoined a small park, where Tony sometimes found time to kick a football with his boys, we kept an eye out in case there were snoopers or intruders.

I also had a lot to do with Tony Blair when as shadow Employment Secretary he wanted an incoming Labour government to abandon the closed shop – not at all a popular move with the trade union movement. It all came to a head at the TUC conference in Blackpool in 1989, when I was SOGAT general secretary, and I managed, just, to swing our delegation vote to support Blair. His new policy just scraped through at the conference.

I am not seeking to namedrop but I am proud to have cooked dinner for three Labour leaders and their wives at our London home. Neil and Glenys Kinnock came in 1991, not long before I accompanied Glenys to Nicaragua. She was president of the charity One World and we both went as observers of the crucial elections taking place there.

We had known John Smith for many years and often dined with him at conferences. Both John and his wife Elizabeth came to dinner with us when John took over in 1993. We were present at the Labour Party dinner in May the following year when John, looking rather weary, we thought, nevertheless managed a rousing speech so that we all left the Park Lane Hotel that night in high spirits.

Next morning was different. On Radio 4 came the news that John had collapsed at his flat in the Barbican and then quickly followed the confirmation that he had died. It was a devastating moment.

As we looked over next morning at the Blairs' house, Keith remarked sadly, 'Tony is probably warning his kids that today it is going to be different at school. And so might be everything else.' Some time later Tony confirmed to him that was exactly what was going through the Blair household after that tumultuous moment of tragedy.

But that was all in the past and now Tony Blair was in 10 Downing Street. We could see that on television. Not that we would know it in Islington. Policemen were swarming everywhere with cars, police dogs and a helicopter overhead. They even decided to take over the park keeper's gardening shed as their command post. Clearly, they wanted to convince Labour that just as

Margaret Thatcher had relied upon them, now there was not enough they could do, nor could they spend or over-staff sufficiently, to convince the incoming government of their vital necessity.

But Blair shot their fox. Within a few hours he announced he would be selling the house at 1 Richmond Crescent 'because of the problems and inconvenience it was going to cause to his neighbours'. While it would be nice to have the new Prime Minister living around the corner, it had to be admitted that it was going to be a real hassle with the over-the-top presence of the police. The real losers, though, were the Blairs themselves, who sold too early, just as London property values were about to soar. The new owners sold about a year later and did rather well, I believe.

In the run-up to the 1997 election I was at a BBC lunch and Jonathan Powell was present. He asked if we could share a taxi back to Westminster. On the way he asked if I would become a trustee of Blair's blind trust, which would handle all monies connected to his office in the election run-up. The trust would ensure there could be no question of people buying forward influence with a possible incoming Labour government. All quite legal, I was assured.

I had never heard of a blind trust and have always trodden carefully where my reputation might be at risk. But two colleagues I respect in the Lords, Lord Merlyn-Rees, former Home Secretary, and Baroness Jay of Paddington, daughter of James Callaghan, were also to be trustees. So I agreed to have my name involved.

The master planner was someone new to me, Michael Levy. I did not even know if he was in the Labour Party but he seemed rather wealthy and apparently was Blair's tennis partner.

The concept of blind trusts had been worked out by Levy's lawyers and seemed safe and sound. Not long afterwards we trustees were invited with our spouses to dinner one Friday night at Levy's home in Totteridge Lane, Mill Hill. Derry Irvine QC, later to become Lord Chancellor, and his wife Alison were also invited. I suppose we were having our first taste of things to come in New Labour.

Over dinner on the eve of the Jewish Sabbath, Levy blessed the meal, and then entertained us well. Tony, Cherie and their three children had joined us and it was an excellent evening. No speeches.

We had the privilege some years later to be invited to dine at Chequers one Saturday evening in a group that included Mo Mowlam and the architect Richard Rogers and his wife. The actors Timothy West and his wife Prunella Scales were also dining companions. Years later we discovered this innocent evening had some shady political inference according to the *Daily Mail* and *Daily Telegraph*. If it did, it escaped us.

But back to the new Labour government. Shortly after my decision on Northern Ireland I received another call from Powell. 'Brenda, are you adamant that you do not wish to be offered a ministerial post?'

I told him that once I had made my mind up I did not prevaricate. I knew I had turned down the Prime Minister and did not expect to get a second chance. I felt I had taken the right decision anyway.

If that was my decision No. 10 had another task in mind for me. I was asked to join the rather hush-hush group that vetted honours to ensure no political impropriety. The team was then chaired by Lord Thomson of Monifieth, a Liberal Democrat, and included the Conservative Lord Pym and for Labour, Lord Cledwyn of Penrhos. The group met on what are known as Privy Council terms and there were never any leaks.

I was to succeed Cledwyn in the group and so would join the Privy Council and would become Right Honourable. This is an obscure honour devoted mostly to politicians though one or two other elder statesmen are occasionally given the accolade. The title is highly rated amongst politicians – rather like earning one's spurs. In the Lords one has seniority over another peer if called to speak though I have never taken up that advantage. There is also a special bench reserved for Privy Counsellors.

This distinction dates back to the small Privy Council that once advised Queen Elizabeth I and was, in a way, the forerunner to our Cabinet system of government. There are occasional meetings even today of the Privy Council to advise our monarch – though she is so experienced she seldom needs much advice. But it is largely ceremonial and members traditionally remain standing in the presence of the Queen.

The secrets of the Privy Council are jealously guarded and never discussed in public. The council enables opposing politicians to meet and hold confidential discussions, and this is what is meant by 'Privy Council terms'. It was on that basis that the three political parties came privately together to look at nominations for honours and to advise the Prime Minister of the day. It was a confidential vetting procedure to protect the Prime Minister, and indirectly the monarch, from potential embarrassment.

Keith was impressed with my unexpected achievement and took me to lunch at Raymond Blanc's splendid Le Manoir aux Quat' Saisons restaurant out in Oxfordshire. It was a memorable meal.

My appointment to the Political Honours Committee was in 1998, when very little was known or heard about its scrutiny. The members met quietly with the people of the Honours Secretariat from Whitehall, who prepared the paperwork and carried out the checking before placing the results before us. The committee in fact dated back to 1922, when there was a scandal involving the sale of honours by the then Liberal Prime Minister, David Lloyd George, and a committee of inquiry was set up. One of its recommendations was 'a committee of three Privy Councillors to scrutinise those nominated for political honours'. But such quiet discussion away from the spotlight all came abruptly to an end a few months later when the Parliamentary Committee on Standards in Public Life asked us to appear before it. I was still very much the new member of the committee and in fact we had not met before we were asked to appear before the committee. I kept my contribution to a minimum.

Not long afterwards John Wakeham, the former Conservative chief whip, Cabinet minister and chairman of the Press Complaints Commission, who has a reputation of being a political fixer, was asked to chair a royal commission and make recommendations on the reform of the House of Lords. I became a member, though I had had my doubts as I had earlier served on the Press Complaints Commission and was not convinced the Wakeham approach would work. But I have to admit that Wakeham achieved the impossible and held the commission together. We consulted widely and held twenty-one meetings for the public to let us have their views.

When our report, *A House for the Future*, was published the cynics were surprised to find our recommendations were unanimous. There had been considerable hard talking on the commission but there was a consensus from the beginning that we wanted to conclude a report which provided a workable solution and stood a chance of being implemented. The only area where there were differences in our conclusions was on the options we put forward on future membership, providing for various ways of evolving an electoral system.

Today there are all kinds of ideas swirling around about the future of the Lords but I emerged from sitting on the commission entirely convinced that the concept of an all-elected Lords would be disastrous. And at some point there would come a challenge to the House of Commons. That would be real trouble.

The House of Lords is already much changed with the departure of the majority of hereditary peers. If the public were able to see the real work of the chamber they could hardly fail to be impressed. There are experts and specialist knowledge on almost every field of activity and debates are of very high calibre, free of petty political knockabout, although there is some hard political bargaining, particularly in the final stages of a Bill.

The trouble is that the media only report the chamber either in terms of defying government, which in a revising chamber is bound to happen occasionally – and is an essential bulwark of freedom – or as a boring, sleepy place of out-of-touch people with one foot in the grave, who do not know what they are talking about. Sadly too many MPs go along with this kind of ill-informed rubbish and too few understand the workings of the House of Lords. Or even wish to.

I believe the media does Britain a grave disservice by this puerile, knee-jerk approach. The BBC tries a bit with *Today in Parliament* but really only looks at what the Lords are saying if they cannot find anything worth reporting in the Commons.

The government accepted a number of our recommendations while reserving its position on our main, more fundamental suggestions. One accepted was forming an Appointments Commission, as Wakeham recommended.

So we still had the Honours Scrutiny Committee but all three of us involved felt it had now been overtaken by events. There was a feeling of duplication of effort and we fed this into 10 Downing Street, suggesting that as the new

Appointments Commission was selecting and vetting crossbench peers it would make more sense for it also to vet the party peers. Eventually this was accepted. Needless to say the press portrayed it as the Prime Minister eliminating the Scrutiny Committee because we had been too much of a problem. This, very definitely, was not the case.

We maintained our rule of not talking to the media so we were not in a position to put the record straight. But we took the opportunity when we appeared before the Commons Public Administration Select Committee, chaired by Tony Wright.

Our chairman was and remains Lord Stevenson of Coddenham, an independent crossbench member. From the former political honours scrutiny committee there is Lord Hurd of Westwell, former Foreign Secretary and Home Secretary, representing the Tories, I am there for Labour and Lord Dholakia represents the Liberal Democrats. The difference is that we are now joined by two independent members, Angela Sarkis and Felicity Houston. I believe this is an excellent improvement and makes us less of a closed society.

At the beginning we commissioned some research into the composition of the House of Lords and made some interesting discoveries. Not surprisingly, all parties were male dominated – the Tories were worst with 85 per cent but Labour and the Liberal Democrats had 78 per cent male and just 22 per cent female. Some 63 per cent of all peers came from London and the South East. Overall, the chamber was dominated by white male Oxbridge graduates (mostly Oxford) aged over 60, and there was a dominance of people with a business background or a career in public service. So hardly a cross-section of the nation.

Six years later there has been a marked change. There are many more women – even a female Leader of the House and the first ever Speaker of the House to be elected is also female. The late Baroness Young has the distinction of being the first woman Leader of the House, appointed by Margaret Thatcher to the post. There is much more racial diversity represented and the new peers now come from all walks of life. So I believe considerable progress has quietly been achieved but one would never know it to hear the barracking from what we know as 'the Other Place' – the House of Commons.

No one I know in the Lords challenges the more senior and representative nature of the House of Commons but it would be helpful if the progress that has been made could sometimes be acknowledged.

The Appointments Commission is responsible for scrutinising and recommending new independent peers and it quickly landed itself in trouble with the media for what they considered a less than inspiring first list of People's Peers. There was no hairdresser listed among them! This was a good example of the mess that spin can land you in. People's Peers was a clever tag thought up in the Press Department at 10 Downing Street and of course initially earned an easy headline. Yet we had held several public meetings around the country, advertised publicly for nominations and received over 3,000 nominations, vetted several hundred people and interviewed dozens in depth. All to fill fifteen vacancies. So when we announced our first list of successful candidates we knew those selected had been put through a gruelling test far more searching than any member of the House of Lords had ever previously endured. Including me.

There was no hairdresser, that was true, though with the best will in the world, I very much doubt if many would have survived the grilling, let alone a lass handy with the scissors. Not even a male hairdresser. And in any case I do not believe any hairdresser actually applied!

In the meantime the Electoral Commission was setting the framework more clearly for funding political parties – although not clearly enough, as it turned out. The sensitivity surrounding nominations for the House of Lords by people who had given donations was rising and the press was continually sniffing around the subject. We already had the requirement that all donations to a political party over £5,000 had to be declared by the party concerned. The chief whip of each of the parties had to sign a certificate for us confirming not only the amounts given to the party by the individual but also that the donation had nothing to do with their nomination.

The reality is that without other sources of funding the political parties are bound to appeal to their wealthy supporters and to their individual members for financial support. Where else is funding to come from?

But the nominations at the end of 2005 turned out to be more controversial than anyone could have expected. First the list was leaked – not by anyone on the Appointments Commission, I believe, which had been operating five years without a leak.

On the list the Prime Minister had given the Green Party one nomination but the problem was that their chief executive had nominated himself – apparently without the knowledge of anyone else in his party. Also Eileen Paisley, wife of Ian Paisley, the Northern Ireland MP, was nominated – by her husband – though this was later cleared with the executive of Paisley's Democratic Unionist Party.

While this was being sorted out the press had ferreted away and come up with the disclosure that some of the nominees, particularly some of those from Labour, had made loans. This was not disclosed to our commission but on reading the Electoral Commission's ground rules it had not been made absolutely clear that it had to be disclosed. We members of the Appointment Commission were quite clear, however, that such disclosure was necessary so that we could do our job properly.

Well, the rest is history. The list turned out to be almost as incendiary as the famous Lavender List in the days of the late Harold Wilson. It was a pretty tough time for members of the Appointment Commission which none of us enjoyed. It highlighted for me that the funding of political parties must have tighter and clearer rules. If the public does not want their politics to be dependent upon wealthy donors then alternatives have to be found and there are not many available.

One obvious source is taxpayer funding. But that would have long-term implications beyond general elections. How are the parties supposed to plan, produce new policies and pay staff between elections? And would the financial limits and transparency apply to local as well as national politics? These are big questions.

Some people always seem to be able to find their way around the rules, however closely defined, and I do not believe it is possible to make any system watertight. Much depends on the will of those involved. What is certain is that this situation has to be resolved, preferably by cross-party agreement, and honoured. Not only in word but in spirit.

Chapter 21

Apart from loving change, I know I am really an organisation person. While I have quite enjoyed having what has become known as a portfolio of roles and in effect working for myself, I do really enjoy leading a team and having executive authority in an organisation.

I suppose that is why I was happy in my trade union career. At branch and at national level I had to carry people with me and show leadership but it was often an opportunity to steer an organisation. And to embrace change. Of course it helps if one knows where one is trying to go . . .

I was enjoying being executive chairman of ICSTIS but by 1997 I had an excellent team in place led by Sarah Harrison and I knew it would soon be time to move on. I am not a believer in keeping a chair warm and after a period of, say, six years, it is time to go. The organisation has by then probably had all it can get from a person and it is time for new ideas.

Tasks such as the Armed Forces Pay Review Body were keeping me busy, as was being a member of the European Sub-Committee of the House of Lords, which scrutinises EU legislation on transport, energy and industry. There are often grumbles that too much legislation comes from Brussels which the British people know little about. Well, blame the lack of reporting, rather than lack of scrutiny.

I understand those in Brussels, including our own diplomatic team, believe that the checking by the House of Lords is very effective and often uncovers flaws which have been missed. Peers can manage to prevent what is known as 'gold plating' – when our own civil service adds to the EU proposals a few extra of their own. Then, when there is uproar, they blame it on Brussels.

But not long after the 1997 general election I was sounded out by a headhunter on becoming the chairman of the Housing Corporation. I did not think it sounded like the road for me but I agreed I would look at the 'job spec' if it was posted to me. Reading it next day in Cornwall I was more than ever convinced. 'I know nothing about housing,' I told the caller who rang from the headhunting firm.

The Housing Corporation was then handling a budget of around £650 million of government funds a year for housing associations, but it is also responsible for regulating the sector. Its role is to stimulate the building of new social housing and to enlist private-sector funding which it is able to match, and which often goes into major developments too big for an individual association to handle.

The days when local authorities built and managed the social housing sector have long gone. Margaret Thatcher's government devastated it really, by encouraging people to buy their council homes cheaply as sitting tenants. Many promptly sold them on at great profit. Either a private buyer came forward or a company snapped it up. Worse, the public sector was then denied the opportunity to reinvest those funds in new homes.

The policy of the Thatcher government was not to get more drive into the building of new council homes but to break the political grip of Labour on the council estates. It worked, but social housing was really the loser. That is the basic reason why today Britain has a desperate, chronic shortage of social housing.

An old trade union friend, Ken Griffin, a former official of the Electrical Trades Union, was a member of the corporation's board and had apparently suggested my name. There was a vacancy because a banker had suddenly quit the chairman's role and the corporation was urgently in need of new blood.

Griffin and I went back a long way – we were together on the Supplementary Benefits Commission back in 1975 and Keith had known him at British Shipbuilders. Griffin arranged for the effervescent chief executive, Anthony Mayer, to phone and we agreed to have coffee at the Langham Hotel, opposite Broadcasting House. He was doing nothing wrong because, as he pointed out, he was ready to brief anyone who might be interested in coming to the Housing Corporation.

Mayer is now the chief executive of the Greater London Authority and I found him an engaging personality. His enthusiasm for working in social housing came through and stirred my interest. Although I had personal knowledge of living in a council house I knew I had a lot to learn. Mayer was really a civil servant from the Department of the Environment but I suspect he was a shade too maverick to reach the top. So he had been happy to take over a big-budget quango.

It came as news to me but there was, it seemed, a big grass roots organisation in housing and those involved, I learned, talked of 'the movement'. Housing had its own jargon and plenty of lively personalities. Interesting parallels with trade unionism were to be found. So I followed up with the headhunters and obtained an application form, which I sent off to the department. Then things started happening quite quickly and I met a team of civil servants for interview. One of them was Mavis McDonald, who went on to become permanent secretary in John Prescott's department. To climb to the top for a woman was still a major achievement in the civil service.

Shortly afterwards I found myself being interviewed and going in to see Hilary Armstrong, then the minister responsible for housing at the Department of the Environment. Armstrong, a future chief whip for Labour, wanted me to start as soon as possible. So I decided to have a go and entered an entirely new world – it was all change again.

The offices were, appropriately perhaps, located in Tottenham Court Road where the once-famous furniture store Maples had been. Many couples had set up their first home from that emporium but the kind of homes we were seeking to build would have required something more modest to kit them out.

Apart from an over-large headquarters I found we also had a London regional set-up and regional offices throughout England and Wales (Scotland did its own thing, as usual). It had the familiar feel of a trade union structure. Up and down the country there were housing associations, just over 2,000 of them, rather like branches, but possessing great autonomy and independence. There were regular major conferences, notably the Chartered Institute of Housing, which gathered for four days at familiar venues such as Harrogate, where speeches were required – nay, expected – and an exhibition. It was one of the biggest events of its kind in Europe.

There was also a vibrant trade press adept at digging out the sector's secrets and a quite incestuous group of people who were making their career in the field of social housing. They were mainly men. Very few women appeared to me to have clawed their way to the top in the housing sector. Yet it is possible to argue very persuasively that women know as much, if not more, about home-making and housing.

What I did enjoy was being on the road again, getting round to meet the ordinary people for whom involvement in their local housing association or the development gave them great satisfaction and pride. In Liverpool I might find myself meeting the local authority and going on to open a new development; in York seeing the amazing experiments in retirement accommodation being pioneered by the Joseph Rowntree Trust; or in Cornwall attending an all-day conference of the local housing association representatives, where, I discovered, they had one of the best self-managed housing developments in the country.

Gradually, from being virtually an unknown organisation with a minimal profile amongst tenants, the people who were our ultimate customers, we started to get it across that the Housing Corporation was a big hitter, had funds and wanted results.

Most of our regional directors reacted favourably to having a chairman who liked to get around, was willing to go on television and was not afraid to meet the local media. In particular I was impressed with Max Steinberg, the director of our North West region, who had an entrepreneurial flair and enjoyed excellent contacts with everyone involved locally in the social housing field.

At head office, I cannot really say it was the same. Redundancies had been declared just before I arrived and morale was tender. But we had some good people, notably Neil Hadden, director of investment, a shrewd operator who knew the sector and investors as well as anyone. Others at head office believed strongly in social housing but were rather set in their ways and perhaps sought a quiet life. Some seemed to have found the corporation a comfortable berth and did not welcome the slightest whiff of change or to be asked why something like a publication, for example, had to be identical with last year's effort. That was how it had always been done!

I felt I needed to open a few windows but as usual proceeded gently. At the DoE I enlisted McDonald's support and made sure she knew what I was about.

I have always believed in a policy of 'no shocks' in my relationship with Whitehall. Good civil servants can cope with change alright – what they do not like is to be wrong-footed and asked by their minister to explain something of which they are totally unaware. Gradually, if they feel comfortable and confident they can be very helpful indeed – after all, a well-performing quango reflects well on those responsible for its budget. And a good appointment reflects well on the minister who approved it.

I decided to meet Unison, the trade union involved at the corporation, and sought to build bridges. I also set out to meet all the staff at Maple House so they could see that I was no threat but intent on careful, controlled, planned change. In particular I wanted to get across that we were a service to people who lived in social housing – or hoped one day to achieve it. They were in effect our customers and I was concerned that they tended to be forgotten in the corporation's high-finance projects or in its policy decisions. As far as I was concerned we were there handling taxpayers' money and we needed to be seen to be more publicly accountable.

I asked one of the board's directors, Eric Armitage of the North British Housing Association, to become deputy chairman and throughout my stay, he was extremely loyal and supportive. In return I always kept him fully in the picture and briefed him before every board meeting. Even so I also felt that we needed on our board people with much more direct experience of social housing. Yvonne Hutchinson, a black lady from Bradford, joined us and became a strong supporter for tenants and change although some of the officials found her hard to work alongside.

When there was a vacancy for what had come to be the rural seat I won agreement that we should have a tenant board member. Until then the seat had always been filled by a prominent landowner. The problem was in finding a tenant with sufficient confidence to become a public director. Jack Dromey of the TGWU, which had absorbed the National Union of Agricultural and Allied

Workers, helped to find Ivan Monkton. Monkton had been active in the farm workers' union and had many interests. He lived in Powys and was a lovely man. He brought to us a great deal of personal experience and some very sound judgement on the way that ordinary people reacted. And he was never afraid to ruffle feathers if he felt that was necessary.

Later, we brought on to the board Julia Fawcett, a dynamic young woman from a sink estate in Stockwell, south London. She really did shake the cobwebs. Fawcett had helped to clean up her estate, confronted drug pushers and knew all about the problems of single mothers through her work at SureStart. And she was only too aware of what it was like living in a tower block where, even if the lifts did work, there was no lighting and people were scared to go in them. Quickly her self-confidence grew, though sometimes she had too much to say. But it was great to have her on board and she was a quick learner. I think she will go a long way.

One objective was to speed up decision-making in the approval of projects and gradually this paid off. It was a big board, thirteen of us in all, but all the members brought in their own angle and experience to make it work. But more immediately I identified three areas in which I wanted to achieve real change: tenant involvement; governance of the individual housing associations, where some were good but others were appallingly managed; and black and minority ethnic housing associations – BMEs as the jargon was quickly established in the housing world. These three objectives were nicknamed the 'Brenda agenda' by the Housing Corporation staff, who quickly got the message that this was where my personal priorities lay.

In the case of BMEs the corporation's record of investment was good but relationships were often poor. I went out of my way to visit housing associations run by the many diverse groups of poor people in British society, including Jews, Muslims, Hindus and Sikhs, and was made very welcome. I also got to know Vietnamese and Chinese – the last of whom still send me a beautiful card each year to mark their New Year.

By the time I handed over the chairmanship the total annual budget had gone from around £650 million to over £1.5 billion. That was big money going into construction and the industry knew it. It no longer regarded the Housing Corporation as stuffy, slow and bureaucratic but a useful partner.

I do not claim this to be my success. There was help from above and from below. Above, Hilary Armstrong, and then the personal drive put into social housing by the Deputy Prime Minister, John Prescott, made all the difference. We were pushing at an open door. And below, when people start seeing results, they get a taste of it and want more. It was again a shift from 'We can't' to 'Why can't we?'.

Different models of ownership started to flourish. Co-operatives had been around a long time but not encouraged much by the Housing Corporation; and arm's length management organisations, ALMOs in the jargon, put forward by the government were not welcome either, because they removed control from the corporation. I did support ALMOs – an awful term. But where local authorities want to pull back from direct management yet not hand an estate over to a housing association, there is a drive now to get the tenants to take responsibility and run their estates themselves. There have been failures but overall this policy by the government has been a great success. Some very poor developments were out of control and had simply become rich pastures for drug traffickers and thieves.

Places such as Castle Vale in Birmingham are now run by their own elected committees of tenants and real local leaders have emerged, proud of their own estates and determined to manage without interference. The government thought so highly of it that when Bill Clinton was here as US President, he was taken to meet the leaders of Castle Vale by Tony Blair.

I personally assessed the corporation's board members and the chief executive. But who checks up on the chairman? No one, I was told.

The DoE had now become the Department of the Environment, Transport and the Regions, but most of the people remained the same. I explained that I had completed assessments of all my board members and now I wanted my appraisal. This had never happened before, they said. But I insisted and eventually my appraisal form was completed by Mavis McDonald. She carried it out formally and in a very businesslike manner. I understand this procedure is now quite widely used across the quango sector and I should think so.

Quangos handle large sums of public money and those who apply for their paid directorships should be assessed and performance-related. After all the public is paying and should get the best.

By the autumn of 2003 my second three-year term as chairman of the corporation was coming to an end. John Prescott wanted to extend it but I declined. However, I did continue chairing a committee of sixteen examining the problems of how affordable housing could be expanded – looking at where the bottlenecks were.

There are no easy answers. The problem with inner cities is that as land costs soar there are people such as nurses, policemen, firemen and social workers who cannot afford to live near their work. They are priced out from where they are really needed.

Both the public and the private sector were represented on what was named the Affordable Home Ownership Task Force and we worked well together despite different backgrounds. It represented a good, wide cross-section of the world of housing. John Prescott picked up our report, which we named *A Home of My Own*. We reported back to him in May 2003 and I am very pleased that a number of our recommendations have now been adopted. We did not solve the housing problem but many of the impediments we identified Prescott made sure were swept away. He particularly initiated the drive we suggested to identify small unused sites in inner-city areas on government-owned property.

So I had enjoyed it all and felt some sense of achievement but it was time for new blood. When one sees the same conference speech invitations coming around again, you know you have said it all. It is time to go.

There was a wonderful farewell party at Church House and a great turnout led by Prescott, who was very generous in his tribute. But the fun came when Keith revealed how he had been asked what present they should buy from a very generous sum collected for my farewell. 'No china, no vases, no silver, no paintings,' he told the Housing Corporation. 'There is no room to put it, she's got the lot and there isn't an inch of cupboard space to spare.' He had a point.

So when he was pressed, he said, 'If you really want to give her something she wants it's a new front door at our house in Falmouth. That's what she really wants.'

Although Keith tried to persuade them that buying the Housing Corporation chairman her own front door would be marvellous publicity, no one would agree. We settled for two garden heaters, in stainless steel, and I must say they transform eating outside in late evening. But a shiny new front door would have reminded me of the happy days at the corporation each time I put my key in the lock. And I still have not got that new one!

Chapter 22

By the time I was closing the door on housing, however, a new world was opening up for me. Quite out of the blue, appropriately enough, I was approached to see if I would take on the chairmanship of a new group to be called Freedom to Fly, or F2F, as it became known. It was a coalition of all the major players in UK civil aviation, who were willing to bury their hatchets – usually aimed at each other's backs – and present a common front.

So here we had the chief executive of British Airways, Ron Eddington, willing to sit alongside Richard Branson of Virgin Atlantic – with no dirty tricks! With them were people such as Mike Hodgkinson, chief executive of BAA, Sir Michael Bishop of British Midland and representatives from the Association of British Travel Agents (ABTA) and Manchester Airport.

The trade unions operating in aviation were involved as were some other main players including Brendan Barber of the TUC, Digby Jones of the CBI and people from the Freight Transport Association and the London Chamber of Commerce. EasyJet had a presence there too and were paying their share – but not of course Ryanair. Their management is strong on taking but poor when it comes to making any contribution for the common good.

But what had brought everyone else together was a common fear. What else would it be?

There was a general view that the aviation industry was about to lose out to the environmentalists over the need for extra capacity in the UK and particularly in the south-east. The government had promised to produce a White Paper to provide a firm statement of policy, the first for twenty years. So aviation urgently needed to get its act together, firstly to try to have an input but most importantly not to allow the government off the hook on its promise finally to produce a policy.

But why me? Where did I fit in?

It seemed to be felt that I had the confidence of them all and would be seen as sufficiently neutral by government to be able to argue their case. I certainly carried no baggage – if that is the appropriate term – in this sphere. When I left SOGAT I was sounded out to become the general secretary of the British Air Line Pilots Association – where Norman Tebbit made his name, incidentally. It was attractive, especially in terms of salary. But at the time I felt my life needed to change course and looking back I think I had taken the right decision.

So it was flattering to be asked but I needed to be sure that everyone really was on side. And was this an argument that really could be won? Not many would have placed a bet in favour at that time.

The more I went into it the easier I felt within myself. No one wants more and more noisy aircraft over their heads, or increased global warming, some of which can be laid at the door of the aviation industry. Aviation in fact, though, only accounts for 2 per cent of global carbon dioxide emissions compared to 18 per cent from road transport, 34 per cent from power stations and a number of other more sizeable contributions.

I believe there is an equally strong case to put forward on why Britain needs to retain a strong aviation industry. It is one of the few real growth industries of recent years which is actually employing more people. It generates half a million jobs. Britain is remarkably good at civil aviation and it is one of our success stories. It has a £10 billion annual impact on the nation's economic health, and many countries, certainly in Europe, would be only too happy if we were to step aside. To a former trade union leader that is a forceful case.

I took some soundings and what I was being told did seem to be the case. All the main players knew they had to close ranks. Lord Marshall, then BA chairman, wrote to me, 'It is important now more than ever that the aviation industry speaks with one voice on the growing demand for air travel. This wide range of support is the main strength of Freedom to Fly and, we hope, will help to articulate the view of the "silent majority" on this issue and provide a powerful and effective voice in the debate on the future of aviation.'

I made my usual condition of proper back-up and here I was fortunate in having Joe Irvine, who had been John Prescott's political assistant, and an official at the TGWU. Irvine knew a lot about transport. He was great on research, invaluable, competent and moved about quietly. I also asked to be able to involve my own personal assistant, Diane Russell, who handled my diary – managed my time – and could ensure that I would be able to fit in all F2F's engagements with my others. Our pay and rations were handled by Ian Reynolds, chief executive of ABTA, with whom I was able to work well.

Everyone must sing from the same hymn sheet in any campaign, and that is where leadership is important. Yet we had a number of big players to get round the table and agree. I did persuade Eddington and Branson to sit alongside each other at our press conference to launch F2F. This caused a big laugh and made a good picture.

We hammered out a common objective, which stated that we wished 'to promote positively the sustainable provision of capacity to satisfy rising consumer demand for air travel and to encourage the adoption of principles by the government'. We listed them carefully and summed up: 'Capacity should be increased in a sustainable way, based on long-term planning, harnessing technological progress and mitigating any adverse environmental effects. Investment should be effective and timely, enabled by a streamlined planning process that takes account of both the national and local needs.' Quite a mouthful but it was important that ministers, civil servants and planners knew what we were about.

We produced good-quality briefing of integrity, containing facts we knew were accurate and thoroughly checked. We did not knock our opponents.

At first the job was intended to last a year but the government put back its schedule for producing the White Paper. It meant we had to continue another year but it also gave us longer to get our case across.

I went to see Alastair Darling, the Transport Secretary, and the relevant civil servants. They welcomed a united approach rather than face a barrage of competing voices from across the aviation spectrum. So the plan to get the case together and argue as one was being effective.

But in the midst of the campaign came the September 11 atrocity at the World Trade Center in New York, which for several months knocked the bottom out of the civil aviation industry. Demand for travel fell like a stone and the thought occurred, 'Are we going to need expansion?' But those well experienced in the flying business predicted it would recover and that the public would not be forced for long to give up travel.

So F2F did certainly open up a whole new world for me. I enjoyed events such as the regular lunch of the Aviation Club, usually held at the Royal Aero Club at the bottom of Park Lane. This was a new venue to me and one I found stacked with the memorabilia of the pioneering years of a new industry. When one realises how a major world industry employing millions and creating wealth for an industrialised society can come from a few people's pioneering enthusiasm – and risk taking – it is a salutary lesson.

For once the Greens were not having it all their way. While I have sympathy with the environmental case I do think their arguments are often too one sided and pitched to play on the emotions of those without the facts. Other people's jobs, and therefore the future of their families, often appear to be of little concern.

F2F was a good example of how business must organise itself and make its case. When the civil aviation White Paper was published in December 2004, F2F's backers were well satisfied. First, regional airports were to be allowed to develop their capacity to full use – something the public had made clear they wanted. Greater capacity would also be located at Stansted – although it was recognised there would be substantial local opposition and planning objections to overcome. But, in effect by careful management, there could be a third runway at Heathrow, which would mean much greater use of facilities. Coupled with the fifth terminal being built on time and able to take all BA facilities from Terminals 1 and 2 it meant considerably more could be squeezed out of what is still one of the busiest and most frequently used airports in the world. I believe we need to keep it that way.

So the job was done. The coalition gave me a great send-off but sadly I knew it would soon disperse. I had many good letters from the new friends I had made in what to me is a dynamic and exciting industry which perhaps not enough Britons appreciate. Several made the point that the industry should have learned a lesson from F2F and should try to show more unanimity. For my part I intended to maintain my interest in aviation.

About this time, in 2003, I had the opportunity to take up two appointments in the private sector. One was with George Wimpey plc, the house builder, and the second was with Dawson Holdings plc, which is in wholesale newspaper and magazine distribution. Both areas which I felt I knew something about and could contribute to the board.

Much of my life since leaving the union world had been in and around the public sector and it was useful to be reminded of the need for the sharply focused business approach on what everyone these days calls 'the bottom line'. Or, more simply, are we making a profit and is it good enough?

I had been sounded out when at the Housing Corporation if I would consider joining Wimpey but I felt there might be a perceived conflict as we were involved in land purchase and major development of homes. But John Robinson, the chairman, who was to serve on my Affordable Home Ownership Task Force representing the CBI, came back when I had left the corporation and renewed the invitation. I am glad I accepted as I have found the competitive world of private house building stimulating. Wimpey builds abroad as well as in the UK and has major operations in Florida, Texas, California and elsewhere in the USA.

The suggestion I should also join a company in which many of my old union's members had been employed was worth a second look. Dawson is the third largest in the field after W. H. Smith and John Menzies. I joined Dawson in August 2004 and it was great to detect the occasional whiff of printing ink on visits to the many distribution plants of the company. Anyone who has ever been in printing will know the buzz that the smell of ink provides. Distribution is very labour intensive and much of the work is done at night, but it was good to turn out in the small hours and talk to our people at Peterborough. Dawson management was surprised when I had no objection to being up all night but it was just like old times to me.

Sadly, union membership has declined sharply in the sector and the GPMU has disappeared into the one of the three general workers' unions, Amicus. Which used to be about engineering! A sign of the times, I suppose.

So these and other activities continued but I also put in plenty of time in the House of Lords. I am classified as a 'working peer' and am expected to be on parade if the government needs voting support. With some contentious legislation going through this has often been the case. I usually am in the House of Lords each afternoon and as Labour peers are split into three 'rosters' I know I am likely to have to stay late each Monday until the house rises.

It is a mistake to speak too frequently but equally an error not to speak enough. The important aspect is to identify issues on which you have concern or experience and concentrate your efforts there. So I tend to watch pensions, housing, armed forces and defence matters, employment and industry.

One view I hold strongly is that there should be a monument to Sylvia Pankhurst within the precincts of Westminster. There is one each for her mother and sister but because Sylvia rocked the boat more I feel she has been frozen out. A campaign, in which I am very involved, is working hard to correct this injustice.

I also like to keep an eye on rural matters affecting the south-west especially as I was asked to chair a working party on regional development recently. It was felt that other regions, notably the north, had got their act together and my area needed to do the same. So a good report was laid on the desk of the Deputy Prime Minister, John Prescott, who opened our conference at Bristol University in April 2006, at which we presented our proposals to representatives from all over the south-west.

A good side of being in the Lords, however, is that having a desk with a computer and the opportunity to book a meeting room in central London means one can carry on with a professional life. This is just as well because in September 2004 came a rather surprising and interesting approach. Sir John Krebs, the chairman of the Food Standards Agency, who I had never met, asked me to carry out an independent review on how well the agency had fulfilled its promises to restore confidence in the nation's food supply. Five years earlier, when set up, the agency had given this pledge and it wanted to honour it.

Some years previously I had had a brief spell on the board of Assured British Meat when an attempt was made to restore the reputation of the industry after the BSE crisis. Actually I was offered the chairmanship but I did not feel I could face up to visits to slaughter houses. I was too squeamish, I suppose. But I knew relatively little about the wider issues. Here was a fascinating opportunity to see what was happening across the whole spectrum of food supply and distribution.

Now that I know more about it, I believe the creation of the Food Standards Agency, taking matters out of the hands of the agriculture department and granting the agency such complete independence, is one of the Labour government's great achievements. But the agency itself was brave enough to ask someone completely independent – and with no axe to grind – to examine it, warts and all. And to publish their verdict. I can think of few, very few, organisations that would have the guts to do that.

The board of the Food Standards Agency meets in public and posts all its decisions immediately on the internet. It is one of the most open organisations ever created in Britain and I believe it is a lesson to us all.

I met Krebs on 16 September and agreed to take on the review. Details of the contract, staff back-up and the work programme were agreed a week later and work started on 5 October. The final report was wanted by February 2006 in time for the board's fifth birthday. A tight schedule. In that time we had pulled together the team – all women as it worked out.

Rachel Maidment was a young woman I had met while serving on the board of the General Insurance Standards Council. I had been impressed with her efficiency and liked her. The council was being wound up and Maidment was going freelance. Chris Woodburn, chief executive of the GISC, agreed to second her in the last months of the council. So she was snapped up, cleared her desk and immediately came on board.

I felt I needed to conduct interviews with 'stakeholders' as they came to be known – organisations likely to have a strong view on how the FSA was working out. Krebs thought it needed to be with about twenty but in the end I met with 125 of them. Diane Russell took on the mammoth organisational task of fixing up appointments and arranging the timing and meeting venues.

We also needed someone to liaise daily within the FSA but who would work totally for the review and maintain our confidences. A difficult task for anyone. Claire Boville was selected by the FSA and she did a brilliant job.

So the four of us set out on a concentrated probe into the world of Britain's food supply: its manufacture, quality, impact on health and media coverage. The full list of people and organisations interviewed filled seven pages of close print of our final report. It ranged from Asda to the Association of Shellfish Growers, the European Commission, Friends of the Earth, the Meat and Livestock Commission, the Women's Institute, assorted journalists specialising in food and consumer affairs and many standards bodies.

We also had interviews with several government departments including two ministers at DEFRA, Larry Whitty and Alun Michael, other ministers at the Department of Health, the Northern Ireland Office and the Welsh Assembly, and the minister responsible in the Scottish Parliament. In addition there were fifty-seven written submissions from such organisations as Marks and Spencer and the Muslim Education Coordinating Council, the Genetically Modified Food News and the Forum of Private Business. We covered participants in Scotland, Wales and Northern Ireland as well as England.

In what became known as the Dean review, though that was not my idea, the terms of reference declared that I would seek to measure how successfully the agency had met its target of firstly protecting public health by promoting a safer food supply and secondly restoring confidence in the way that decisions on food matters were taken in Britain. We were also asked to assess whether the agency had met its core values – to put consumers first, to be open and accessible, and to act as an independent voice.

We met representatives of all political parties, journalists such as Felicity Lawrence of the *Guardian* and John Mason of the *Financial Times*, and Peter Vicary-Smith, chief executive of *Which?*.

If we had any difficulty it was in trying to pin down the Department of Health to give a view. I tried coming in at several levels but there was an ominous silence, it seemed, coming from that quarter. Eventually, though, I was able to obtain a session with Melanie Johnson, minister for public health, who then was very helpful. But I did wonder if the old rivalry between Health and Agriculture in the past had had anything to do with it.

If we missed anybody, all I can say is that it was not for the want of trying. Generally people responded magnificently and thoughtfully. Politicians came off the fence and various trade associations tried hard to be objective and not just to grind the axes of their members.

I found it heartening that when people are approached in all sincerity and seriousness, then they can and will respond positively. Having set off with an open mind it was uplifting. After all, it was a world completely new to me, though I had read many reports and papers beforehand and had the help of several in-depth briefings from senior FSA officials.

Much midnight oil was burnt in the closing sessions but with my energetic young team we hit our deadline and delivered a 61-page report to the Food Standards Agency in time for its board meeting on 10 February; Rachel Maidment and I attended and gave an oral presentation on the findings.

In my personal letter to Krebs enclosing the report I wrote, 'Everyone I approached was prepared to put forward their views in a free and unfettered way. The result is, I assess, one which any organisation would take satisfaction in. The agency has come out of the review with the overwhelming support of the stakeholders. Of course there are criticisms, some more serious and urgent than others, but generally the stakeholders have confidence that FSA is capable of dealing with these.'

In his response Krebs wrote back a formal letter with a handwritten postscript: 'Thank you once again for producing such a thorough, perceptive and constructive report.' And Dr John Bell, the chief executive, wrote to say, 'You have given us plenty to think about for the future. Thank you for agreeing to brief the staff. I know they will appreciate it.'

Krebs stood down as chairman a few weeks later. He left in the knowledge that he had done an excellent job. It would be a brave politician who now decided to tamper with the FSA, I felt.

Well, that seemed to be that for food – the paperwork could all go into the filing cabinet now that my report was concluded. Our little team had lunch together at the House of Lords and we all went back to where we had been before the sudden call of FSA.

But two months later that experience with food turned out to be highly relevant because my name was in the ring to become the chairman of the Covent Garden Market Authority. Nothing to do with opera or with *My Fair Lady*, I must emphasise. This Covent Garden is at Nine Elms, near Vauxhall on the south side of the Thames. Here much of London's fruit, vegetables and magnificent flowers are moved from wholesale to retail.

They are handled on an area of over 50 acres, prime value land, in one of the most congested cities in Europe. The market had been moved there by central government in the 1970s. The area between the Strand and Long Acre had become congested, making it almost impossible for the huge trucks to bring in the fresh produce. The colourful sight of a market porter with a score of wicker fruit baskets on his head hid a scene of mounting chaos. Unable to get agreement with the traders on moving, the government finally bit the bullet and financed the move to Nine Elms. But it was as if the government then forgot all about the market and so changes that have long been needed have been put on the back burner and pushed aside by successive governments.

Yet food distribution has changed with the emergence of supermarkets which buy direct, and much clearly has to change if New Covent Garden Market is to have a future. I believe it does but it is going to be a major task turning things around.

The other personal development has been an appointment to the board of the National Air Traffic Service, responsible for air traffic control in the United Kingdom. So that background at Freedom to Fly is likely to turn out to be very useful.

*

In my lifetime I have seen women make substantial progress in gaining equality but I believe they have a long way to go. It is wrong that it is still rather rare for a woman to achieve the top job. In the examples I have given – the Covent Garden Market Authority, the Housing Corporation, the Armed Forces Pay Review Body – I am the first woman to hold these posts. But is that right? Women will have made it when sometimes a man gets a job, sometimes a woman and nobody even comments.

Among the top FTSE-100 companies the lack of women on the board is a disgrace. I do not accept that women are not sufficiently able to run a top company. The FTSE-250 companies do have a better record but in the top echelon it is basically a man's club. There is a still a view that the serious stuff is for the boys. That is maybe why they sometimes make such a mess of it!

In the public sector I think women have been faring better but the sector is better geared to the whole issue of diversity. It thinks and plans ahead because it is embedded in the system. That does not happen in the private sector. It all depends on top management – they set the pace and climate. If they want to use women properly – who often have achieved better educational results than their male rivals – then the top brass must make a genuine decision to use that talent.

Sir Peter Davis, when he was at Prudential and then Sainsbury's, personally put a great deal of effort into a programme called Opportunity 2000, trying to persuade companies to use more women – as did Baroness Howe of Idlicote, the first chairman of Opportunity 2000, of which I was proud to be a member. I regret that this seems to have faded away in the City of London. It is a backward step and lets companies off the hook. Yet business is the real loser.

Still, we have come a long way and that is good. Women are much more confident, and rightly so, but too many young women lack confidence. Their ambition is to get married – to have a man to look after them. Now I am not against getting married. But a look at the divorce rate, the figures for separation and at longevity clearly shows marriage, as the totally consuming element, is not always the wisest course for a woman. They have got to be able to look after themselves and for that they need to set their sights higher. And why not?

Today some young women want nothing to do with this kind of thinking. If there is a glass ceiling, they can punch their way through, they claim! Well, good luck to them, if they can manage it, but there are millions who cannot and need role models and leadership.

In my own case life has been good to me. But it did not come on a plate. I worked hard, always read my papers and prepared well. So I was ready to seize my chances as they came along. The world is not for wilting wallflowers – in business, commerce or even politics. Looking back there might be some things I would have done differently but taken in the round I have been thoroughly privileged and lucky, and I have had plenty of opportunities. So I cannot complain.

And there is more to come, I hope.

Of one thing I am now certain – I would never consider a full-time job again. The concept of having a variety of differing tasks is much more stimulating and one meets so many interesting and varied people. I also love having the chance to bring about changes which benefit people in their working lives. I have had much greater satisfaction in that field than in anything else I have done.

I recall when general secretary of SOGAT my big task of the year was negotiating the general print agreement for a quarter-million members. And some good things were achieved in those long hours of negotiations, sometimes going through the night. Yet I am much prouder of our proposal for a national cancer screening programme for all women in the industry – not just my members – which the employers accepted. That was a real breakthrough of which I am still very proud.

But I am also very happy to think that of all the people I have met in a pretty active life, not all necessarily in agreement with me at the time, today I can count on half the fingers of one hand those that I actually detested. Set that against the hundreds from all walks of life who have been such great fun to know and to work with, who have opened up doors on life for me I might have missed, and whose company I have really enjoyed. Now that's been the fun of it all and I would not exchange that for anything.

As I told my union when I left . . . no regrets.

Index

The following abbreviations are
used in this index:
BD = Brenda Dean; EETPU =
Electrical, Electronic,
Telecommunications & Plumbing
Union; NGA = National
Graphical Association; SOGAT =
Society of Graphical and Allied
Trades

affordable housing 253, 256, 262
air force 226–9
air traffic control 267
air transport 258–62
Amalgamated Engineering Union
　20
Amicus 263
Amos, Baroness (Valerie) 216
Anne, Princess Royal 222
Any Questions 44
Apple, R. W. (Johnny) 57
Ariel 189–90
Armed Forces Pay Review Body
　225–30
Armitage, Eric 253
Armstrong, Hilary 251, 255
Armstrong, Jill 100
army 226–9
Ashworth, Professor John 236
Associated Society of Locomotive
　Engineers and Firemen 126
Association of Cinematograph,
　Television and Allied
　Technicians 127
Assured British Meat 264
Atherton, Candy 238–9
aviation 258–62, 267

Bach, Paul 234
Bailey, Walter 114
ballots
　decision to strike (January
　　1986) 80, 82–3
　Murdoch offer (May 1986)
　　147, 150–2
　improved compensation offer

(October 1986) 168
SOGAT general secretary 55
special levy (December 1986)
　163–6
Bank of Scotland 161
Banking, Insurance and Finance
　Union 115, 116
banks, charges to SOGAT 161–2
Barber, Brendan 258
Barclays Bank 161
Barnet, Colin 21
Bartlett, Denis 109, 160–1
BBC 119, 148, 149, 189–90
Beattie, George 107
Beckett, Margaret 108–9
Beckett, Sir Terence 196, 197
beds 41
Begrie, Janet 115
Bell, Dr John 266
Bell, T. 114
benefit claims 137–8, 161, 182
Benn, Tony 147, 149
Bickerstaffe, Rodney 107–8
Bishop, Sir Michael 258
Blair, Tony 213, 240–3
blind trusts 242–3
Blom-Cooper, Louis, QC 211
Blunkett, David 235
Bonner, Arthur 204
Booth, Albert 196
Booth, George 2–3
Boville, Claire 265
Bradbury Wilkinson dispute
　61–2
Bradshaw, Keith 223–4
Braine, Sir Bernard 118
Branson, Richard 258, 260
'Brenda's Rule' 34
'Brenda's time' 10, 107
Brinton, Tim 118
British Printing Industries
　Federation 176
British Shipbuilders 196, 198
British Telecom 211–12
Britton, Michael 174
Brown, Cyril 68

Brown, Jane 163
Bryan, Lyn 107–9
Buckton, Ray 63, 126
Burgh, John 40
burglary 162–3
Butler, Eric 86

C. Nicholls printing firm 11
Cabinet Policy Unit 36–7
Callaghan, James 239
Canada 68–9
cancer screening 23–4, 269
Carr, Robert 114
cars
　BD's 11, 16, 30, 111–12
　impounding of 110–11
Castle, Barbara 24, 38
Challen, Rev. Peter 185–8
Chalmers, Sandra 31
Chapple, Frank 47, 48
Chard, Ted 68, 93, 174, 205
Charles, Prince of Wales 222–3
Chennel, John 219
Cherrill, Charlie 174
Chicago Sun-Times 117
Chiddick, Professor David 237
ChildLine 211–12
Chitty, PC 190–1
Christianity 185
Citrine, Walter 41
City University 236
Civil and Public Services
　Association 126
civil aviation 258–62, 267
Clarke, Charles 64, 208, 213
Clarke, Kenneth 117, 225–6
Clarke, Tony 127
Cledwyn of Penrhos, Lord 243
Clement, Barrie 86, 181
Co-operative Bank 95
Cohen, Barbara 171
collective bargaining 168
Collier, John 139
Collins, Jack 32–3
Colman, Tony 41
Coltrane, Robbie 165

270

Committee on Standards in Public
Life 244
Commonwealth War Graves
Commission 230–4
compensation, for strikers 137,
141–2, 147, 167–8, 175
Confederation of British Industry
196, 197, 213
Conran, Shirley 21
Conroy, Harry (SOGAT
committee) 16, 30–1
Conroy, Harry (*Times*) 85
Cornwall Combined University
215
Costello, Mick 120–1, 123
Covent Garden Market Authority
267
Crowther, Jim 53
Crowther, June (née Swinbourne)
40, 53
Cudlipp, Hugh 59

Dahrendorf, Lord 221
Daily Express 70, 141
Daily Mail 71, 196, 243
Daily Mirror
on employment laws 100
industrial relations problems
59–60
and Labour Party 64, 65, 141
TUC reception 195–6
and war graves 230
Daily Star 195
Daily Telegraph 71–2, 243
Danby, Barbara 50
Darling, Alastair 260
Davidson, Ian Hay 41
Davies, Justice Michael 93–4
Davis, Sir Peter 268
Dawson Holdings plc 262
Dean of Beswick, Lord (Joe) 220
Dean, Bobby (brother) 1, 54–5,
184, 217–18
Dean, Hugh (father) 1–2, 27, 57,
184, 217–18
Dean, Lillian (mother) 1, 17, 57,
184
Dearing, Sir Ron 235–8
deaths ix, 169
Delaney, Michael 169
Dennison, William 113
Department of Employment 196
Devney, Barrie 56
Dholakia, Lord 246
dismissal, strikers 121–4
distribution 81, 87–8, 93, 96–7,
262
see also TNT
Donnison, David 37–8
Dromey, Jack 253–4
Dubbins, Tony
and EETPU 102, 159–60
and Graphical, Paper and

Media Union 202, 203–8
Murdoch's view of 76
negotiations 140, 150
and Wapping test run 77, 82

Economist 212
Eddington, Ron 258, 260
Edmonds, John 208
EETPU
and SOGAT 'poaching' 46–8,
78, 159
TUC and 48, 102–3, 158–60
Wapping production 78, 158
Electoral Reform Society 55, 205
electricians *see* EETPU
Elton, Ben 165
The End of the Street 158–9
Ennals, Lord 221–2, 223
Erridge, P. 127
Evans, David (Lord Evans of
Watford) 163
Evans, Judith 236
Evans, Sir Harold 71
Express Newspapers 195

Fairclough, Ian 190
Fallshawe, Tony 189–90
family life 1–2, 30, 49, 184,
256–7
Farrer & Co. 96, 121–3, 173,
174, 176
Fawcett, Julia 154
Feather, Vic 19
Fellows, John 68
Felton, David 86, 181
Financial Times 143, 179–80,
265
Finch, Bob 92, 128
Fish, Peter 227
Fisher, Allan 96–7
Fitzpatrick, Barry 136–7
'Fledgling Policy' 35–6, 54
Foley, Gerry 32
Food Standards Agency 263–6
Foot, Michael 196
Freedom to Fly 258–62
Freeman, Bill 105, 133, 143, 174
Freemasonry 7

Gavron, Bob 212
general election (1997) 238–9
General Insurance Standards
Council 264
George Wimpey plc 262
Geraghty, Sean 46
Gill, Ken 63
Gillespie, Bill 120, 121, 124, 139
Glass, John 4–5
Goodman, Geoffrey 66
Gorst, John 118
Goudie, James 102
Gould of Potternewton, Baroness

(Joyce) 217
Graham, Alastair 126
Graham of Edmonton, Lord (Ted)
220
Graphical, Paper and Media
Union (GPMU) 202–9
Gray's Inn Road 136–7, 139,
141–2, 147
Greater London Council (GLC)
114
Green, Michael 181
Griffin, Admiral Sir Anthony 198
Griffin, Ken 250
Griffiths, Bryn 77, 82
Groves, Mick 165
Guardian 143, 159, 180, 265
Gunning, Roy 92, 164

Hadden, Neil 252
Hague, Helen 179–80
Hain, Peter 201
Haines, Joe 60
Haldane Society 190, 191
Hamilton, Nigel 94, 111
Hammond, Eric 47, 48, 78,
158–60
Hanshaw, Patrick 112
Harding, Mike 165
Harris, John 89, 101, 172,
174–5, 177
Harrison, Sarah 249
Harvey-Jones, Sir John 118–19
Haskel, Lord (Simon) 217
Hattersley, Roy 40
Haworth, Christine 228
Heseltine, Ken 28
Hicks, Michael 105, 143–4, 174
High Court 93–4, 109–10, 139,
173–4, 175
higher education 235–8
Hill, Dennis 39, 43–4, 46, 55,
93, 163
Hinchcliffe, Nick 102
Hodgkinson, Mike 258
Holland, Sir Geoffrey 237
Holmes, George 68, 105–6, 112,
170, 177
Home Office 116–17, 149
honours 244, 245–8
Hoon, Geoff 228, 230, 231
Hope, Brian 99–100
Horsman, Mike 225, 226, 228,
232, 233
hospitals 215–16
Hourston, Gordon 226
House of Lords
Appointments Commission
245–8
BD accepts peerage 217–21
BD as working peer 220–1,
230, 240, 249, 263
membership 245–9
reform 244–8

Housing Corporation 250–7
Houston, Felicity 246
Howard, Anthony 132
Howarth, Valerie (*later* Baroness
    Howarth of Breckland) 212
Howe of Idlicote, Baroness 268
Howell, Noel 116
Hurd of Westwell, Lord 246
Hutchins, David 68
Hutchison, Dave 76
Hutchison, Yvonne 253

ICSTIS (Independent Committee
    for Supervision of Telephone
    Information Services)
    210–11, 249
Imbert, Peter 192
immigration 116–18
Independent 181
industrial relations 88, 121–3,
    183, 214
Industrial Relations Act (1971)
    18
Institute of Occupational
    Therapists 222, 223
International Women's Year
    (1975) 20–4
Inveresk plc 212
Irvine, Derry, QC 102
Irvine, Joe 260
Isaacs, Tony 120

Jackling, Sir Roger 231, 234
Jackson, Glenda 165
Jay of Paddington, Baroness 242
Jean (work colleague) 5–6
John Marshall Hall 185, 187
Johnson, Boris 132
Johnson, Melanie 265
Jones, Digby 258
Jones, Michael 103
Jones, Tim 179
Jones, Wynn 106, 148, 171, 189,
    192
Jordan, Bill 208
journalists 71, 85–6, 116–17, 177

Kay, Stefan 212
Kellaway, Richard 232
Kellogg's 33–5
Keys, Bill
    and BD 18–19, 36–7, 39,
        49–50, 55–6
    Bradbury Wilkinson dispute
        61–2
    and EETPU membership 46,
        48
    and Fleet Street 180
    retirement 51–2, 74–5
King, Andrew 190
Kinning Park, Glasgow 147
Kinnock, Glenys 241
Kinnock, Neil

and BD 241
and Labour Party 213
and Robert Maxwell 64
Wapping dispute 103, 130–2,
    171
Kirkpatrick, Eddie 178
Knapp, Jimmy 126
Knox, Amy 5–6, 7, 8, 9
Krebs, Sir John 263, 264, 266

La Bamba boat 199
Lady Chatterley's Lover 11–12
Lamont, George 92, 95, 115, 164
Lang, Ian 117
Laurillard, Professor Diana 236
Lawrence, Felicity 265
Leighton, Ron 117
Levin, Bernard 85
Levy, Michael 242–3
Literacy Trust 236
Litherland, Bob 117
Livingstone, Alan 215
Lloyd, John 179
London Gazette 217, 218
London Post 121, 159
London School of Economics 236
Lord, Terry 89
Lynch, Kenny 165

McDonald, Mavis 251, 253, 255
McDowall, Keith (husband)
    and BD 196–9, 214, 219,
        239–40
    career 196–7, 213–14, 239
McKenzie, Kelvin 183
McWhirter, Fred 7
Maidment, Rachel 264, 266
Major, John 225, 226
Manchester Evening News 21, 28
marches *see* rallies and marches
Mardell, Mark 81–2, 181
Marsh, Lord 198
Marshall of Knightsbridge, Lord
    259–60
Mason, John 265
Mason, Sir Ron 215
Matthews, Bruce
    negotiations 57–8, 77, 79, 139,
        141
    new technology report 69
    predetermined plan 120,
        121–3
Mawhinney, Brian 215
Maxwell, Elizabeth 65
Maxwell, Robert 59–67, 72–3
Mayer, Anthony 250–1
media
    and BD 56–7, 97–100, 107–8,
        152–3, 163–4
    end of strike coverage 177,
        179–81
    and Parliament 245
Meltzer, Albert 194

Melvern, Linda 158
Mentorn Films 214
Merlyn-Rees, Lord 242
Michael, Alun 265
Miles, Bill
    and BD 30, 45, 52, 75, 145,
        195
    negotiations 77, 78–9, 82, 120,
        140
    in secret 82, 133, 172–3
    new technology visit 142–3
    and TNT distribution 96–7
    and union divisions 142–3
miners 116, 126
Mitchell, John 48, 109
Molloy, Mike 160–1, 205
Monks, John 103, 140
Monkton, Ivan 254
Morning Star 120, 143
Morris, Christopher 189
Morris, Pamela 236
Morrison, Bill 9
Morrison, Sara 237
Moss, Doris 54
motor vehicles
    BD's 11, 16, 30, 111–12
    impounding of 110–11
Mowlam, Mo 239, 243
Murdoch, Rupert
    and BD 57–8
    and NGA 76, 83
    negotiations
        Heathrow (May 1986) 146–7
        Los Angeles (March 1986)
            133, 135
        New York (January 1987)
            vii–xi, 172–3
    on the end of the strike 179
    pre-strike 57–8, 78–9, 82
    political lobbying 193
    UK newspaper acquisitions 59
    US citizenship 58, 135
    see also Matthews, Bruce; News
        International; O'Neill, Bill
Murray of Epping Forest, Lord
    220

Nash, Roy 197
National Air Traffic Service 267
National Union of Printing,
    Bookbinding and Paper
    Workers 5–9
National Union of Railwaymen
    126
National Union of Seamen 126
National Westminster Bank
    161–2
navy 226–9
negotiation skills 7, 12–13, 131,
    135
negotiations
    end of strike 174–9
    Heathrow (May 1986) 146–7

Hyde Park (April 1986) 139–42
Los Angeles (March 1986) 135
New York (January 1987) vii–xi, 172–3
pre-strike 57–8, 77–9, 82
Neil, Andrew 85
New York Times 57
News International
  concern for reputation 175–6
  demands 81
  journalists 71, 85–6, 116–17
  predetermined plan 120–4, 131
  see also Murdoch, Rupert; Wapping
News of the World 59, 97, 120, 139
newspaper industry 68–9, 70–2, 158
Newspaper Proprietors Association (NPA) 32–3
NGA
  Bradbury Wilkinson dispute 61–2
  car loan to BD 111
  Murdoch view of 76, 83
  negotiations 140, 150
  and SOGAT 75–7, 83–4
    financial assistance to 89, 167
    merger 200–3
  and Wapping test run 77, 78, 79
Nickson, Sir David 197
Northern Ireland Office 239–40
Norwood, Eve 68–9
nursing homes 223–4

O'Brien, Ted 52–3, 55, 68
Office of Manpower Economics 225, 228, 232
O'Leary, John 47, 55
O'Neill, Bill
  legal costs 182–3
  negotiations 78–9, 167–8
    secret meetings 146, 172–3, 174–5
  predetermined plan 120, 121–3
  SOGAT v. NGA 83–4
Open University 236
Opportunity 2000 268
Osborne, Billy 112, 124
Oxburgh, Sir Ronald 236
Oxford University 132

Paisley, Eileen 248
Paisley, Ian 248
Palin, Michael 231
Pankhurst, Sylvia 263
Parish, Alf 77, 140
Parker, Sir John 198
Parsons, Nicholas 31

Patel, Chaim 224
Paterson, Marie 24
pension funds 175, 212
pensions 138
picketing 93, 96, 104–5, 156–7
Pole-Carew, Christopher 158, 159, 167
police
  means of identification xii, 149–50
  violence xii, 105–6, 132, 147–50, 170–1, 189–94
Police Complaints Authority 190, 191–2
Police Complaints Commission 150
Police Federation Journal 193–4
Political Honours Committee 244, 245–6
political parties, funding 247–8
Post Office 214–15
Post Office Engineering Union 201
Potter, Dr David 236
Powell, Albert 31, 43, 44, 50–1, 57–8
Powell, Jonathan 240, 242
Prescott, John 255, 256, 263
press *see* media
Price Commission 40–2
Printers' March for Jobs 130
Printing and Kindred Trades Federation (PKTF) 11
Private Eye 198
Privy Council 243–4
Pym, Lord 243

Question Time 119

rallies and marches
  anniversary at Wapping (January 1987) 170–1
  Methodist Central Hall (May 1986) 144–6
  Printers' March for Jobs (April 1986) 130
  Trafalgar Square 19, 24–5, 133–4
  Wembley (March 1986) 130–2
Rama, Denys 191
Rantzen, Esther 212
Redhead, Brian 22–3, 72
redundancy 137, 141–2, 147, 155
Reynolds, Ian 260
Rice, Tom 158, 159
Richard (Wapping resident) 113
Richards, Geoffrey 120–3, 173, 174–7
Richards, Sheelagh 223
Rifkind, Malcolm 226
Riley, John 113–14

Rirma (Revisers, Ink Rollers & Manufacturers' Assistants) 76
Ritchie, Tony 114
Robbins, Chris 174
Robert Horne Paper Co. 144, 145
Roberts, William 94
Robertson, George 228
Robinson, John 262
Rogers, Richard 243
Ross, Ian 181, 197
Routledge, Paul 86
Royal Bank of Scotland 115
Royal British Legion 230
Royal Mail 214–15
Russell, Diane 35, 260, 264

SAGA magazine 230–2, 234
St Andrew's Junior School 2–3
St Ives plc 212
Salvation Army 54–5
Sapper, Alan 127
Sarkis, Angela 246
Scales, Prunella 243
Scargill, Arthur 23
Scotland, Patricia (*later* Baroness Scotland of Asthal) 211
Scotsman 100
Sear, Nancy 22
Searby, Robert 121
secondary action 88, 126, 183–4
Senior Salaries Review Board 228
Sergeant, Danny
  and BD 152–3
  hesitancy 82, 90, 204
  SOGAT executive 55, 90, 142, 145–6
Shaw, Alan 55
Shaw, Giles 149
Shephard, Gillian 235
Shepley, Ernie 14
Sheridan, Joe 6–8, 9, 12–13, 16, 26–9
  lessons learnt from 12, 131, 173–4
shoe industry 223
Shore, Peter 112, 114, 171
Skinner, Dennis 171
Slater, Jim 126
Smith, John 22, 197, 216–17, 241
Smith, Tom 13, 18
social housing 253, 256
Socialist Workers Party 147
SOGAT
  conference (1968) 14–15
  conference (1976) 26
  conference (1984) 53–4, 57
  conference (1986) 152–6
  divisions within union 142–4, 153–4, 177, 179
  donations 89–91, 95

executive
  decision to end strike 176–81
  general secretary campaign
    52–7
  president campaign 44–51
  succession 43–4
  financial cost of dispute 160–2
  financial problems 155, 163–6
  Manchester branch 13–23,
    28–32
  merger with NGA 200–3
  sequestration 93–5, 109–12,
    114, 174
    costs 160, 161, 182
    release from 138–9
  strike headquarters 91, 95
  Union Jack Committee 92–3,
    94, 128
  see also ballots; Graphical, Paper
    and Media Union
Solanki, Baz 189
South Africa 125–6
Southwark Borough Council 114
Sporting Life 59, 65–6
Squires, Dorothy 115
stamps 214–15
Standards in Public Life,
    Committee 244
Steinberg, Max 252
Stevens, Jocelyn 195
Stevenson of Coddenham, Lord
    246
Stone, Bert 11
Stretford High School 3
strikers
  compensation 137, 141–2,
    147, 167–8, 175
  dismissal 121–4
  statistics 180–1
Suckling, Maurice 55
Sun 58, 75, 97, 116, 127, 183
Sunday Times 83, 97
Supplementary Benefits
    Commission 37–8
Swinbourne, June 35–6
  see also June Crowther
Switzer, Barbara 63
Sykes, Sir Richard 236

Tabachnik, Eldred QC 101–2,
    174, 177
Takare plc 223–4
Taylor, Mr Justice 110, 114
Taylor, Noel 191–2
Taylor, Steve 190
Tebbit, Norman 46, 82
technological change 33–5, 56,
    68–70
telephone information services
    (ICSTIS) 210–11, 249
telephone operators 210–12
telephone tapping 144, 193
Templeton, Harry 66

Thompsons 89, 100–1, 172, 174
Thomson of Monifieth, Lord 243
Thornton-le-Fylde 27, 219
Times
  end of dispute coverage 179
  Gray's Inn Road plant 136–7,
    139, 141–2, 147
  journalists 85–6
  photograph of BD 152–3
  and war graves 231
TNT
  delivery problems 114
  drivers 127–8
  establishment of 96–7
  picketing 96, 104
  violence at depots 147, 157
Todd, Ron 127
Tothill, Margaret 90, 99, 144,
    205
Tower Hamlets Borough Council
    113
Townshend, Pete 165
trade unions
  for armed forces 229
  and charity 209
  function 87
  recognition 76, 140
  support for Wapping dispute
    95, 126–7, 131
Trades Union Congress 48,
    102–3, 158–60
Transport and General Workers'
    Union 20, 127, 230
TUC 48, 102–3, 158–60
Tuffin, Alan 200–1
tuition fees 237–8
Tuppen, Ken 83, 111, 145, 181,
    205, 208

unemployment benefit 137–8,
    161, 182
Union Jack Committee 92–3, 94,
    128
Union of Communication
    Workers 127
Union of Postal Workers 200–1
Union of Shop, Distributive and
    Allied Workers 20
Unison 253
United States
  Chicago Sun-Times 117
  newspaper production 68–9,
    158
universities 236–8
University College London
    Hospital 215–16
Upcroft, Michael 30

Vicary-Smith, Peter 265
Vint, George 190
violence
  increasing 156–7
  police xii, 105–6, 132, 147–50,

    170–1, 189–94
  troublemakers 104, 150, 193
Vodafone 211–12

Walsh, Tony 92–3, 164
Walters, Ian 185–7, 189
Wapping dispute
  cost 80, 182–3
  installation and testing of new
    machinery 58, 69–70, 76–7,
    83
  local authority reaction 113–14
  local residents 112–13
  support from individuals
    114–17, 165
  support from trade unions 95,
    126–7, 131
  transfer of editorial functions
    85
  union recognition 76, 140
  see also ballots; negotiations
war graves 230–4
War Widows' Association 234
Warren, Phil 189
Washington, David 163
Washington Post 68
Watson, Allan 68, 203
Watts, Tom 165
Welfare Fund 133
Welland, Colin 165
West, Timothy 243
Which? 265
Whitelaw, William 239
Whitty, Lord (Larry) 265
Wilby, Peter 86
Wilkins, Baroness 223
Williams, John 165
Willis, Norman 102–3, 146, 159,
    164, 171
Willoughby, George 46
Wilson, Charles 69–70, 121
Wintour, Charles 132
Wintour, Patrick 180
Wishart, Ruth 100
women
  equality 45, 56, 267–8
  Fledgling Policy 35–6, 54
  glass ceiling 28, 268
  International Women's Year
    (1975) 20–4
Wapping demonstration 124–5
Woodburn, Chris 264
work permits 116–18
Wright, Tony 246
Wyatt, Woodrow 158, 193
Wyrko, D. J. 191–2

Yokoyama, H. E. 133–4
Yorkshire Bank 161
Yorkshire Post 100